A Hieroglyphic Vocabulary to the Theban Recension of the Book of the Dead

E. A. Wallis Budge

I0895951

Routledge
Taylor & Francis Group
Routledge Revivals

First published in 1911
by Kegan Paul, Trench, Trübner & Co. Ltd

This edition first published in 2014 by Routledge
2 Park Square, Milton Park, Abingdon, Oxon, OX14 4RN
and by Routledge
711 Third Avenue, New York, NY 10017

Routledge is an imprint of the Taylor & Francis Group, an informa business

Publisher's Note
The publisher has gone to great lengths to ensure the quality of this reprint but points out that some imperfections in the original copies may be apparent.

Disclaimer
The publisher has made every effort to trace copyright holders and welcomes correspondence from those they have been unable to contact.

A Library of Congress record exists under LC control number: 11029270

ISBN 13: 978-1-138-77891-7 (hbk)
ISBN 13: 978-1-315-76471-9 (ebk)
ISBN 13: 978-1-138-78965-4 (pbk)

Routledge Revivals

A Hieroglyphic Vocabulary to the Theban Recension of the Book of the Dead

Containing a comprehensive dictionary of hieroglyphs to all the texts of the *Theban Recension of the Book of the Dead*, and also to most of the supplementary Chapters of the Saïte and Graeco-Roman period that are usually appended to it, this volume will prove to be a staple part of a rounded appreciation of Ancient Egyptian literature.

First published in 1911, the index includes all English equivalents to the Egyptian words. Phonetic values for each symbol are provided, the arrangement of the words and their various forms is arranged alphabetically throughout, and each hieroglyph is printed clearly: a user-friendly and concise tool for all enthusiasts, students and researchers.

Books on Egypt and Chaldæa.

A HIEROGLYPHIC VOCABULARY TO THE THEBAN RECENSION OF THE BOOK OF THE DEAD

WITH AN INDEX TO ALL THE ENGLISH EQUIVALENTS OF THE EGYPTIAN WORDS

BY

E. A. WALLIS BUDGE, M.A., LITT. D., D. LITT., D. LIT.

KEEPER OF THE EGYPTIAN AND ASSYRIAN ANTIQUITIES
IN THE BRITISH MUSEUM.

NEW EDITION. REVISED AND ENLARGED.

LONDON

KEGAN PAUL, TRENCH, TRÜBNER & CO. LTD.

DRYDEN HOUSE, 43, GERRARD STREET, W.

1911

PREFACE TO THE SECOND EDITION.

THE following pages contain a Hieroglyphic Vocabulary to all the texts of the Chapters of the Theban Recension of the Book of the Dead which is printed in this Series (Vols. XXVIII—XXX), and also to most of the supplementary Chapters of the Saïte and Graeco-Roman period which are appended thereto. The whole work has been comprehensively revised, and in the case of characters to which the values given in 1897, when the first edition was compiled, are now obsolete, special care has been taken to place them in the order in which they have since been proved to belong. The arrangement of the words and their various forms is usually alphabetical, and it is hoped that the few exceptions to this rule will cause the reader no difficulty. A very considerable number of words and forms have been added to this edition, and it was necessary, for reasons of space, to omit all references.

A new feature of this edition of the Vocabulary is the Index to all the English equivalents of Egyptian words printed herein. This was prepared in answer to the requests of many who had used the first edition of the Vocabulary.

For the care which Mr. Adolf Holzhausen has given to the printing of this work my sincere thanks are due.

E. A. WALLIS BUDGE

BRITISH MUSEUM,
February 4th, 1911.

VOCABULARY.

 A.

aatā, atitā 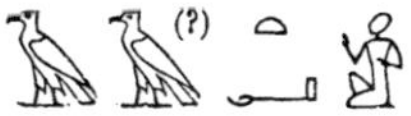 ministrant, celebrant, a kind of priest.

aȧr  to bind, tie together, to put under restraint, to coerce, to persecute, to oppress.

au  to make a gift or offering, to present.

ait 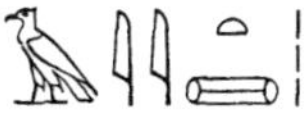 bread-cakes, loaves of any shape offered for funerary oblations.

aut  offerings of meat and drink, sacrifices, bread-cakes, etc.

aut  light, radiance.

au  to be long, length, the opposite of  *usekh* breadth, to extend, be extended, *e. g.* extended (*i. e.*, lavish) hand, length of the back, extended of years, long of strides; compare also .

au  to expand, to dilate (of the heart), hence , joy, gladness, pleasure, delight.

au  fully, exceedingly, to the utmost, to the full extent.

Au-ā 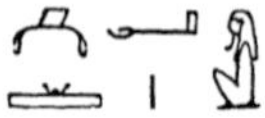 the "god of the extended arm".

au  children, youths, the young, unmarried men, synonym of *sheriu* children.

ausek 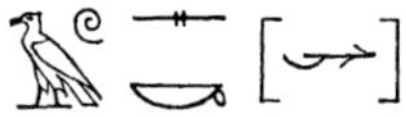 stick, staff, sceptre, symbol of high position and dignity.

abit  an insect which brought the deceased into the Hall of

Osiris, identified with the praying mantis. A variant gives *bai* .

abu — cessation ceaselessly, unremittingly.

Abu — Elephant-city. The Island of Elephantine and the town and district of Syene. The region of the First Cataract.

abka — to shine.

abtu — maternal and paternal ancestors. Heb. אבות.

Abt-ṭesi-ruṭu-neter — a proper name.

apṭu — geese, ducks, water-fowl in general, and finally birds of any and every kind offered for sacrifices.

afiu — fish offered at funerary feasts.

afu — to injure, to harm.

Amm — flame, fire, heat, blaze, to scorch, to burn, to shrivel up. Var. .

Am[m]u — the Fire City of the Other World.

amm  to grasp with the hand, to hold in the fist, to seize, take by violence, snatch at, fist, grasp.

amu 

ames  the name of a sceptre, or staff, associated with Ȧmsu, or Menu, the god of generation and fertility.

Ani  a scribe and treasurer of holy offerings.

Arthikasathika  a proper name.

ah  to be troubled, injured, suffering.

aha  evil, injury, harm.

Ahat  an ancient goddess, who was identified with Hathor, and appeared in the form of a cow or a woman.

Ahit 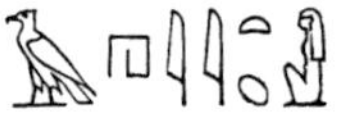 a goddess who supplied the dead with food.

Aḥu  a god who was connected with offerings.

Aḥui (?)  the name of a canal (?).

aḥu 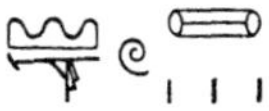 food, bread-cakes, offerings of all kinds.

aḥet  fields, estates, farm, cultivated land.

akh  to bloom, to blossom, flower, bloom.

akhakh  flowers of the sky, *i. e.*, stars.

akhi  reed, water-plant, rushes, marsh flowers.

akhet  the first season of the Egyptian Year.

akhaā  to enter, to penetrate.

akhab  to give to drink.

Akhabiu  a class of divine beings, or gods, who were associated with the Akeru-gods .

akhetu  *i. e.*, , things, objects, food, bread-cakes.

Aseb  the name of a Fire-god in the Other World.

asbiu		sparks of fire, flames, fiery spirits.
Aseb-ḥer-per-em-khetkhet		a god with a face of fire which advanced and retreated alternately.
askh		to cut a crop, to reap.
asta		to hasten, to hurry, be swift or rapid.
asta ȧb	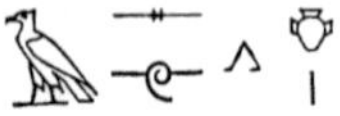	to hurry the heart, to arrive at a hasty judgment.
astu		water in motion, a stream or canal.
Ashu	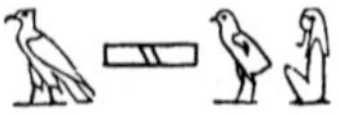	name of a god.
Ashbu	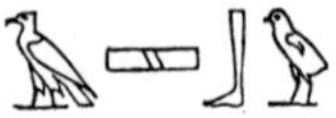	name of the warder of the 5th Ārit.
Asher		name of a city, or temple district, or god.
ashert		roasted flesh of animals, or birds, grilled meat, steaks, joints, etc.

akit  a chamber, or hut, or small house.

Aker  a very ancient name of the Earth-god.

Akeru  The two gods who guarded the western and eastern ends of the tunnel through the earth which the Sun-god passed through nightly. They were the ancestors of the Akhabiu gods, 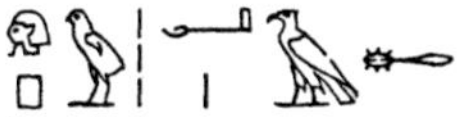
, and also of Rā 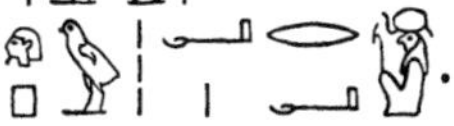.

Akeriu  a group of earth-gods who appeared in the form of serpents.

aqa  *i. e.*,  dirt, filth, what is filthy.

Aqeṭqeṭ 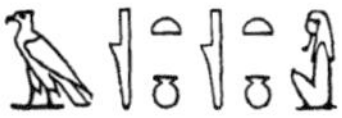 one of a group of seven gods or spirits associated with Osiris.

Aḳab
Aḳb  the great celestial ocean and the god who presided over it, water, flood, celestial Nile.

Aḳbȧ	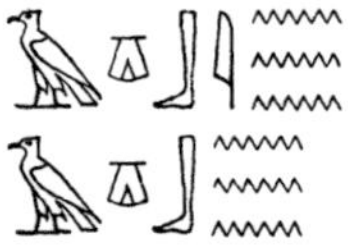	the great celestial ocean and the god who presided over it, water, flood, celestial Nile.
at ***atu***		injury, assault, attack.
at		a support of a god, a perch for a bird, etc. The word is also written with a wrong determinative .
at		the vertebrae, back, the middle of something.
at	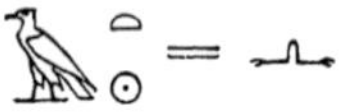	not
at		moment, a period of time, season.
Ati		The ninth nome of Lower Egypt; its capital was Per-Ȧsȧr (Busiris).
atiu		evil beings, fiends, enemies.
atutu		a kind of wood.
atep		a load, a burden, something carried on the head, to carry, to bear, to support.

atef, *atefu*	name of one of the principal crowns of Osiris.
Atef-ur	a proper name.
aṭ	to be wounded, injured.
aṭȧu	a ceremonial garment with magical properties.
aṭu	crocodile, or water lizard. Plur.
Ȧtes ḥer-mer (?)	a proper name.
aṭet	the vertebrae, back. Also written

Ȧ.

A	The god Thoth. The form is common in the later period.
ȧ	Personal pronoun. I, me, my.
ȧ	O! Hail!
ȧ	praise, acclamation.

àa		boat.
àa		standard, perch for a sacred bird.
àaa		plants, flowers, growing crops.
àaau		he of the two feathers, plumed one.
àaat		standard, perch for a sacred bird.
àau ***àaut***		aged one, old age, old man, senior; plur. .
àait		aged gods, divine old men.
àau		to praise, to applaud, to ascribe glory to, to acclaim, to rejoice.
àaiu		praise, praises, acclamations, rejoicings, glorifyings.

ȧaiu  }
ȧaut  } praise, praises, acclamations, rejoicings, glorifyings.

ȧait  tombs, or funerary domains under the charge of priests, sepulchres.

ȧaiti  the gods who preside over the Ȧats; see Chapter CL.

ȧamḥet  see 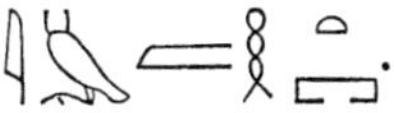.

Ȧaru   a region in the Other World which formed a portion of the abode of the blessed.

ȧarret  eyes (?).

ȧarret  milk.

ȧaret  vine, vineyard.

Ȧaheṭ 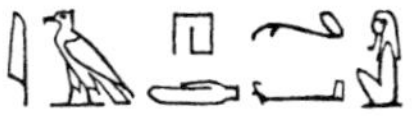  a god whose functions are undefined.

ȧakhu  light, splendour, radiance, brilliance, rays, the god of light or splendour.

Ȧakha-bit  the name of a goddess.

Àaku 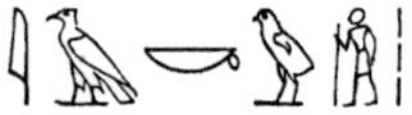 the name of a group of gods or of deified human beings.

àakebi, *àake-bit* 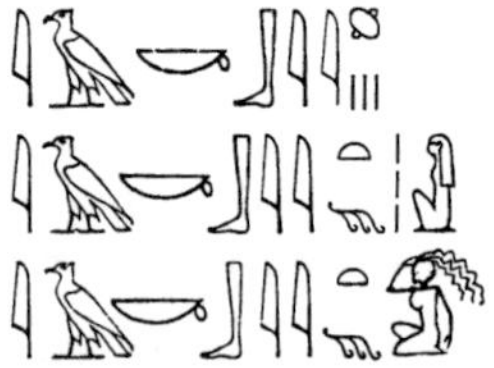 women who wail and pluck out their hair, professional wailing women or mourners.

àakebu  groans, lamentations, mourning, wailings. Another form is 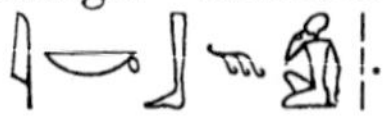.

àaqet  flowers, grass, herbs.

Àaqeṭ-qeṭ  "He who revolves", name of a god.

àat   dignity, rank, grade of honour, position, preferment. Plur. .

àaat  things possessing a bad or strong smell.

àat  an article of dress, part of a girdle (?).

àat  the vertebrae, back.

àat  to split, to cleave asunder, to break.

àat  standard, perch, pedestal.

Àat ent Ɐp-uat  "Standard of Àp-uat", name of the lower deck of the magical boat.

àat  domain of a god, tomb of a god, funerary district; plur. . The kingdom of Osiris contained 14 Àats :—

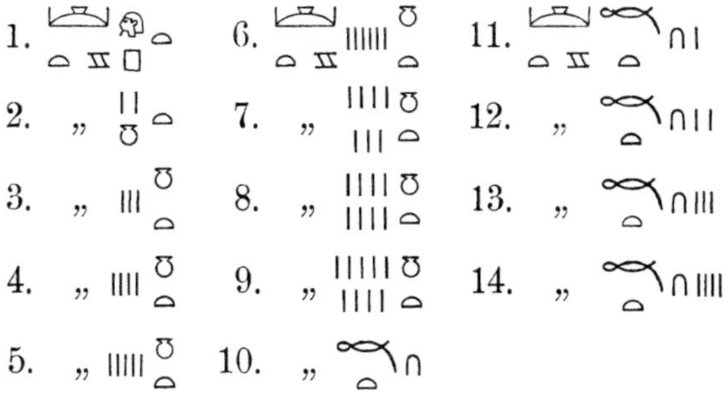

àat Àmentet  the funerary domain of the West (Àmentet).

àat khu  the Àat of blessed souls.

àat en khet 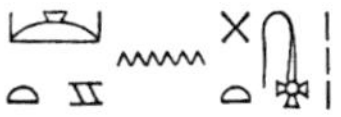 the Àat of fire.

àati  The two Àats, *i. e.*, the Àat of Horus and the Àat of Set, or the two Àats of Osiris.

Àat-urt  the god of the Great Àat.

Åat ent Kher-āḥa  The Åat of Kher-āḥa, *i. e.*, the ancient Egyptian city which stood near Old Cairo (Fusṭâṭ).

åatu  praise, praisings, adorations.

åati, ***åatu***  slaughter houses, chambers of tortures; places where the enemies of Rā and Osiris were punished.

åaṭ  child, male or female, youth.

åaṭeb  flood, storm, rush of water.

åaṭet  net for snaring birds or fish, the net in which the Enemy snared souls.

åaṭet 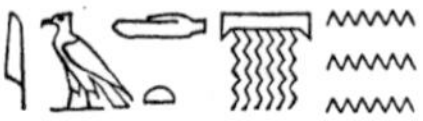 rain-storm, dew, moisture.

åaṭti  oppression, injury, oppressor.

åā 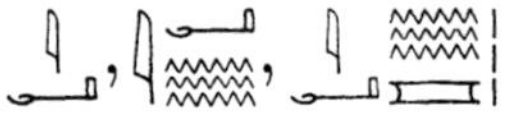 to wash, to cleanse, purify,  to wash the heart, *i. e.*, to cleanse the heart by taking vengeance.

ȧāu — a washing, a cleansing.

ȧā — a sinful act. to sin against the god.

ȧāāu — apes, incarnations of the spirits that praised the rising sun.

ȧāb — to come towards, to meet, to present an offering, one opposite, an offering.

ȧāb, **ȧābet** — an offering, oblation, ceremonial gift, a vessel of offerings.

ȧāb — an offering of a libation.

ȧānu — praise, adoration, words of glorification; plur. , .

ȧār, **ȧārt**, **ȧārtu** — serpent, snake, cobra. The Greek form is οὐραῖος, uraeus.

ȧārāt — snake goddess; plur. .

ȧārti — the Two Snake-goddesses, *i. e.*, Isis and Nephthys; the Four Snake-goddesses.

ȧārtu ānkhu — the "living uraei" which lived on the cornice of the shrine of Osiris.

ȧāḥ, ȧāḥu — the moon.

ȧāḥu — the Moon-god, in later times called Khensu.

ȧātu ent khert — name of a part of the magical boat (Chap. XCIX).

ȧu — praises, rejoicings.

ȧu — old man.

ȧu — used in later times for *er* from, to, into, for, at, in, etc.

ȧu — to be, to exist; I am, thou art, he is, we are, she is; as an auxiliary , etc., and see *passim*.

ȧu  to be shipwrecked,

 the shipwrecked man.

ȧu  offence, sin, crime, iniquity, wickedness, defect, breach of the Law.

ȧui 

ȧuit 

ȧut 

evil, harm, injury, defects, deceit, to commit wickedness, or sin.

ȧu  to speak, cry out, utter words.

ȧu  to conceive a child, be pregnant.

ȧua  ox (of the Earth-god Seb).

ȧuai  roof of a building.

ȧuȧu  dogs, jackals.

Ȧuu-ba  a proper name.

ȧuāu  the living body.

ȧuā 

ȧuāu 

flesh and bone, joint of meat, haunch of an animal, carcase.

ȧuā 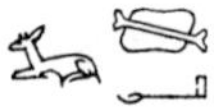

ȧuāā 

ȧuāu 

to be flesh and bone of some one, to be the heir, inheritance, the divine Heir.

ȧuāu 

heir.

ȧuāt 

heirship, inheritance.

ȧuāu  heirs, kinsfolk, people of one's own flesh and blood.

ȧuiu  those who lacerate or cut.

àuur  to conceive, conception, pregnant.

àuurt  a pregnant goddess.

 heir.

àuf  flesh, limbs, members.

Àuf-ānkh  a proper name.

àumes  false or deceitful speech, exaggeration in speech, lies.

àun  colour, skin, hair.

àuna  certainly, assuredly.

àunt  a garment, clothed, dressed.

Àuràu-àaqer-sa-ànqrebathi 

 a proper name.

àuhet  to utter words.

àuheṭ  name of a god or divine being.

àuḥ  to be submerged, sprinkled.  steeped in something.

àukhemu  a group of gods, stars.

àukhemu urṭu 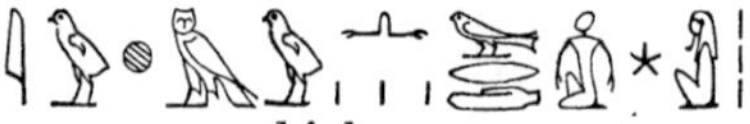 stars which never rest.

àukhemu seku  circumpolar stars which never set.

àukhemu Pen-ḥeseb (?)  stars of the god Pen-ḥeseb.

àukhekh 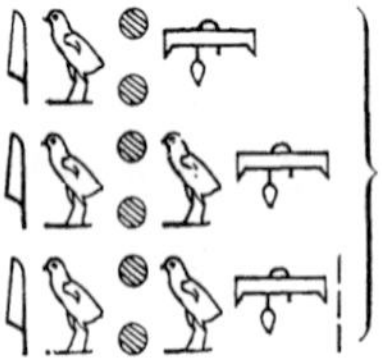 night, evening, darkness.

àusu  scales, balance.

Àuḳer

Àuḳert  the name of the Other World of Heliopolis (Ànnu).

Àuḳeru 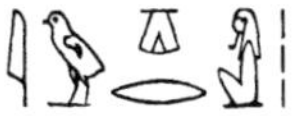 the gods of the Heliopolitan Other World.

Àuḳert  the goddess of Àuḳert.

Àuḳert-khentet-àst-s  name of one of the seven sacred cows.

àuṭ  to travel.

àu-t  thou art.

àu-ten 

àu-then  ye are.

àuti  fiends, enemies, foes.

àb  desire, wish.

àb  pegs, stakes.

àb  thirst.

àb  thirsty man.

Ȧb = Abtu Elephantine.

ȧb = name of a fish.

ȧb , left side.

ȧb cessation.

ȧb , the physical heart, will, wish, love, desire ; plur. ,

to judge hastily.

to do as one pleases.

"great of heart", bold, brave, arrogant, boastful.

of joyful heart.

to eat the heart, *i. e.*, to lose the temper, be sorry.

valiant.

be brave.

to fill the heart, to satisfy, be satisfied.

within.

with heart's desire.

with prompting of the heart, desire.

the amulet of the carnelian heart.

àba heart-soul.

àbu drink.

àbu the desired one.

Àbu-ur a proper name.

àbu , or to stop, to cease.

cessation.

àbui left side.

àbi panther or leopard skin.

àbit the praying mantis.

àber a kind of unguent.

àbḥu tooth. Plur.

àbekh  to penetrate, to make a way through.

àbsit 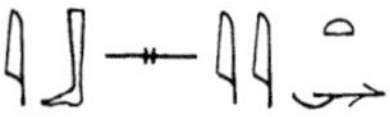 hull of a boat.

Àb-ka, **Abt-ka**  a proper name.

àbku  grief, to grieve, to weep.

àbt  middle hall, or chamber, of a house.

àbt  coffer.

àbt  thirst.

àbt  left hand side, the east.

àbt, **àbti** 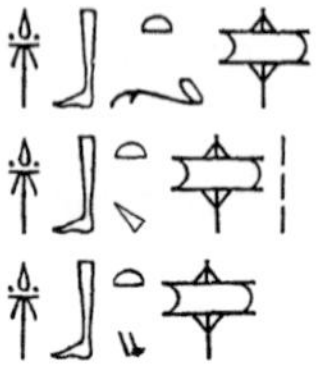 east wind.

àbt, **àbti**  eastern country, or region. 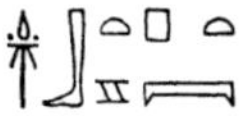 eastern sky, east of heaven;  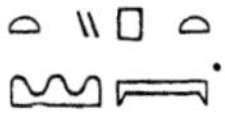.

àbti 

***àbtet* (*àbti*)** 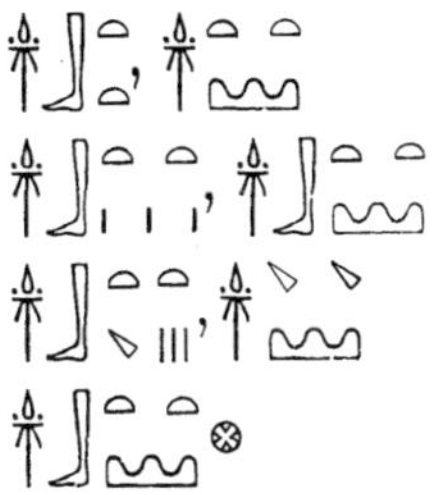 east, eastern country, or region.

àbtet 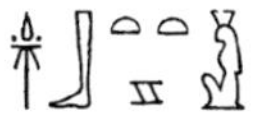 goddess of the east.

àbtiu  gods of the east, eastern deities.

àbt 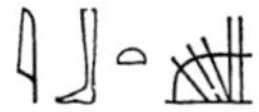 net.

àbtu  slaughter, slaughterings.

Àbṭ 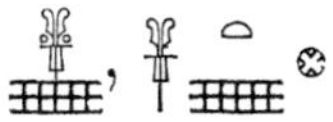 the nome of Abydos.

Àbt 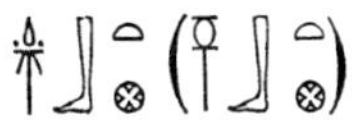 the city of Abydos.

Àbṭu  the city of Abydos.

Àbṭu the city god of Abydos.

àbeṭ the month of thirty days, plur. ; the monthly festival, plur. .

the second month of the season Pert, the last day of the second month of this season.

àbṭ, ***àbṭu*** a mythological fish which swam before the Boat of Rā; its companion was the *ànt* fish.

àp to count up, to reckon, to consider, a reckoning, a counting, reckoner of years, counter, numbered, counted.

àppet reckoning, account.

àp to judge, to be judged, to decree, be decreed, judgment. great judgment.

àp — judge of dooms.

judged. — judge.

àp, *àpu* — to judge, to dispute or argue with someone, to award, be awarded, to bring a message, to announce tidings. — a judge of words or affairs, — *àp maāt* righteous judge.

àpt — decree, judgment, sentence of doom.

àput mitu — sentence of death.

àp, *àpu*, *àpi*, *àpt* — to open. — open! — opened.

àp re, *àpu re*, *àpt re* — the ceremony of "opening the mouth".

Ȧp-uat
Ȧp-uati
Ȧp-uatu  "Opener of the roads", a name of a wolf-god who was supposed to conduct the deceased over the roads which lead to the Sekhet Ȧaru, or Elysian Fields. Ȧp-uat was a companion of the jackal-god Ȧnpu, with whom he is sometimes confounded.

Ȧp-uat meḥt sekhem pet 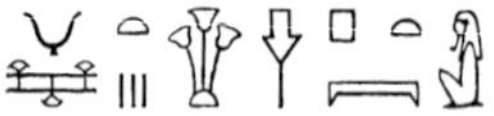 The god Ȧp-uat of the north as guide to the roads of heaven.

Ȧp-uat resu sekhem taui  The god Ȧp-uat of the south as guide to the roads of earth.

Ȧp-ur  "great opener", name of a god.

ȧp ḥer  except. 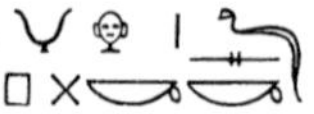 except thyself.

Ȧpu  A city, the Panopolis of the Greeks, the Akhmîm of the Arabs.

ȧpu
ȧpiu  these,  these gods,  these who dwell in.

ȧpiu — openers, those who make a way.

ȧputi — messenger, envoy, ambassador; plur.

two envoys.

ȧppiu — judges.

ȧpen — (see) these. these gods who dwell in.

Ȧpsi — a name or title of a god.

ȧpt — sacred chamber of a temple, private apartments of a house, sacred or profane *ḥarîm*.

ȧpt — stick, staff, sceptre.

ȧpt ȧst — name of a portion of Eastern Thebes, Karnak (?).

ȧpt — message, envoy.

ȧpt — messengers.

ȧpt	brow, forehead, top of the head (?).
	the hottest part of the fire.
	top, surface (?) of the waters.
	brow of the god Qaḥu.
ȧptu	these.
ȧpten	these.
Ȧp-shāṭ-taui	a name of Osiris.
ȧf, afu	flesh, limbs, members.
ȧfṭ	to rest, to sit down.
ȧfṭu	four.
ȧfṭet	four.
ȧfṭi	a kind of cloth or garment.
ȧm	in, into, inside.
ȧm (?)	a standard.
ȧm	a boat.
ȧm	to arrive in safety.

ȧm — flax, a kind of cloth.

ȧm — not, do not.

ȧm, **ȧmu** — to eat, to consume, swallow up, devour.

ȧmi — eating, eater; plur.

ȧmti — eater.

ȧm baiu — eater of heart-souls.

ȧm besku — "Eater of Livers", or intestines.

ȧm sāḥu — "Eater of mummies".

ȧm snef — "Eater of Blood"; one of the Forty-two Judges in the Hall of Osiris.

ȧm (un) — to eat, to consume.

ȧm — bread-cakes, food.

drink.

Ȧm-ḥauat-ent-pehui-f  "Eater of the offal of his body"; the name of the doorkeeper of the Third Ārit.

ȧmt, **ȧmtu** 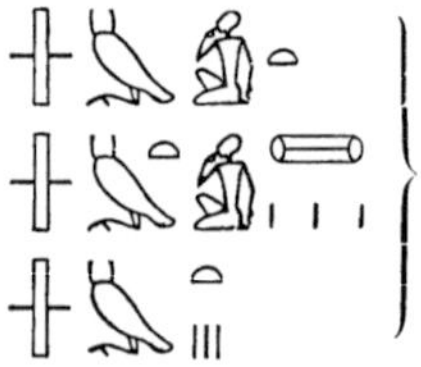 food, something fit or used for food.

ȧm, **ȧmt** 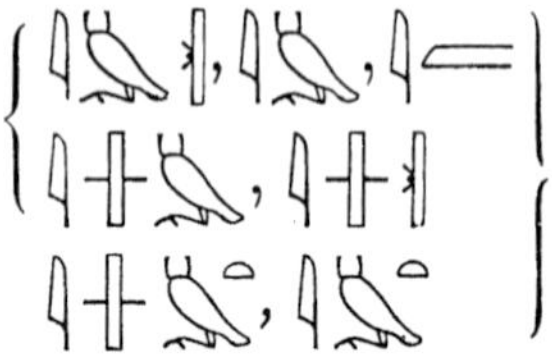 in, among, with, through, upon, by, around, there, therein.  in it (or him),  in it (or her),  by the back of.

ȧm, ȧmt 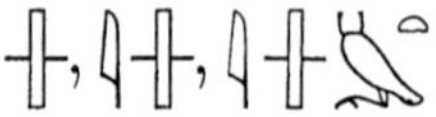 dweller in.

ȧmi 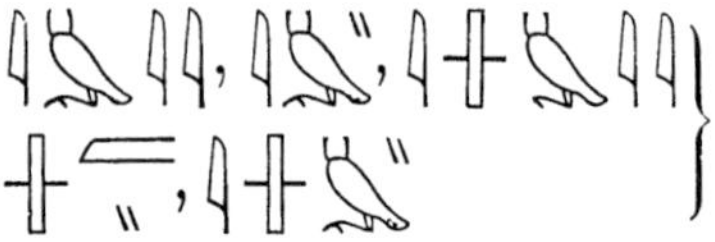 he who is in, dweller in; plur. ,  those who are in.

ȧm-ā — a title of a priest or ministrant.
ȧm ȧst-ā

ȧm-uḥet (?) **neb ta Tchesert** — "he who is in the embalmment chamber, Lord of Ta-tchesert", a title of Anubis, the divine physician and embalmer.

ȧmi-at — one in, or at, the supreme moment.

ȧmi ȧb — he who is in the heart.

ȧm-ȧten-f — he who is in his disk, *i. e.*, Rā.

ȧmi-uȧa-f — he who is in his Boat, *i. e.*, Rā.

ȧmi mu — he who is in the water, *i. e.*, Sebek.

ȧmi unnut-f — he who is in his hour.

Ȧmi-meḥen-f — he who is in his Meḥen serpent, *i. e.*, Rā, or Ȧf; plur.
ȧmi-meḥent-f

ȧmi-ha-f  he who is in his time, or place.

ȧmi-hem-f  he who is in his fiery serpent, *i. e.*, Rā.

ȧmi-khet  he who is in his fiery disk.

ȧm-khet 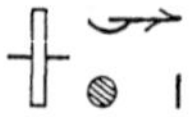

ȧmi-khet 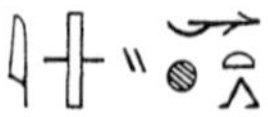 he who is in the following of.

ȧmi-suḥt 

ȧm-suḥt  he who is in his egg, *i. e.*, Rā.

ȧmi-mer-nesert (?) 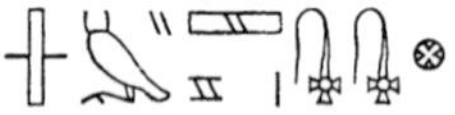 he who is in his fiery Lake, *i. e.*, Rā.

ȧmi-karȧ-f  he who is in his shrine, *i. e.*, Rā or Osiris.

ȧmi-ṭebtu  he who is in his coffin, *i. e.*, Osiris.

ȧmi-tchetta  he who dwelleth in eternity.

ȧmiu-ȧat-sen  the gods in their domains.

ȧmiu Ȧbṭu  those in Abydos.

àmiu-Ànu  the gods in Ànu (Heliopolis).

àmiu-àḥ-ur 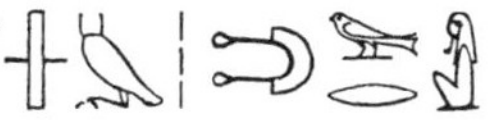 those in the Great Field.

àmiu-āāui  those in the hands.

àmiu-baḥ  the gods who are in the presence.

àmiu-beḳa  those who are in a weak state.

àmiu em-baḥ  the gods who are in the presence.

àmiu-hru-sen  those who are in their days.

àmiu-Nekhen  those who dwell in Nekhen.

àmiu Kher-neter  those who are in the Other World.

àmiu Neṭet  those who dwell in the city of Neṭet.

àmiu khet 
àmiu khet  those who are in the following of.

àmiu khuti  those who are in the two horizons.

ȧmiu sāḥu — those who are in their mummied forms.

ȧmiu-sut-sen — those who are in their hair.

ȧmiu seḥu-sen — those who are in their halls.

ȧmiu-shems, ***ȧmiu-shemsu*** — those who are in the following of.

ȧmiu-karȧ-sen — those who are in their shrines.

ȧmiu-ta — those who are in the earth.

ȧmtu, ***ȧmth***, ***ȧmith***, ***ȧmithu*** — among, between; Chap. CIV. 1, CIV. 1.

ȧmt — in

ȧm ȧb — what is in the heart, thought? prayer?

ȧm khent — title of a priest.

ȧma tree.

ȧmam date-palm.

ȧmakh serf, servant, one who venerates another, or is venerated, a beatified being.

ȧmakhi partic. masc. partic. fem.; plur. A late form is

ȧmu divine beings.

ȧmu trees, plants.

ȧmu flames, fire.
gods of fire.

ȧmu colour, pigment.

Ȧm-urt a proper name.

ȧmi shrine, chamber.

ȧmuhettu, *ȧmihettut* apes, incarnations of the spirits of the dawn.

ȧmuti image, figure.

ȧmem palm-tree.

ȧmem to putrefy.

ȧmem skin, hide.

ȧmmā grant, give, let there be, prithee, give I pray, open I pray, give water and air, give thy hand, let me pass, give (*i. e.*, incline) thy face.

ȧmmu beams, rays of light, splendour.

àmmu  boats.

àmmeḥet 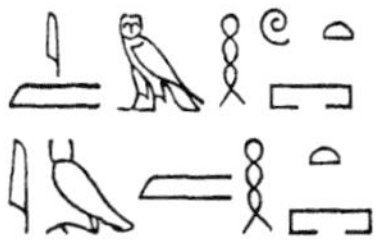 a portion of the Other World of Seker.

àmm ḳeḥu  those who are in a state of weakness.

Àmen 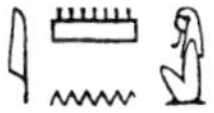 a god of generation and conception, who symbolized the invisible creative forces of Nature.

 "Àmen which art in heaven".

 "Àmen the prolific Bull".

Àmen-nathk-ruthi-Àmen  A Sûdânî form of Àmen.

Àmen-nau-àn-ka-entek-Sharu  A Sûdânî form of Àmen.

Àmen-Rā 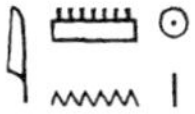 the great god of Thebes, chief element in the triad Àmen-Rā, Mut and Khensu.

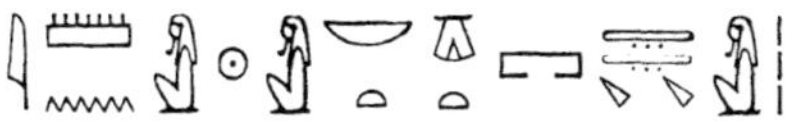 "Àmen - Rā, Lord of the throne of the Two Lands".

"King of the South and North, Ȧmen-Rā, king of the gods".

Ȧmen-Rā Ḥeru-khuti Ȧmen-Rā Harmachis.

Ȧmen-ruti Ȧmen and the two lion-gods Shu and Tefnut.

ȧmen to hide, be hidden, hidden one, something hidden. , those who hide, hider, secrecy, in secret, the hidden gods.

ȧmenu-ā those whose arms are hidden.

he whose name is hidden.

those whose bodies are hidden.

those whose mysteries are hidden.

ȧmenḥiu the divine butchers, or gods of slaughter.

Ȧmen-ḥetep 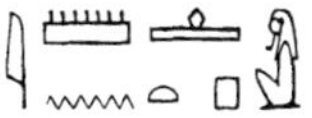 a proper name.

Ȧment ***Amenti*** ***Ȧmentet***  the "hidden" place, or land, the West, the abode of departed spirits, the name of the first division of the Other World. A late form of the name is .

 the "beautiful Ȧmentet".

Ament 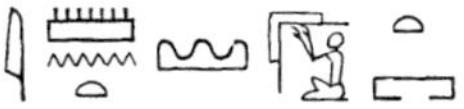 hidden place; plur. .

ȧmentiu  divine beings who live in Ȧmenti, or the West;  Ȧmenti deified, 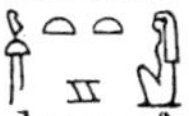 the goddess of the West, or Ȧmenti.

ȧmenti 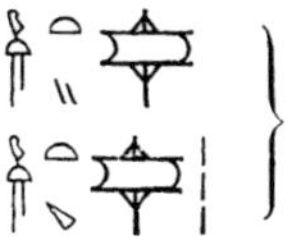 the west wind.

ȧmsi — a god of generation, fertility, fecundity, etc. Probably a form of Menu.

Ȧmseth — one of the four sons of Horus. The reading appears to be a mistake made by the Egyptians in reading *Ȧmseth* instead of *Ȧḳesth*. See Ḳesthȧ.

ȧmt — chamber, house, abode.

ȧmt — possessions, goods of a house.

ȧmt — the title-deeds of a house or property.

ȧmt — tree (?), or tent, camp.

ȧmt — light, radiance, splendour.

ȧmt — that which is in. what is in the waters. , etc.

Ȧmt-ṭehen-f — a proper name.

ȧmtiu — . . . .

àn 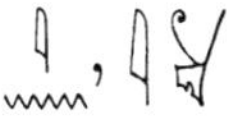 a mark of emphasis or interrogation, used sometimes as a preposition, behold! lo! cf. 

àn ķert  lo moreover.

àn (*n*)  no, not, mark of the negative. 
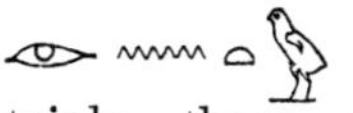 most certainly there cannot be done.  I am not.

àn às  except, unless.

àn àbu  ceaselessly.

àn urṭ  unresting.

àn petrà  unobserved.

àn maa  unseen, invisible.

àn maa-n-tu  unseen, invisible.

ȧn maa-n-tu, ***ȧn maatu*** — unseen, invisible.

ȧn mu — waterless.

ȧn meḥ, ***ȧn meḥ-f*** — undipped (?), unwashed (?). Also

ȧn nifu — airless.

ȧn netchnetchet — not to be discussed or gainsaid.

ȧn rekh, ***ȧn rekhtu*** — unknown.

ȧn kheper — never was.

ȧn sep — at no time.

ȧn smȧ — untold.

ȧn sek — indestructible,

ȧn seṭ — unsplit.

ȧn shenārtu — unturnable.

Ȧn ȧruṭ-f
Ȧn ȧarruṭ-f } the place where nothing grows.

Ȧn-erṭā-nef-bes-f-khenti-heh-f name of one of the Seven Spirits with Osiris.

Ȧn-ḥeri-ertisa name of a god.

ȧn
ȧnu } to bring, to bear, to carry. to bring, bringing, brought, those who bring; something brought.

ȧnu what is brought in, gifts, increase.

ȧntu offerings; peace-offerings.

Ȧniu name of a god.

Ȧn name of a god.

Ȧn- {*ṭes* / *ṭemt*} — a proper name.

ȧnit — a dwelling, chamber, house.

ȧnuk — I.

Ȧnu — On, Heliopolis.

ȧnnu — skin.

ȧnnuit — skin, hair, plumage.

Ȧn-ȧtef-f — "Bringer of his father", a proper name.

Ȧn ā-f — "Bringer of his arm"; the name of one of the Forty-two Judges in the Hall of Osiris.

Ȧn-urt-emkhet-uas — name of the mast in the magical boat (Chap. XCIX).

ȧnb — to dance, to rejoice.

ȧneb — wall; plur.

ȧneb mason.

ȧnep region, estate, ground.

Ȧnp

Ȧnpu The god Anubis, son of Set and Nephthys, a jackal-god who embalmed the dead, and guided the souls of the blessed to the Other World. Titles: , , .

Ȧn-mut-f "The pillar of his mother", title of a ministrant or priest.

ȧnem

skin, hide.

ȧnemsit a kind of garment.

ȧnenit a proper name?

Ȧn-ruṭ-f the god of the place where nothing grows.

Ȧnrerutṭ-f the place where nothing grows.

àner  stone.

 "Stone of Maāt", a proper name.

àner 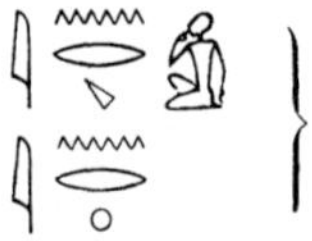 a proper name.

ànhetet 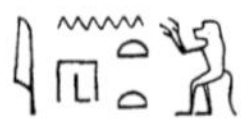 ape.

ànḥui 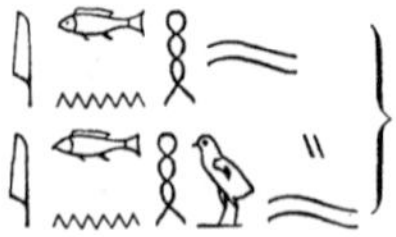 the two eye-brows.

ànḥu-tu  surrounded.

Àn-ḥer  "Bearer of the sky"; an ancient god of Upper Egypt who is often associated with .

Àn-ḥer  name of the warder of the Sixth Ārit.

Àn-ḥetep  one of the Forty-two gods in the Hall of Osiris.

ànes, **ànsi** 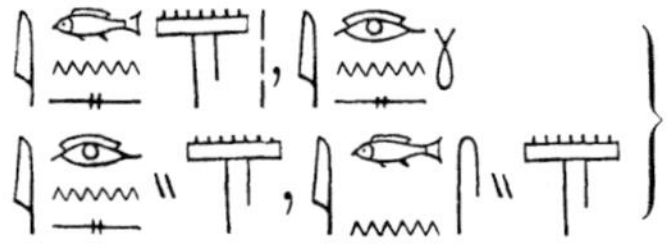 name of a ceremonial garment.

ànset 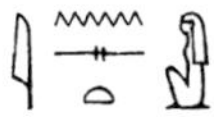 a goddess (?).

ȧneq 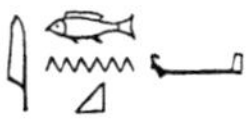 to bind, tie on, to fasten.

ȧnqet  to embrace, to surround.

ȧnqet 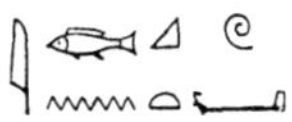 name of a tool, or instrument, "clincher", rope (?).

ȧnt 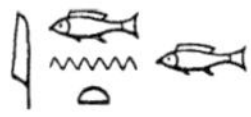 name of a mythological fish which swam before the boat of Rā.

ȧnt 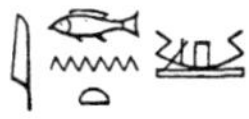 name of a solar boat.

ȧnt 
ȧntet, ȧnti 
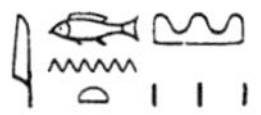
} a valley, especially a funerary valley.

ȧnti  pillars, columns.

Ȧnti 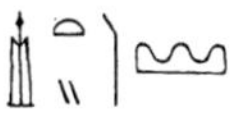 the hill-folk who lived in the Eastern Desert of Ta-sti 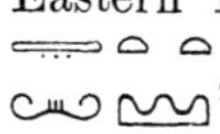, or Nubia.

ȧnti 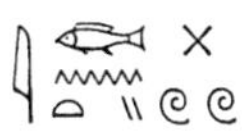 a hindrance, obstruction.

ȧntiu  those who have nothing, the destitute, those who are not, or do not exist.

ȧntet 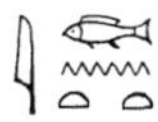 to go back.

ȧntet  cord, fetter, chain.

Ȧn-ṭebu  the name of a god.

ȧnetch 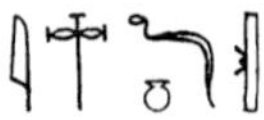 to incline, to bow.

ȧnetch ḥer 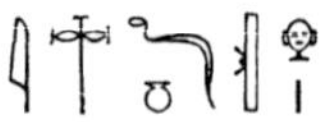 to incline the head to a suppliant, to turn the face towards.

ȧr  to tie together.

ȧr  if, now.

ȧr sa 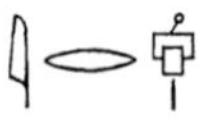 if after, now as for.

ȧr ḳert  if moreover, however.

ȧr, **ȧru**, **ȧrit** 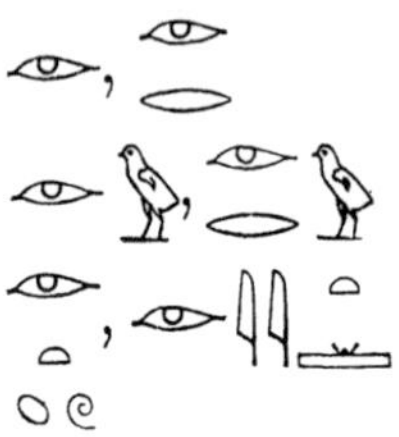 to do, to make, to create, to form, to fashion; ,  doing, making, creator; ,  made, wrought,  made;  make ye;  things done.

àrit  to work the heart, to think.

 to make or prepare a path or road.

 to prepare food.

 to celebrate the Haker festival.

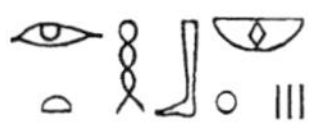 to keep festivals.

 to make protection, to perform ceremonies for the protection of some one.

 to work for successful results, to strive for peace.

 to perform a transformation.

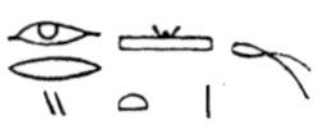 to make, or write, or recite, a book.

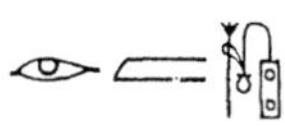 to do into writing, to make a copy, to write.

àriu 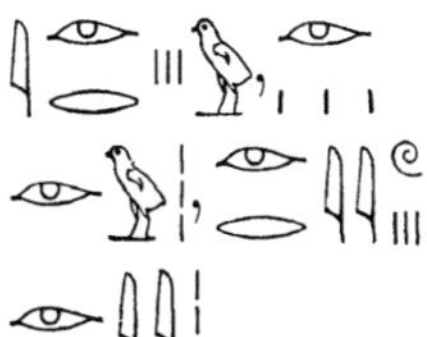 doers, makers, workers.

àriu  workmen; fem. .

årit work, something done.

actions, deeds, labours, works, things done or to be done.

år, åri used as an auxiliary verb, see *passim*. "Maker of truth, or righteousness", a title of Osiris, Hathor, and other gods.

åri-Maāt

Åri-em-åb-f the name of one of the Forty-two Judges in the Hall of Osiris.

Åri-en-åb-f

Åri-nef-tchesef name of a plank or peg in the magical boat.

Åri-entuten-em-meska-en-Mer-ur uṭebtu-en-Suti name of the leather bands in the magical boat.

Åri-ḥetch-f a proper name.

Årisi a proper name.

åru form, attribute, figure, image; plur. .

ȧri belonging to: their name; their seat; their bull (var.); their length.

ȧri a person in charge of, or belonging to, or attendant upon something, watcher, porter, guardian.

guardian of my flesh.

guardian, or guardians, of the sky.

keeping watch about, or around.

keepers of my mouth.

watching the limbs.

keeping guard over the neck.

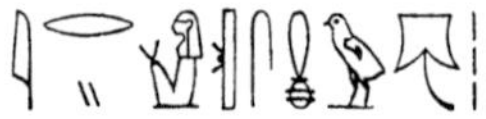 belonging to the leathers.

 guarding the earth.

ȧri āa  porter, doorkeeper, guardian ; plur. .

 porter of the door of Ȧmentet.

ȧriu ārrtu 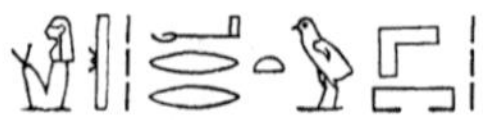 warders of the Ārits.

ȧri mākhait  warder of the Scales.

ȧri ḥemit 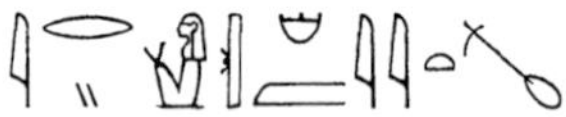 warder of the oar, *i. e.*, steersman.

ȧri ḥenbiu  warder of the cultivated lands.

ȧru khut  guardians of light, *i. e.*, beings of light.

ȧri sȧpu  keepers of the records, or books of doom.

ȧri sebkhet-f  keeper of his pylon.

ȧri qeb en meru en khet 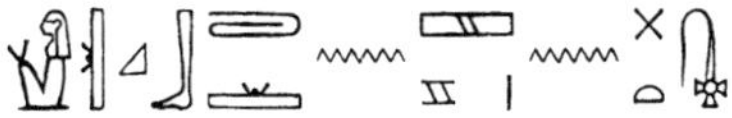 keeper of the Bend of the Lake of Fire.

ȧrārti 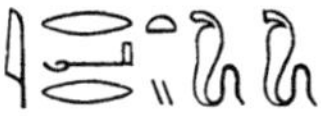 two uraei.

Ȧruhut  a proper name.

ȧrp 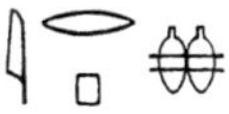 wine.

ȧrpu  ... Chap. CLXIX. 1.

ȧref  an emphatic particle.

ȧrmā  with.

ȧrek  a particle.

ȧrt  to flow, what flows.

ȧrt  Chapter LB. 1.

ȧrtet 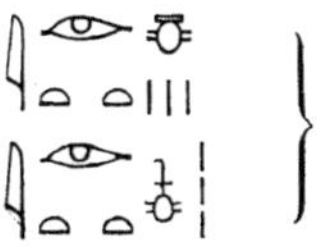 milk.

ȧh  calamity.

ȧhabu  joy, gladness, cries of joy.

àhen  a kind of wood.

àhehi  rejoicings, cries of joy.

Àḥ  the Moon-god,

àḥ  ... Book of Breathings II. 22.

àḥ  collar, embrace, to ward off.

àḥ, àḥu  ox; plur.  oxen, .

àḥai  a sistrum bearer.

àḥāu 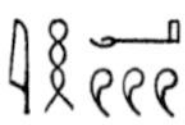 members.

àḥi 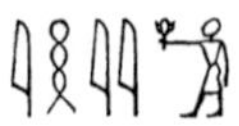

àḥu  the name of one of the Forty-two Judges in the Hall of Osiris; a proper name; .

àḥu  fields (?), measuring cords.

àḥu  wooden tools or instruments.

àḥui  the two *àḥui* gods = 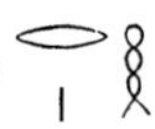 .

Àḥibit name of a god.

àḥunnu youth, child.

àḥemu (?) ... Chap. XCII. 13.

àḥti throat.

Aḥti a name of Osiris.

Àkh O!, would that, O tell me.

àkhabu grain.

àkhib to speak.

àkhemu urṭu a class of stars.

àkhekhu, ***àkhekhui*** darkness, night.

Àkhsesef a proper name.

Às a proper name.

ȧs — behold, to wit, namely, , , , , , , .

ȧsu — intestines.

ȧsu — winds.

ȧsu (?) — ... Chap. CXXVII B. 17.

ȧsi, ȧsu — , tomb, sepulchre.

ȧsu — recompense or in return for, in place of.

ȧs — , to pass forward, to advance.

ȧsu, *ȧsi* — to decay, to rot, destruction. decay,   incorruptible.

Ȧsȧr — the god Osiris, son of Seb and Nut, husband of Isis, and father of Horus. The deceased is usually identified with Osiris and is called by his name.

Ȧsȧr Ȧnpu — Osiris-Anubis.

Ȧsȧr ānkhti — Osiris the Living One.

Ȧsȧr Unnefer — Osiris Un-Nefer.

Ȧsȧr Utetti — Osiris the begetter.

Ȧsȧr-ba-erpi — Osiris, soul of the divine Image.

Ȧsȧr-bati-erpit — Osiris, twin soul of the divine image.

Ȧsȧr Ptaḥ neb ānkh — Osiris-Ptaḥ, Lord of Life.

Ȧsȧr-em-pesuru — Osiris in Pesuru.

Ȧsȧr em pesṭ ent nut-f

Ȧsȧr em Seḥnen

Ȧsȧr em Ṭenit

Ȧsȧr nub ḥeḥ Osiris, gold of eternity.

Ȧsȧr neb ānkh Osiris, Lord of Life.

Ȧsȧr neb er tcher Osiris, Lord to the boundary, *i. e.*, of All.

Asȧr Netchesti Osiris the Less.

Ȧsȧr Ḥenti Osiris of the two crocodiles.

Ȧsȧr Ḥeru Osiris-Horus.

Asȧr Ḥeru-khuti Tem Osiris-Harmachis.

Ȧsȧr ḥer ȧb semt Osiris in the funerary mountain.

Ȧsȧr ḥer shāu-f Osiris on his sand.

Ȧsȧr khent Ȧbṭu Osiris, President of Abydos.

Ȧsȧr khenti Ȧmenti Osiris, President of Amenti, or the Other World.

Ȧsȧr khenti Ȧmentiu  Osiris, President of those who dwell in the Other World.

Ȧsȧr khent Un 

Ȧsȧr khenti 

Ȧsȧr khenti Nefer (?) 

Ȧsȧr khenti nut-f 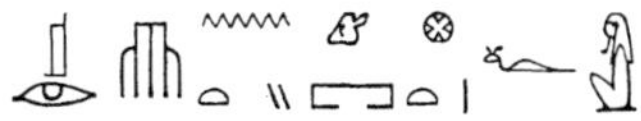

Ȧsȧr khenti nestu 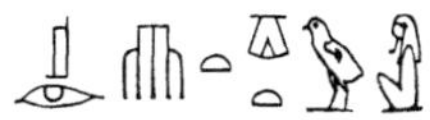

Ȧsȧr khenti Ru-stau 

Ȧsȧr khenti seḥ ḥemt 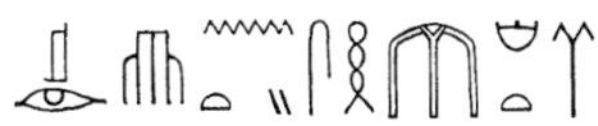

Ȧsȧr sa Nut 

Ȧsȧr saa 

Ȧsȧr Sab (or *Ḳeb*?) 

Ȧsȧr Saḥ 

Ȧsȧr Sekri	
Ȧsȧr Taiti	
Ȧsȧr tua	
Ȧsȧr Ṭem ur	
Ȧsȧr Teḳaiti	
Ȧsȧrtiu	beings like unto Osiris.
ȧsi	who?, what?
ȧsp	grief (?), misery, wretchedness.
ȧsfet	faults, sins, evil deeds, sinners, evil ones.
ȧsfeti	faults, sins, evil deeds, sinners, evil ones.
ȧsfetiu	evil fiends, sinners.
ȧsentu	cords, ropes.
ȧser	tamarisk (?), plants, herbs, grass.
Ȧsert	name of a city.

àsha  linen, some kind of woven stuff.

Àses 
Àsest  a city in the seventh Àat.

àses  to rope in, to bind.

àsstu  a rope.  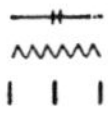 those whose heads are tied.

àsk  behold, lo!

àst, àstu 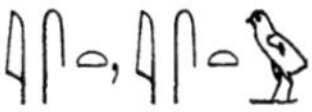
àsth  behold.

Àst 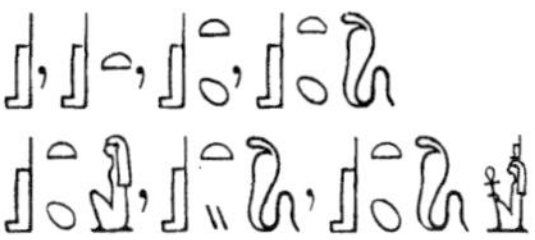 the goddess Isis.

àst 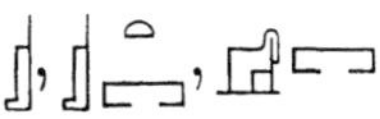 seat, place, habitation, abode, shrine; plur. 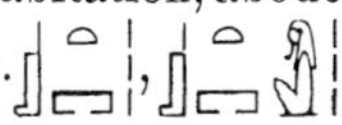.

àst àb 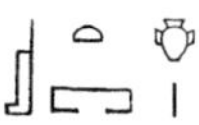 place of the heart, heart's chosen place.

àst āāui 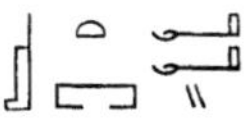 place of the two hands.

ȧst urt  great place, *i. e.*, the sky.

ȧst utchat 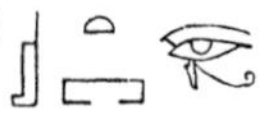 seat of the Utchat, resting place of the Eye of Rā.

ȧst maāt  the place where the Law is administered.

ȧst ḥert  heaven.

ȧst ḥeḥ 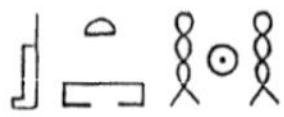 everlasting abode.

ȧst Ḥeqet 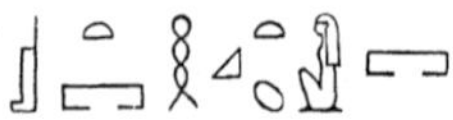 shrine of Ḥeqet.

ȧst ḥetep 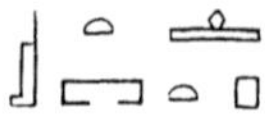 place of repose.

ȧst ḥetep ȧb 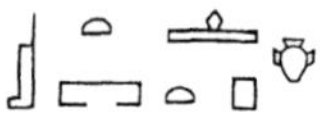 seat of rest of the heart.

ȧst shetau en Ḥeru 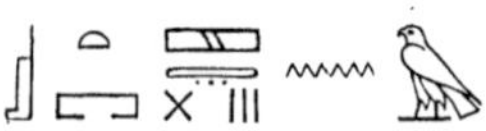 the secret abodes of Horus.

ȧst qebḥ  place of cool water, bath.

ȧst taa  place of fire in the Other World.

ȧst tchesert 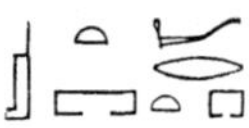 shrine, sanctuary, holy place.

ȧsṭ 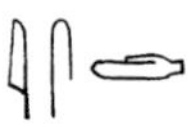 to tremble, make to shake.

Ȧsṭenu  name of a god.

ȧsteḥ (?) — to beat down.

ȧstheḥt (?) — to beat down.

Ȧsṭes — name of a god.

Ȧstcheṭet — name of a district.

ȧshāt — knife, slaughter.

ȧshep — light, radiance.

ȧshpit — chamber, hut, house.

ȧsheset — see ȧqeset.

ȧshesh — to be carried away.

ȧshet — subsistence, oppression, oppressor (?).

ȧshta — tree.

ȧsheṭ — persea tree, trees, plants.

ȧk — injury.

ȧkebu hair.

ȧkeb, ȧkebu , ***ȧkebet*** lamentation, wailing, weeping.

ȧkebit wailers, mourners.

Ȧkeniu a proper name.

Ȧkentaukha-kheru the porter of the Sixth Ārit.

Ȧkenti a proper name.

Ȧksi a city of the Ninth Ȧat.

Ȧqen name of a god.

Ȧqeh name of a god.

ȧqer perfect, strong, complete, skilful; plur. , a skilful scribe.

Ȧqrit a goddess.

Ȧqert-khenti-ḥet-set the name of one of the Seven Cows.

ȧqḥu to enter.

ȧqeset who, what, where,

ȧqet wine, beer.

ȧqeṭu builders, masons, architects.

ȧqeṭs bad, wicked, evil.

Ȧḳau name of a god.

ȧḳap
ȧḳep } rain-storm, tempest.

Ȧḳeru
Ȧḳeriu } gods of the Other World.

Ȧḳert
Ȧḳertet } the name of the Other World of Heliopolis.

Ȧḳert-khent-Ȧset-s the name of one of the Seven Cows.

ȧḳeḳit a kind of garment, robe.

ȧt father.

àt (for ***ànt***)
àti (for ***ànti***)
àtet
— negation, no, none, not, cannot, without, impotence, plur. things which are not, evil beings; without, destitute, abjects.

àti ākhem — unquenchable.

àti uteb — immutable.

àti men — painless.

àti maa — invisible, not seeing, blind.

àtu rekh — unknown.

àtu khesef — irresistible.

àtu àsi — incorruptible.

àti sek — undecaying.

àti shes — impassable.

àt — emanation.

Àtaru-àm-tcher-qemtu-renu-par-sheta — a proper name.

àteb	territory, region.
àtef	father; dual , ; plur. , father gods, Father Osiris, Father Kheperà.
Àtem	see under Tem, Temu.
àten	the solar disk.
	the god of the solar disk.
	the two-horned disk.
àtennu	appellations.
àter, **àtru**	river, canal, water-flood, stream; plur.
àtert	one half of the sky, or world.

ȧtert meḥt 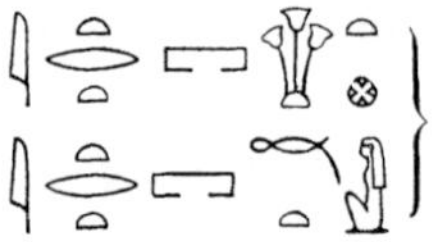 the northern half of the sky.

ȧtert shemā 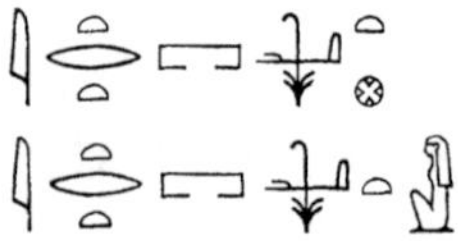 the southern half of the sky.

ȧterti

ȧturti  the two halves of the sky.

Ȧthabu  name of a city.

ȧthḥu 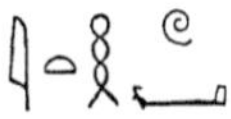 to drag, pull, draw.

Ȧtektaukehaqkheru 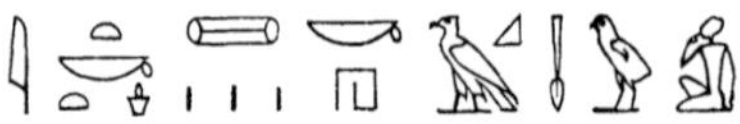 a proper name.

ȧṭ  oppression, oppressed one.

ȧṭ  to be deaf.

Ȧṭu  a city of the Eleventh Ȧat.

ȧṭu  children.

ȧṭeb  region, domain; plur. 

ȧṭmȧ 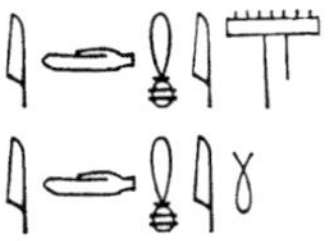 a kind of cloth, a ceremonial garment.

ȧṭen 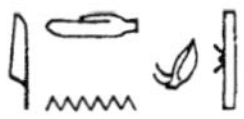 deputy, vicar, chief?

ȧṭent  division, a separation.

ȧṭerit 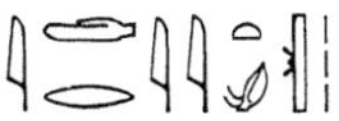 misfortunes, calamities.

ȧṭḥu  papyrus swamps, the Delta generally.

ȧṭeṭiu  those who injure.

ȧthi (**ȧti**)  prince, sovereign, king.

ȧthen 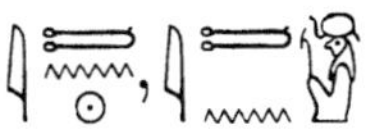 the solar disk, the god of the solar disk.

ȧtheth 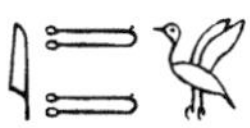 to hover, to alight.

ȧtcha  robber, man of violence, violence.

Ā.

ā hand, arm, paw of an animal; dual , , ; plur. , power ; at once, straightway, immediately, ancestor (see ṭep ā); "Eater of the Arm", name of a god, a flight, action of battle, place of yesterday, before.

Āāiu, etc. the name of the posts of the magic net (Chapter XCIX).

ā, āa house, dwelling.

āa , to advance, journey onwards.

āa, **āatu** , , , door, gate; plur. , , , , , , ; the two leaves of a door , , .

gods of the doors.

the two doors of the sky.

the two doors of truth.

the two doors of the sky.

the two doors of Ta-qebḥ.

āa — great, large, mighty, to be great;

āat

great one, great god, great goddess; plur.

āaui — twice great.

āaāa

āati — two great goddesses.

āa-ȧb — great of heart, *i. e.*, proud, arrogant.

great forms, *i. e.*, possessing many forms.

āat ur sep sen  most exceedingly great.

āa baiu  great of souls, *i. e.*, most valorous.

āa mertu 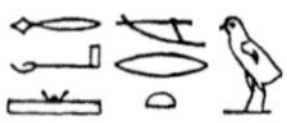 greatly beloved.

āa neruȧ 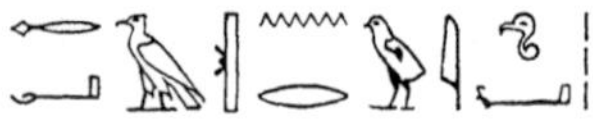 greatly victorious.

āa rennu  possessing many names.

āa khāu  possessing many crowns.

āa kheperu  of many transformations.

āa senṭ  he who is greatly feared.

āa sekhemu 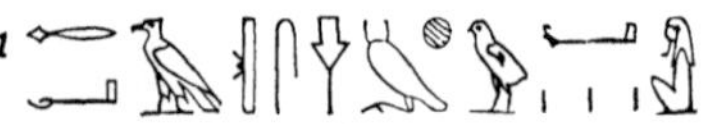 great one of powers.

āa sheps  most holy.

āa shefshefit  most terrible, or awful one.

Āa-kheru  "mighty of speech", the warder of the Seventh Ārit.

Āat-em-khut  "great one in the horizon", a proper name.

āā 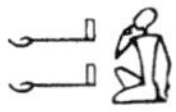 to eat?

āā 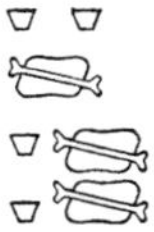 heir, inheritance, heritage, to inherit.

āat  stone amulet, plur. 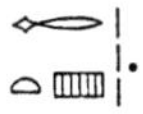.

āt, āāt  members, limbs, body.

āātu-pu-ent Kher-neter 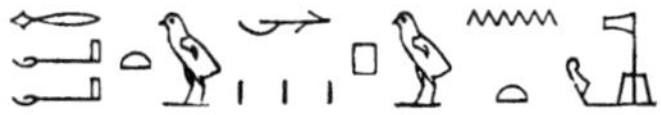 name of the oar-rests in the magic boat (Chap. CXIX).

Āaṭi  the name of one of the Forty-two Judges in the Hall of Osiris.

āu, āāu  ass.

āān 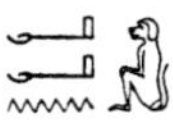
āānā 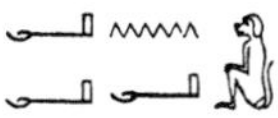
āānāu  ape, monkey.

āu 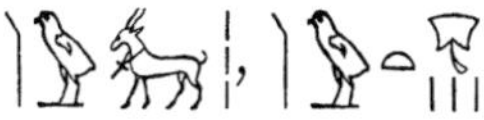
āut  animals, quadrupeds.

āu  sins, offences (vol. II, 148, 4).

āua
āuau — to be strong, to act violently, to plunder, to rob, to oppress, vanquish, etc. , violence, wrong, evil act, evil doer, robber; ill treated, oppressed; (Chap. XVII, Nebseni, l. 25).

āuai — violence.

āun
āunu — , to be strong, violent, fierce.

āun-ȧb (?) — to be of a fierce disposition, violence.

āuq — pool, marsh, watery ground.

āb — , with , opposite, before, in front of, thus; , , , , , .

āba (**uba**) — opposition.

āb altar, table of offerings.

āb to present offerings, to offer up a sacrifice.

ābuaa to bring before, to present.

āab, **āabet, ābet** offering, sacrifice; plur.

ābai (**āabai**) sacrifice, offering, a priest who read the Liturgies.

āb (**uāb**), **ābu** (**uābu**), **ābet** (**uābet**) clean, pure, holy, to be pure, to purify, to sprinkle or wash ceremonially.

āb (**uāb**) libation, purification; plur.

āb (**uāb**) libationer, a man ceremonially pure.

āb (*uāb*) pool of water used for purificatory purposes.

ābu (*uābu*) clean raiment, holy apparel.

ābet (*uābet*) water-house, bath, clean place; plur. ; great pure place

ābti (*uābti*) double holy place.

āb (*uāb*) **āāui** , clean-handed.

āb (*uāb*) **ru** clean-mouthed.

āb (*uāb*) **ḥeru** clean-faced beings.

ābu (*uābu*) propitiatory offerings.

Āb-ur (*Uāb-ur*) a title of Osiris.

āba (*uba*) , to open or force a way, or passage, through something.

āba (*uba*) **ru** to open the mouth.

āba (*uba*)
ābet (*ubet*)
ābata (*ubata*) — entrance, opening.

āba — to see.

ābat (*ubat*) — fore-court of a temple.

Āba-ta (***Uba-ta***) — "Opener of the Earth", a name of a god.

Ābau-taui — the name of a god.

āb — horn; , two-horned; plur. ; broad-horned; *neb ābui* "lord of two horns" = Dhu 'l-Ḳarnên, a title of Alexander the Great.

ābiu — divine ancestors.

ābeb — to see.

āp (*āap*) , — to fly.

Āpep	the arch-enemy of Rā. Copt. ⲁⲫⲱⲫ "giant".
Āpef	name of a fiend.
āper	to be equipped or provided with, furnished with; provided.
Āper / ***Āpert***	the name of a city and city-god.
āpesh	tortoise, turtle.
āpshait	a kind of beetle. Perhaps the weevil, the Muta Jambi, or "head of God", of the Bakuba of the Kasai District in the Congo Free State. (See T. A. Joyce in *Man*, vol. IX, No. 1, p. 3.)
āfa	filth.
āfau	food.
āfent	wig, headdress; plur.
āftet	place, abode, chest.

āfṭet place, abode, chest.

ām to eat, consume, devour; eaters.

āmam to eat, to understand, to comprehend.

āmt what is eaten, food.

ām àb "to eat the heart", *i. e.*, become angry and rage.

āmam-àrit "Eater of the Eye"; name of a god.

Ām-āu "Eater of the Ass"; name of a fiend and enemy of Rā.

Ām-àsfetti "Eater of Sinners"; name of a god.

Ām-baiu "Eater of souls"; name of a fiend.

Ām-ḥeḥ "Eater of eternity".

Ām-khaibitu "Eater of Shades"; the name of one of the Forty-two Judges in the Hall of Osiris.

Āmām "Devourer"; the name of the Eater of the dead.

Ām-mit "Devourer of the dead".

Ām-mit a consuming serpent goddess.

Ān a proper name.

ān, ***āni*** tablet, board, writing palette.

ān to turn back. Partic. plur. those who turn away, or return.

ānu a mythological fish.

Ānpet a name of the city of Mendes.

ānkh to live, to live upon, to feed upon, life, living one, living; alive. Copt. ⲱⲛϩ. the living one, a name of Osiris.

ānkhu,
ānkhiu — the living, men and women, title of the blessed dead.

ānkh tchetta — the living for ever. — life from death.

ānkh user — life and power.

ānkh utcha senb — life, strength and health.

ānkhet — life.

ānkhet — victuals.

Ānkhti — a name of Osiris.

ānkh — a kind of unguent.

Ānkhet pu ent Sebek neb Bakhau — a proper name.

Ānkh-em-bu — "Eater of abominable things".

Ānkh-em-fentu  "Eater of worms"; name of the warder of the Fifth Ārit.

ānkhui 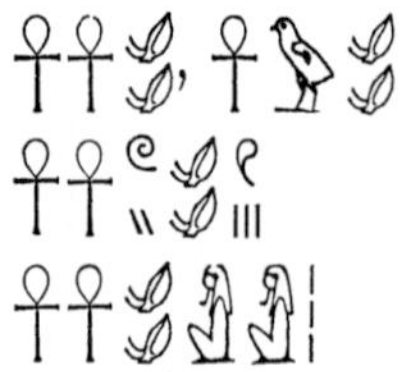 the two ears.

ānkhȧmu  flowers, or aromatic plants.

ānt  ring.

ānt  to be covered with something.

ānt  claw, talon, hook, nail of the hand or foot, "Claw  of Ptaḥ"; a proper name.

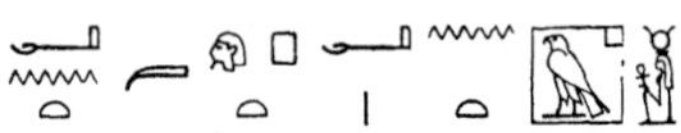 "Claw on the hand of Hathor"; a proper name.

ānti 

ānṭ 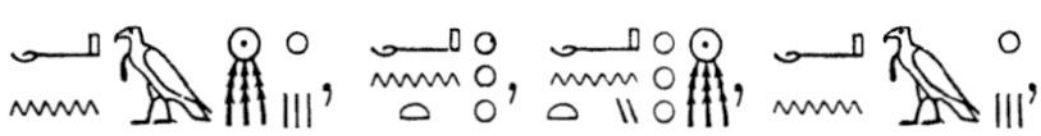

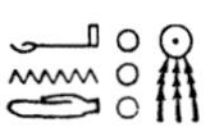 myrrh, unguent (?).

ānti — a preparation of myrrh used by women.

ānṭu — light, radiance.

ānṭ — evil.

ānṭu — darkness.

Ānṭi — the name of one of the Forty-two Judges in the Hall of Osiris.

ār — an animal of the goat species.

ār — to approach, to bring, to come, to arrive; ; divine beings who approach.

āra — to find (?).

ārār — jawbone.

ārārt — uraeus.

ārāti — two uraci goddesses.

two very large uraei.

the living serpent goddesses.

ārit tool, lintel of a door.

ārit hall, chamber; plur. .
The Seven Ārits .

ārfi bundle, purse.

ārrt
ārrit hall, mansion; plur. .

Ārq to bind, to tie, girdle, to be completed.

ārq to swear.

Ārq-ḥeḥ name of a city.

ārq end; end of the earth.

ārqi last day of the lunar month.

ārt jaw, jawbone.

ārti the two jaws.

ārtu houses, abodes, mansions.

āḥ moon.

āḥ 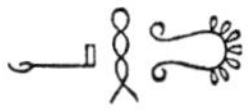 to surround, embrace.

āḥa 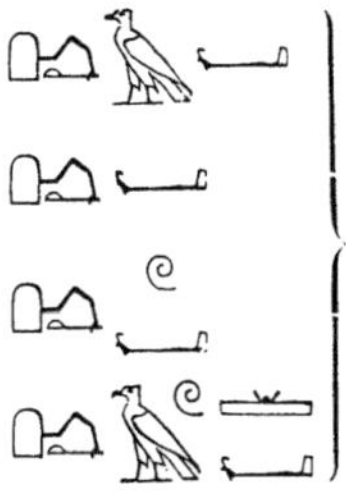
āḥau
to fight, do battle, wage war;  fighter,  fightings.

āḥa-ā  to fight bravely (?).

āḥa-tu  fight, contest, struggle.

āḥau  fighting implements, weapons.

āḥaui  the two Fighters, *i. e.*, Horus and Set.

Āḥau ḥeru  "Fighting faces", a name of certain gods.

āḥāt 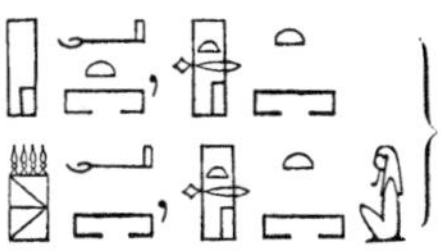 great house, palace.

āḥā 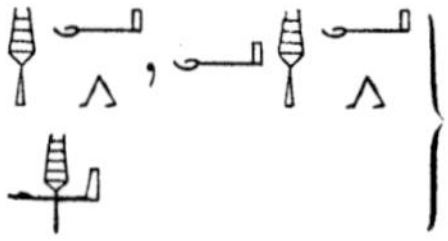 to stand up, to withstand. 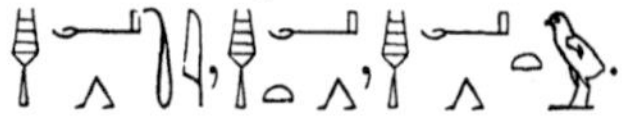.

āḥā  as an auxiliary verb:   and see *passim*.

āḥā 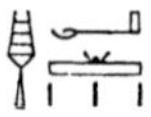 stability.

āḥāu  condition, state, position.

āḥā
āḥāu
āḥāt 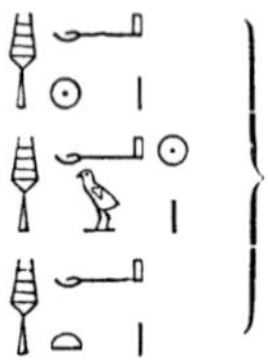 time, season or duration of life, life, a contemporary. 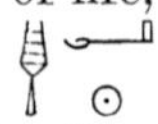  .

 period from life, or in life.

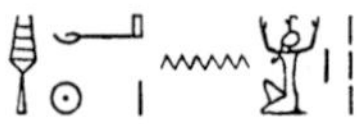 period of eternity.

āḥāu  noon-day.

āḥāu 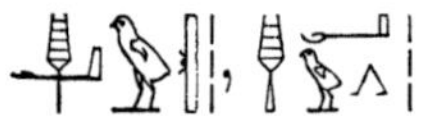 supports.

āḥāu  stores, food, provisions.

 folk who are provisioned.

āḥāit boat.

āḥāt tomb.

ākh to spread out the heavens, or sky.

Ākhtuset a class of divine beings. The variants are:
ākhmiu.
àukhu-seku.
ākhsemiu.

ākha to fly, to soar; *ākhai* flying.

ākha to sleep.

ākhan
ākhanet } to close the eye.

ākhu fire-altars.

ākhem
ākhemu } to quench, to extinguish; quenched.

ākhemu 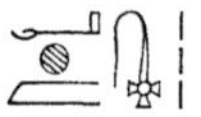

ākhmiu  } quenchers, those who extinguish.

ākhem  figure of a god.

ākhemu  figures of gods.

ākhmet  river banks.

Ākhen-åriti (?)**-f** 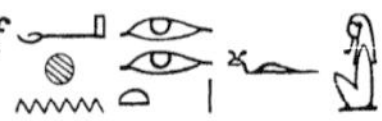 a proper name.

ākhekhau  serpent-fiends, monsters.

ākhekhu  "Darkness"; a proper name.

āsha 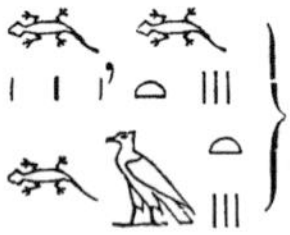 to be much or many, manifold.

 many reeded.

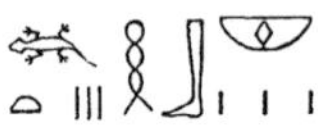 of multitudinous festivals.

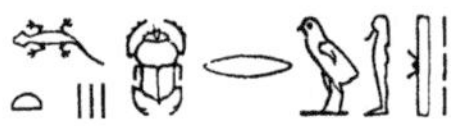 of many forms.

 loud voiced to speak.

āshau 

āshat  } crowd, multitude.

āshat  crowd, multitude.

āsh  to call, to invoke, to cry out.

āshu 

 evil speech.

āsh 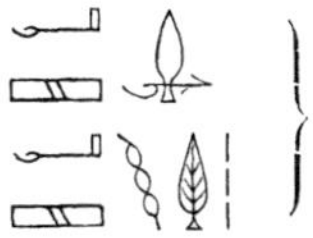 cedar, or acacia, tree, cedar gum.

āshāsht 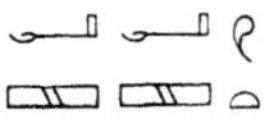 part of the body.

āshāt 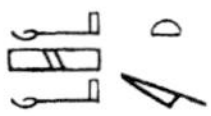 knife.

āshem  the forms in which the gods appear upon earth.

āshemu, *āshemiu*  crocodiles. A variant gives 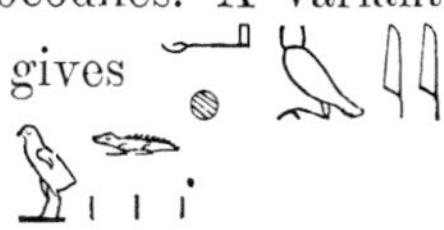

āshashat  gullet.

Ākesh  name of a city.

āq  to enter, go in.

āqiu those who enter.

āqet things which enter.

āq pert entrance and exit.

Āq-ḥer-àmi-unnut-f "He who enters in his hour"; a proper name.

āqu cakes, loaves of bread.

āqa to present bread (?). Chap. XCIX, 3.

āq maāt (?) exact truth (?), just.

āqa to keep the mean, right, exact, true, just, truth, to be in the middle.

to be exactly over the heart.

āqau truth, right, justice.

Āqan the name of a god.

āqi part of a boat.

āq, āqa  rope, cordage, tackle of a boat.

Āqennu  the name of a city.

āḳa  unguent.

āḳu  to be burned.

āt  domain.

āt 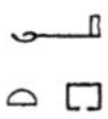 hall, palace.

āt  member, limb; plur. , 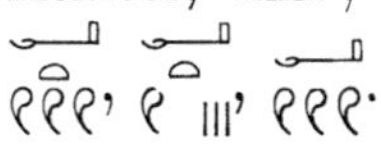.

Āti 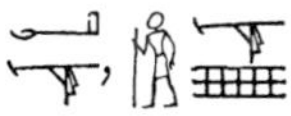 name of the ninth nome ot Lower Egypt.

āteptu  grain, seeds.

āter  provisions.

āṭ (*ānṭ*) 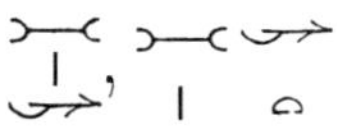 pole of a net with curved ends.

Āṭ (*Ānṭ*)  name of a god.

āṭ (*ānṭ*)  domain, territory, soil.

āṭ (**ānṭ**) to split, to divide.

Āṭ (**Ānṭ**) the morning boat of the sun.

āṭu name of a mythological fish.

āṭurtu (a mistake ?)

Ātch-ur "Great splitter"; name of a god.

ātchet (**āntchet**) fixed, firm.

U.

. . . . Chap. CLXVIII. Circle X, 14, 2.

u they, them, their.

u district, region.

Ua a proper name.

ua, **uau** to depart, go away, be afar off; remote.

ua, ***uau*** way, path, road; plur.

uau waterway, stream.

uauau radiance, light.

uau flame, fire.

uau chains, fetters.

uauu to speak evil, blaspheme.

uauiuait hair.

uai to destroy, overcome, gain the mastery over.

Uaipu a cow-goddess.

uab flower, blossom.

Uamemti the name of one of the Forty-two Judges in the Hall of Osiris.

uart ropes, cordage.

Uarekht (?) a mythological region.

Uart-neter-semsu a proper name.

uaḥ to place, to set, to fix, to add to, permanent, abiding.

to add to something.

uaḥit libation vessels.

uaḥuu mummy bandages.

uaḥtu to mummify.

uakh
uakhet } "Green"; the name of a pool in the Elysian Fields.

uas sceptre.

uas contentment, happiness.

Uast Thebes.

uash to worship, be adored; two-fold worship.

Uaḳ the name of a festival.

uat way, road, path; plur. , great roads, good roads, all roads, ways of the dead; the two roads.

eastern roads.

western roads.

northern roads.

southern roads.

uatch sceptre, staff, stick.

uatch tablet of green faïence, amulet.

uatch unguent, sulphate of copper eye-paint.

uatchu sulphate of copper.

uatch shemāt sulphate of copper of the south.

uatchet a kind of linen.

uatch to make to flourish, be green, vigorous, to blossom, be new, fresh.

uatchet green.

uatchet green things, plants, herbs.

uatchu *q. v.*

Uatch-ȧriti (?) "Green Eyes"; a proper name.

Uatch-ur
Uatch-urȧ "Great Green Sea"; *i. e.*, the Mediterranean.

Uatch-nesert "Green Flame"; the name of one of the Forty-two Judges in the Hall of Osiris.

Uatchit a goddess of fire.

the two fire-goddesses, Isis and Nephthys.

uatchit abode, house.

uȧ I, me.

uȧa — boat, boat of Rā.

uȧaui — the two boats of Rā, the boats of morning and evening.

uȧa en Maāti — the boat of Maāt.

uȧa en ḥeḥ — "Boat of Millions of Years".

uȧn — to become worms.

uā, *uāu* — One, the One, *i. e.*, God. One of the gods;

One God (Osiris); One (fem.).

uā — one; fem. ; , being one, or alone; to be one .

uā—ki one ... the other; one embraced the other; fem. ... ; one in one; one of one.

uā = indefinite article ,

uā neb any one, each one, every one.

uā uāu one alone, only one.

uāu alone. Also and .

uāuti solitude.

uā with at once, all at once; and compare , .

uāt in a piece of cloth.

Uāau the herald of the Third Ārit.

uār passage.

uār to depart.

uārt passage, the name of a place.

uārt thigh; the two thighs.

"thigh" of water.

"thigh" of the lake.

"thigh" surrounding.

"thigh" of iron whereon is the station of the gods.

that "thigh" of Kher-āḥa.

that "thigh" whereon is the House of the Moon.

uārt stream.

uu evil, evil one.

uu region, district;

ui sign of the dual. two very mighty gods.

Ui a proper name.

uit chamber.

uben to rise (of a luminary), to shine; rising and setting;

ubennu, ***ubentu*** rays of light.

ubennu to flow.

ubekh, ***ubekht*** to shine, light up, shining, blazing.

ubes water-flood.

ubesu beings of fire, sparks (?).

Ubes-ḥer-per-em-khetkhet "Fiery face, coming forward in retreating"; a proper name.

ubeṭ to be scalded, to set fire to, to burn up.

ufa — to chance on, to light upon.

umet — a garment.

umet — the middle (?).

umet — walls, fortifications, building.

un — lightness, defect.

un, unen — to be, being, existence, to become, to exist; as an auxiliary verb see *passim*.

unt, *unent* — being, existence; plur. those who are, things which are.

uniu — human beings.

un maā — in very truth.

un — to open, opener, opening; opened.

uniu, ***uneniu*** } openers, scatterers.

un ḥer to open the face, *i. e.*, show the face, to appear; ; to open the mouth , .

un shrine.

un shaved.

un, ***unnu*** } to pull out the hair.

un, uni, unt , , to walk, run, rise upright; runners.

unun, ***unn-unn*** , , } to run, stand up.

unun to sow seed.

Unȧset name of a city.

unām unguent.

Uniu, or ***Unniu*** name of a city.

unini light.

uni light, defective.

Unen-em-ḥetep a division of the Sekhet-Ȧaru.

unb flower, bloom; plur.

unpet flowers, blossoms.

Unpepet ent Ḥet-Ḥeru "Flower of Hathor"; a proper name.

unef , to remove, to uncover, to unloose.

unem
unemi
unemt
the right side, the right as opposed to left.

unem , , to eat, see *Ȧm*.

unnu evil, wrong, defect.

Unnu Hermopolis, the city of Thoth.

unnuiti sacrificer.

unnut a brief space of time, a moment, an hour, a season, interval. Plur.

Unnut goddess of the hour.

Un-Nefer, ***Unen-nefer***, ***Unen-Neferu***, ***Unen-Neferu*** A title of Osiris, meaning something like "the well-doing Being". Coptic forms of the name are ⲟⲩⲉⲛⲉⲃⲣ̅ⲉ, ⲟⲩⲉⲛⲟⲃⲣ, ⲟⲩⲉⲛⲟⲃⲣⲓ, ⲱⲛⲟⲫⲣⲉ, etc.

Un-Nefer-Rā.

Un-Nefer, son of Nut.

Un-ḥāt a proper name.

unkh, ***unkhu*** to dress, to array oneself, to put on a garment.

unkh to tie, untie, set loose.

unkh a garment.

Unes the metropolis of the XIXth Nome of Lower Egypt.

unshu wolves.

Unt a city of the Twelfth Ȧat.

Unti the name of a god.

un tini be ye.

unṭu mankind, people, kinsfolk, relatives.

Unth name of a district or country.

ur to be great, great, mighty, supreme, powerful.

ur, uru great one (God); plur.

urt great one (fem.), goddess.

uru dual masc. "two great".

urti dual fem. "two great goddesses".

two very great goddesses.

ur great man, chief, prince, nobleman, master; princess. Plur. masc. ; plur. fem.

ur sep sen × doubly great.

ur as comparative, ... greater than.

ur as superlative, greatest of 5 gods.

ur in titles etc.:

ur  a joint of meat, haunch, carcase;  

Ur-at  "great of moment", a proper name.

Urit  name of a city.

urit  hall, house, room.

Ur-ȧrit-s 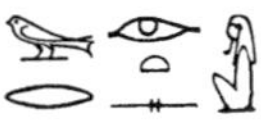 a proper name.

Ur-peḥui-f  a proper name.

Ur-ma  title of the high-priest of Heliopolis (?).

Ur-maat  a proper name.

Ur-mertus-ṭeshert-shenu 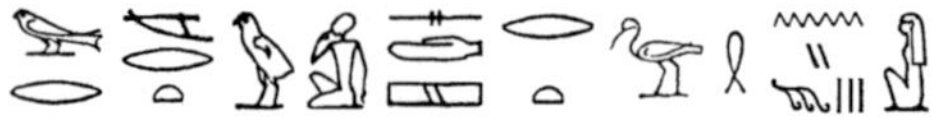

Ur-mertis-ṭeshert-shenu  "The red-haired one who is greatly beloved"; name of one of the Seven Cows.

Ur-ḥekau  a deity who is mighty in words of power, a god or goddess of magic.

Ur-kherp-ḥem 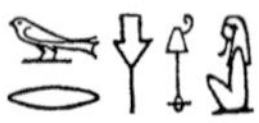 "chief master of the blacksmith's tool"; a title of the high-priest of Memphis.

Ur-senu  chief of the physicians.

urer 

urert 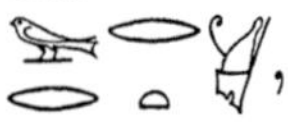, 

urertu 

the name of a crown.   the gods who wear the *urert* Crown.

urḥ 

urḥu 

to smear or rub with unguent, to anoint.

Urḥetchati  two goddesses of Heliopolis.

urs  a pillow, head-rest.

ursh 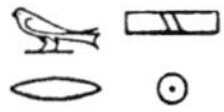 to pass the day, to watch; 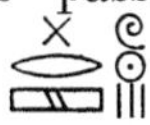 watchers.

Urek 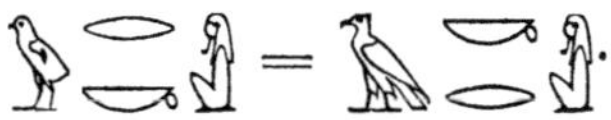

urt 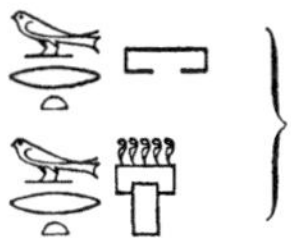 hall, palace.

urt  funeral chest, or coffer.

urt 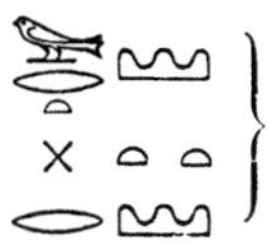 funerary mountain, cemetery.

urt 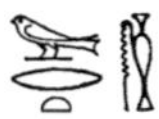 flood.

urt 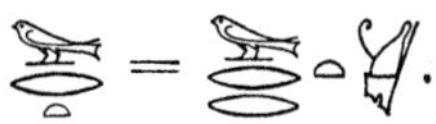

Urt-urt  a proper name.

urṭ, urṭu  to be inert, motionless, helpless, to rest.

Urṭ-àb  "He whose heart is still"; a title of Osiris.

urṭu , see .

uh to be troubled?

uhau to supplicate.

uhaȧu to fail.

uhem

uhemu to repeat, to report, to narrate; , to repeat; .

uhemm

to speak again.

to renew life, live again.

a new form.

to renew protection.

, with , a second time, again.

uhem-ā anew, afresh.

Uhem-ḥer a proper name.

uhen  decay, failure.

uhen 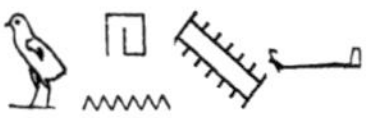 to overthrow; 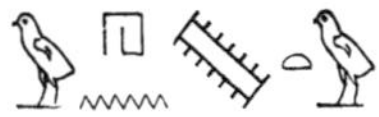 be overthrown.

uḥā 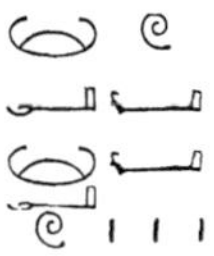 to unloose, be set free from, to return (in the evening).

uḥā  cord, rope.

uḥā  to catch fish, to snare game, fisherman, fowler.

uḥeset 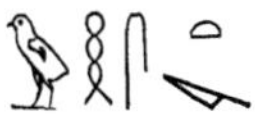 to beat down, to slay.

uḥet  baked meats, stew (?).

ukha  to lay down, set down, to seek after, search for.

ukha  darkness, night.

ukha  pillar.

ukhakh  to seek after.

ukheb  to shine.

ukhert  wooden implement.

ukheṭ  to be angry, be pained, disgusted.

ukheṭet 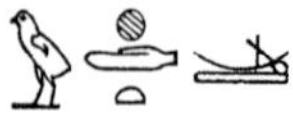 boat.

us 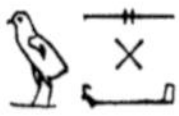 to do away with.

usfau  idle, lazy.

user  to be strong, mighty, strength, might, power, strong; 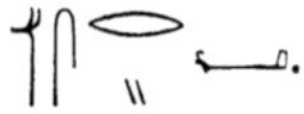.

useru  powers, mighty beings (human or divine).

usert  strength.

usert 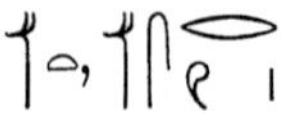 skull, top of the head; plur. 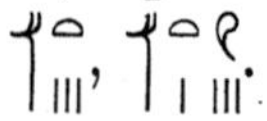.

User-àb  "Strong-heart"; a proper name.

User-ba  "Strong-soul"; a proper name.

useru  oars, rudders, steering poles.

useru  to steer a boat.

Usert  the name of a goddess.

useḥ 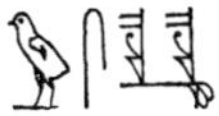 to advance.

usekh 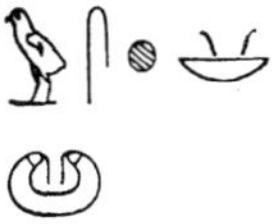 collar, neck ornament, pectoral.

usekh  to be in a wide space, to be wide or spacious, breadth, broad.

Usekh-nemmet  "He of the long stride", the name of one of the Forty-two Judges in the Hall of Osiris.

Usekh-ḥer  "Broad Face", a name of Rā.

usekht  the wide space of the sky, a large hall or room; 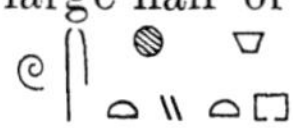 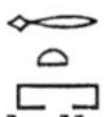 the great double hall.

Usekht Maāti 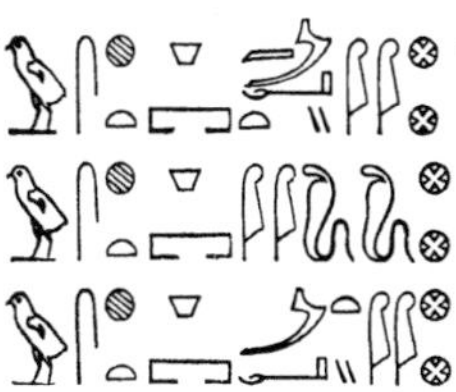 the name of the double Hall wherein Osiris judged the dead.

Usekt Shuu the Hall of Shu, *i. e.*, heaven.

Usekht Ḳeb the Hall of Ḳeb, *i. e.*, earth.

usekhu plated (?).

usesht urine.

usesh to micturate.

usten, ***ustennu*** to walk, to follow.

Usṭ a proper name.

ush to cry out.

ush misery.

ushau night, darkness.

ushā te eat, to gnaw, crunch bones.

usheb to answer, to eat (?).

to make an answer at the right time.

usheb to beget, begotten.

ushen	to net, to snare.
ushenu	feathered fowl.
uḳ	to burn, be burned.
uḳa	name of a festival.
uḳaiu	wooden pegs or legs.
ut	the city of embalmment, the abode of Anubis.
utu	embalmment.
utu	the god of embalmment, *i. e.*, Anubis.
ut	coffin, mummy bier.
uta	to embalm, swathe a mummy.
Ut** (**Uḥet**?) **meḥt	the Northern Oasis (Baḥrîyah).
Ut** (**Uḥet**) **res	the Southern Oasis (Khârgah).
Utau	a class of divine beings.

utu to set out on a journey, to make an expedition.

utu, *uteṭ* to issue an order or command, to decree, to ordain.

utet, *uteṭt* commands, behests, things ordered or decreed, records, documents, deeds, copies of deeds.

Utu-nesert the name of one of the Forty-two Judges in the Hall of Osiris.

Utu-rekhit The name of one of the Forty-two Judges in the Hall of Osiris.

utu =

utu flowers.

utuit oar rest.

Utent the name of a country.

utet 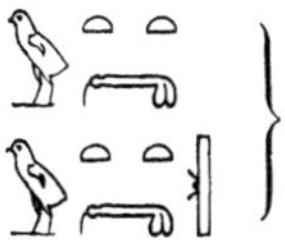 to beget.

 begetter.

Utet 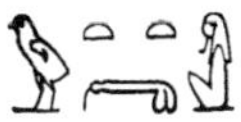 "Begetter", a name of Osiris.

Utet-Ḥeḥ  "Begetter of millions of years"; a proper name.

uṭ, *uṭet* 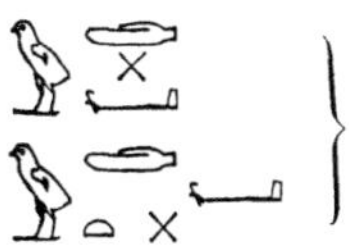 to cast down or out, to shoot out, dart forth, to utter a cry.

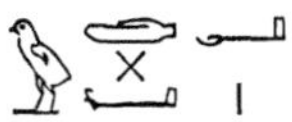 to lay violent hands on some-one.

uṭaiu  strong ones.

uṭit  chamber.

uṭebu  mutable.

uṭeb  to go round, turn about.

uṭeb, *uṭebu* 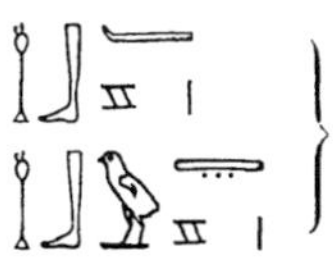 furrow; plur. , .

uṭebtu 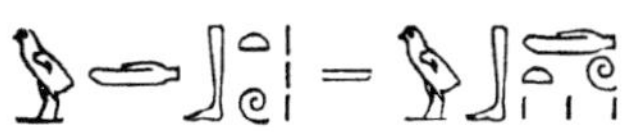 burned.

uțen, *uțenu* — to bring something as a gift, to make an offering; .

uțenu, *uțent* — offerings, things given as offerings.

uțeḥ — altar, table of offerings; plur. .

uțeț — to void, shoot out.

uthes — to raise up, to lift up, support.

utcha — to go out, set out, to begin a journey.

utchat — a journey, a going forth.

utcha — to be in a good state or condition, sound, healthy, well.

utchau — strength, power.

utchau  amulet, object of power.

 magical powers.

Utcha-re  "Strong-mouth"; a proper name.

utcha sep  strong with good fortune.

utchat  the "strong", *i. e.*, the Eye of Rā, whence came all power, strength, health, protection, etc.

utchat  the Utchat with legs und wings.

utchat  the Utchat of Sekhet, the great lady, the mistress of the gods.

utchati  "the two Utchats", *i. e.*, the two Eyes of the sky, or the Sun and Moon.

utchā — to weigh, to estimate, to consider, to reckon up, to decide.

to consider or weigh deeds or words.

utchā senemm — to weigh hair?

utchā — making the water to balance his throne, or making his throne to balance on the water.

utchāiu — to estimate the fields; weighers, those who try something in a balance.

utchāt — judges.

utchāti — judgment, decision.

Utchā-aābet — "computer of the offering", name of a god.

utchfau — to delay, to tarry.

utcheṭ — to walk.

I.

i, *iu* — to come, come, come!

i-tu, *iu-tu* — coming, a coming, advance.

it — a coming.

iu — comers; comers with glad tidings.

iu — to end (of a book) it has gone out in peace.

iu āq — going in and coming out, entrance and exit.

Iu pastu — a class of divine beings.

i, it — hail, O.

iu — O verily.

iumā — sea, lake, river, any large collection of water.

Ir-qai — a name of Ȧmen-Rā.

ikh to stretch out the heavens.

isu abodes, chambers.

B.

ba one of the two souls of man, the heart-soul, which was intimately connected with the *ka* and the heart, as opposed to the spirit-soul *khu*. Plur. , , , .

ba mentioned with and ; with , with , with and .

a perfect soul.

an equipped divine soul.

a living soul.

a living heart-soul and a perfect spirit-soul.

soul of souls.

my soul is the souls of the gods.

soul of eternity.

soul in the body.

soul of life.

a soul [made] of gold, an amulet.

thy soul is to heaven, thy body is under the ground.

ba the divine Soul, or soul of God.

ba soul of Osiris;

of Rā;

ba soul in Shu;

ba soul in Ḳeb;

ba soul in Tefnut;

Holy Soul, a name of Osiris.

Holy Soul, a name of Osiris.

the Soul which is in Nut.

 the Soul of the gods who exist in the body of Osiris.

 the Soul of the Great Body which is in Saïs, Neith.

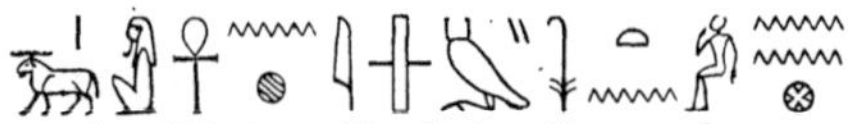 the Living Soul in Suten-ḥenen.

 the Soul of Àmenti.

baiu  divine souls, souls of gods.

 the souls in the gods.

 the souls of the gods of the East.

 the souls of the gods of the West.

 the souls of Heliopolis.

 the souls of Pe-[Ṭep] (Buto).

 the souls of Nekhen.

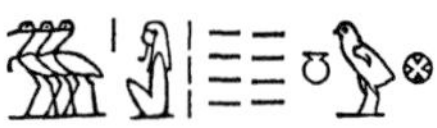 the souls of Hermopolis.

 living souls.

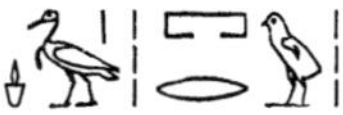 souls who have appeared.

 souls of the dead (*i. e.*, damned).

 souls of his father (Osiris).

baui  the double soul.

 the double soul in the Tcha-fui, *i. e.*, the souls of Osiris and Rā.

Bai  the Soul-god, or the Divine Soul, or the Ram-god;  the double-soul god.

Bati  a name of Osiris.

Ba  divine soul with plumes .

Ba 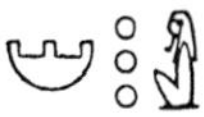 the metal-god; a proper name (?).

ba  to be endowed with a soul.

ba  to cleave, make a way through something.

Bau  a proper name.

baba  to work.

babau  cavern, cave, den or lair; plur. 

Baba  the name of the first-born son of Osiris.

Ba-neb-Ṭeṭṭeṭ 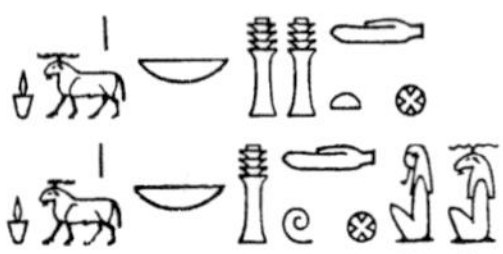 Soul-god, or Ram-god, lord of Ṭaṭṭu (Mendes), a title of Osiris.

Barekathȧ tchaua  a proper name.

baḥ , or , with  before, in front of.

Bakhau  the Mountain of sunrise.

Bast  the city of Bubastis in the Eastern Delta, the modern Zaḳâziḳ.

Bast  the goddess of Bubastis.

Bast  Bast dweller in Thebes.

Basti  the name of one of the Forty-two Judges in the Hall of Osiris.

bak  to work, to toil, to serve.

 works, labours.

baq  olive tree.

baḳ  to be weak, weary, feeble, helpless.

baḳ  weak one, the helpless one (*i.e.*, the mummy); plur. .

bat / *båat*  plants, boughs, branches.

Bati 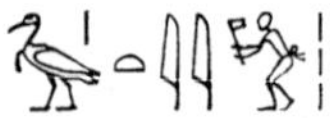 name of a fiend, or of a group of fiends.

båa 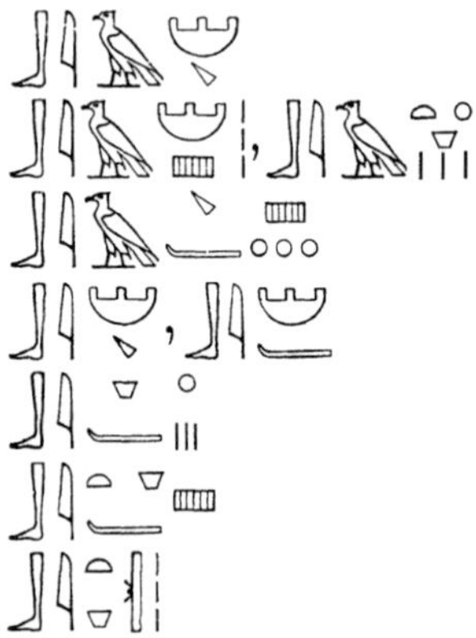 the ore of a metal, iron, copper, etc., a metal tool, a name of the sky or firmament.

båa en pet 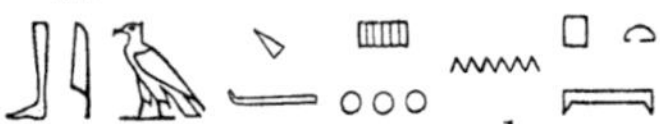 metal of the sky, meteoric iron (?).

 that iron in the sky.

båat shemāu 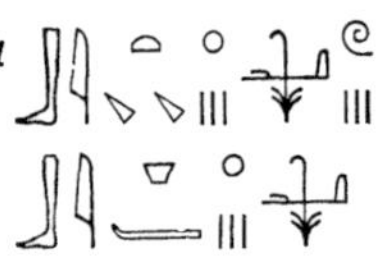 "the metal of the south", iron.

bȧat shemāu 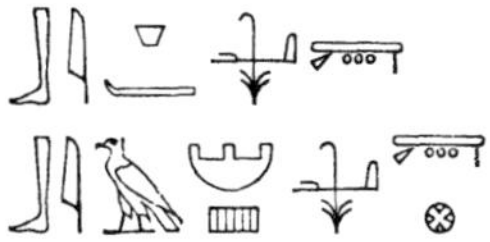 "the metal of the south", iron.

bȧau  } wonders, wonderful things.
bȧat 

bȧaq  a kind of grain, or fruit.

Bȧbȧ  the name of a god, Baba (?).

bȧbȧ  a cry of joy.

bȧn  evil, wickedness.

bȧk  hawk; plur. .

 the double divine hawk.

Bȧket  the city of the divine hawk.

bȧt, bȧti  king of the north.

Bȧti  a proper name.

bābāt  water-flood, stream.

bāḥ  to be flooded, inundated.

Bāḥ 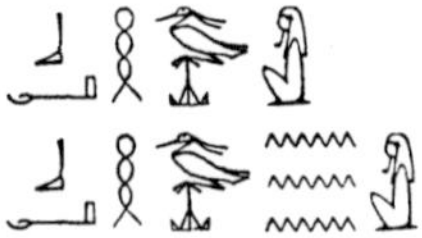 the god of the Inundation.

bi  name of a fiend.

biu  strength.

bu 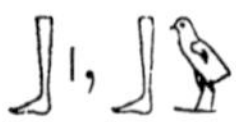  purity,  oneness (?), altogether, 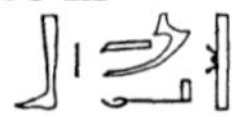 lawfulness, legality, truth,  this place (?).

bu neb  everywhere, every place.

bu nebu  all men, all people, everyone, folk in general.

bu nefer  prosperity, happiness.

bu ṭu  evil thing, calamity.

bu, *bu-pu* — not, it is not; […] (?).

but — evil thing, abomination.

buṭ — offering.

bebait — the mantis.

bebuu — strong.

Bebi — the name of a god.

bebet — flowers.

bebet — fountain head.

bebet — hollow place, cavity.

ben — not.

benānā — to bathe.

benben — a kind of wood.

benben — bier, funerary couch.

benbent 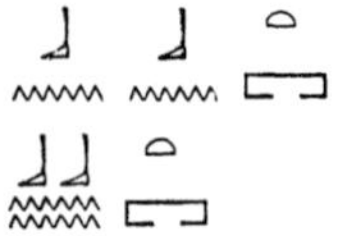 hall, pylon chamber.

ben  to pass away, to dissolve, to go on.

ben 
benen  to beget, to be united with, union.

benen  ring.

benen 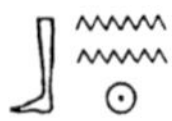 a kind of wood.

bennu  a bird commonly identified with the phoenix.

 the Bennu, the Soul of Rā.

bennut   matter, pus.

bennu 
bennut  cakes (?), bread.

Bener  the name of a city.

benrȧ  to be sweet, pleasant.

benrȧu	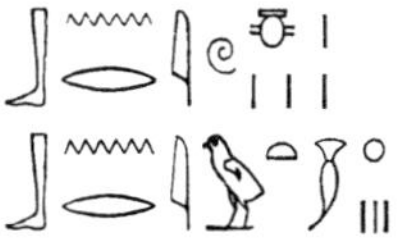	sweet things, dates, date wine, pleasant, nice.
benshu		bolts.
bent		divine apes, incarnations of the spirits of morning.
benti	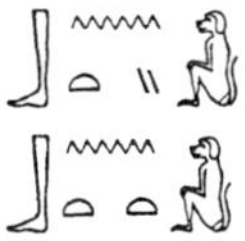	
beḥ		to cut, to split.
beḥen		baleful one.
beḥen	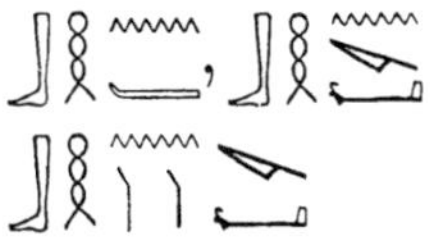	to cut, to pierce; 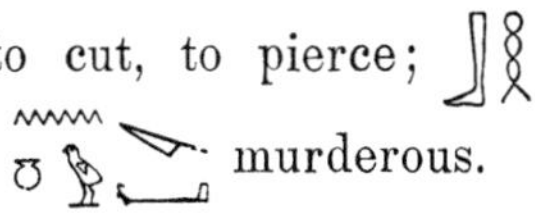 murderous.
beḥennu		animals of the wolf or dog species.
beḥes	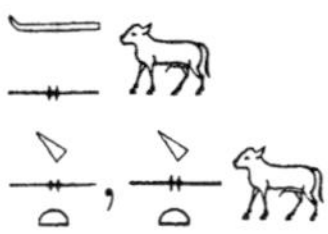	calf.
Bekhennu		a proper name.
bekhekhu		fire.
bes		form (?).

bes — to enter, to pass in, to rise (of the river).

increase.

bes, ***besu*** — flame, fire, blaze.

Besu-Aḥu — a proper name.

Besu Menu — a proper name.

bessu — humours, excretions, filth.

Besek — = Sebek, the Crocodile-god.

besek — internal organ of the body; plur.

besh — to vomit.

beshu (?) — (?) metal plates, scales.

beka — pregnant.

beka — to shine, the dawn, to-morrow.

bekau — weakness.

beq — olive tree, olives; the olive tree in Heliopolis.

beq — a proper name.

beqsu — eyeball, skin (?).

beqsu — balance, scales.

Beqtui — a proper name (?).

beḳ — misery.

beḳi — helpless one, sinner.

beḳa — defect, sin, crime, evil, sinner; plur.

beḳa, *beḳai* — evil man, sinner.

beḳasu — . . . .

beḳsu — part of a boat.

beḳset — . . . .

bet — place, every place, everywhere.

bet — incense.

bet — grains, seed.

bet — flower.

beta — to sin, commit a fault, do wrong.

betau, *betu* — sin, wrong, abominable thing; plur.

Betȧ — name of a city.

betennu, *betnu* — swift.

beṭ — incense.

beṭ, *beṭ-ti* — barley.

white barley.

red barley.

beṭesh  to be weak, powerless, but disposed to do evil.

beṭesh 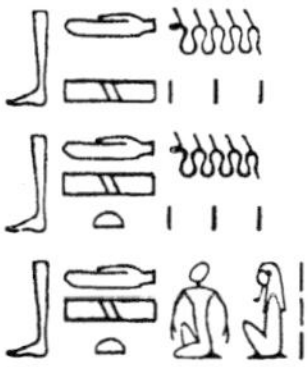
beṭeshet } impotent fiends; fem. sing. .

Beṭshu  the name of a city.

Beṭ-ti 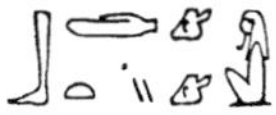 a proper name.

bethet (?) 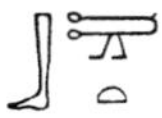 brought.

betcha 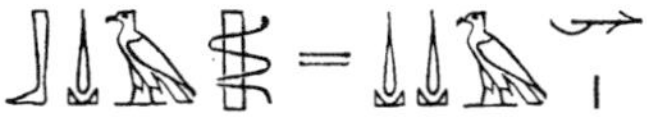 a tool or instrument.

P.

Pe 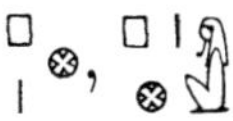 One half of the city of Buto (Per-Uatchit).

Pe . . . . .  the little Pe (?).

p  the.

pa  } the;  the one who;   the one who is between.

pai-ȧ  my.

pai-f  his.

pa, ***pai***  to fly, flight.

pait  bolt hole.

paut  stuff, substance, matter, cakes, offerings in general.

paut 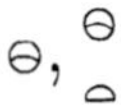 primeval matter, the material out of which the gods and the universe were formed.

pauti  the god of primeval matter, the chief Egyptian god of the Predynastic Period.

paut neteru the whole company of the primeval gods, *i. e.*, . The = the names of Nu.

= or

the Great Company of the gods.

the Little Company of the gods.

the complete Company of the gods.

paut-ti the Great and Little Companies of the gods.

pan = = this.

Par, or ***Pal*** a proper name.

Parehaqakheperu a proper name.

pas an ink jar.

pasekh = .

Pashakasa a proper name.

pat (?) light.

pā spark, flame, fire; plur. .

pāt men and women, people, a class of people.

pāit ḥer-f human-faced.

pu , a mark of emphasis: ; .

puȧau cakes.

pui a demonstrative particle.

Punt, ***Punṭ*** the region whence came *ānti* (myrrh) and other aromatic gums and spices, a region in Africa near the southern end of the Red Sea. The district of Punt proper was probably situated some distance inland.

putrȧ (Nebseni Papyrus), an interrogative particle. What is this then? *i. e.*, what does this mean?

pef, ***pefa***, ***pefi***, ***pefat*** a demonstrative particle.

pefes, ***pefses*** to burn, be hot, fiery, a spark, to cook, bake.

pefsit baked.

Pen, ***Pen-ḥeseb*** (?) a proper name (?).

penā to overturn, capsize (of a boat), to invert a matter.

peni land (?).

penu rat, mouse.

pens . . . . . .

penq 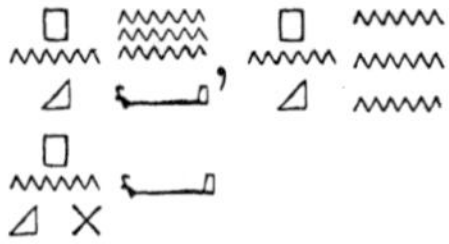 to beat to pieces, to macerate.

Penti  the name of a god.

pert  a season of the Egyptian year.

per  house, abode, temple, habitation; plur. 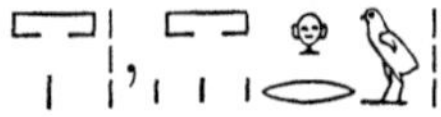 celestial mansions.

perui  double house.

per āa  "great house" פַּרְעֹה.

Per-ȧbu 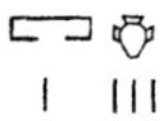 the temple of hearts, *i. e.*, the judgment hall.

per Ȧsȧr 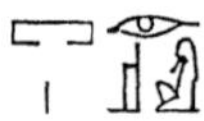 temple of Osiris.

Per-Ȧst 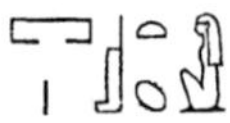 the temple of Isis.

Per-Ȧsṭes 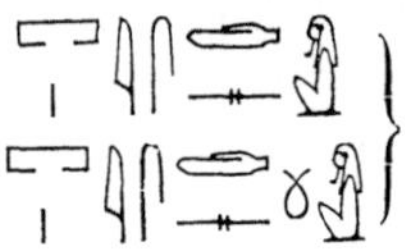 the temple of Ȧsṭes.

Per-Unnut  the temple of the Hour-goddess.

Per-ur 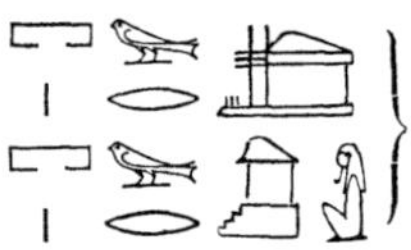 the "great House", *i. e.*, the tomb.

Per-Ptaḥ — the temple of Ptaḥ at Memphis.

Per-Menȧ — the house of coming into port, *i. e.*, the tomb.

Per-Menu — the temple of Menu.

Per-neḥeḥ — the house of eternity, *i. e.*, the tomb.

Per-neser — the house of fire.

Per-neter
Per-neter-āa — the temple of the god, *i. e.*, Osiris.

Per-Rerti (?) — the temple of Shu and Tefnut.

Per-Ḥapṭ-re — the temple of Ḥapṭ-re.

Per-ḥāt — the temple of hearts, *i. e*, the judgment hall.

Per-Ḥepṭ-ur — the temple of Ḥepṭ-ur.

Per-Ḥeru — the temple of Horus.

Per-Ḥetch — the "White House".

Per-Khenti-menȧtu-f the temple of the "President of his dead".

Per-Sabut the house of Sab (or Ḳeb), the earth (?).

Per-Sati the temple of Sati.

Per-suten the house of the king, *i. e.*, palace.

Per-seḥeptet the temple of Seḥeptet.

per-shāt (?) the house of books, *i. e.*, library.

Per-Kemkem the temple of Kemkem.

Per-Keku the temple of darkness.

per qebḥ the house of coolness, *i. e.*, bath (?).

Per-tep-ṭu-f the temple of him that is on his hill, *i. e.*, Anubis.

Per-Tem the temple of Tem.

Per-Ṭeḥuti the temple of Thoth.

per, *peru*, *perr*, *perru*  to come forth, to rise up, to appear, to make oneself manifest;  to come forth retreating;  to appear in the presence.

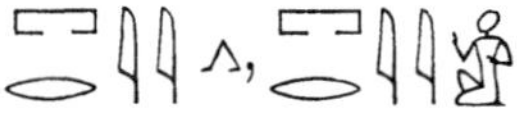 comer forth; plur. 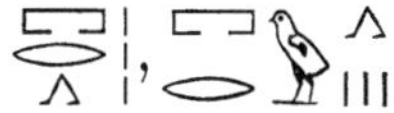 things which appear, manifestations;  to come forth; 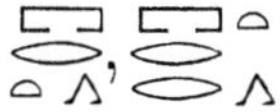 appearance, exit.

per-ā  to come forth boldly, brave.

per ḥer ta 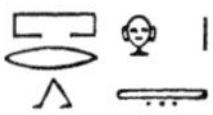 to be born on the earth.

pert em hru  to come forth by, or in, the day; the title of several groups and Chapters of the Theban Recension of the Book of the Dead.

pert  offspring.

pert, *pertu*  things which appear, *i. e.*, offerings.

pert er kheru 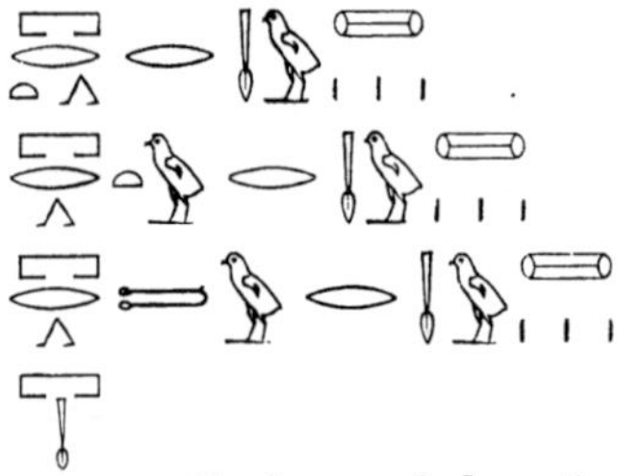 "things which appear at the words", *i. e.*, sepulchral offerings of bread, beer, oxen, geese, unguents, etc. Determinatives of these objects are usually added to  thus: 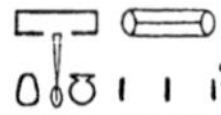, 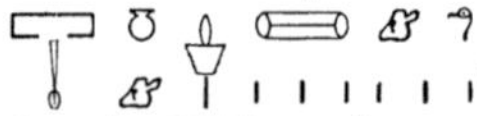, 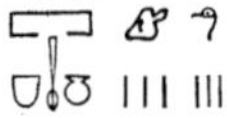, 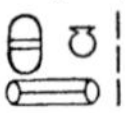, 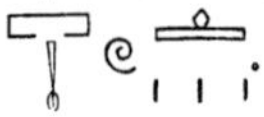.

perit  temples.

peri  strip of linen, bandage.

persen 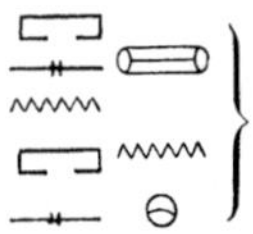 a kind of cake; plur. 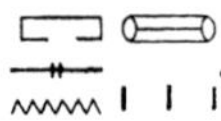.

pert 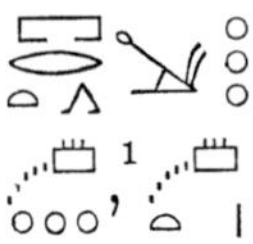 corn, grain in general.

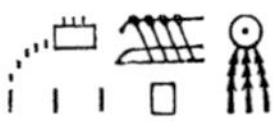 white grain.

1. Perhaps "measures of grain" *ḥeqat.*

black grain.

red grain.

peḥ

peḥu

peḥuut — to arrive at, attain to, to reach the end.

peḥt

peḥu — the back part, the end.

peḥi

peḥui — the lower part of the back, the buttocks, thighs.

peḥti

peḥuit — stern of a boat.

peḥu — swamp, marsh.

peḥrer — to run.

peḥreru runners, a class of beings.

Peḥreri "Runner", a name of Rā.

peḥti strength of the thighs originally, then strength, might, power, in general.

pekha to separate.

Pekhat the name of a goddess.

pekhes to cover over, fall on.

pes ink-jar.

pesaḳes a mistake for to spit.

peseḥ to eat, to bite (of an insect or animal), to sting.

Peskheti a divine envoy.

pesesh to divide, to cleave, to allot.

divisions.

pesḳ to spit.

Pesḳ-re a proper name.

pesṭ (*pestch*) nine, ninth.

pesṭ to shine, to illumine.

pesṭ, *pesṭtu* rays of light, radiance, brilliance.

Pesṭu the god of light.

pesṭ to spread out like light.

pesṭ, *pesṭu* back, backbone;

pesṭ tep to move the head.

pesh to spread out.

peshen 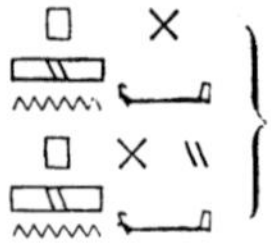 to divide, to cleave.

Peshennu  name of a city.

Peq  a region near Abydos.

pequ, *peqt* 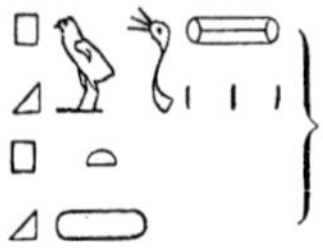 cakes, food.

peqt  apparel of fine linen.

peḳ 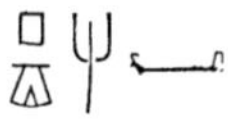 to explain.

peḳ  byssus, very fine, semi-transparent linen.

Peḳa  name of a city.

peḳes, *peḳas*  to spit upon.

Peḳes 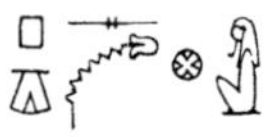 name of a city and a god.

pet  the sky, heaven; 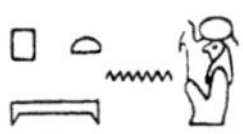 the heaven of Rā.

pet 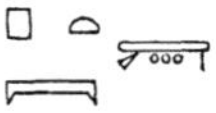 heaven and earth.

 heaven, earth and the Other World,

petti  heavenly beings, denizens of the sky.

pet  eastern heaven, or sky.

 western heaven, or sky.

 northern heaven, or sky.

 southern heaven, or sky.

petpet 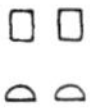 to crush, break.

Peti  a proper name.

pet 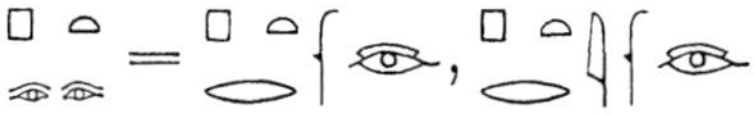 to see.

peti 

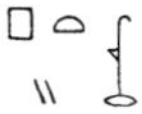

peter 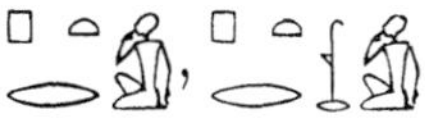

who? what? an interrogative particle.

what then is it? *i. e.*, what does this mean?

peter

petrȧ 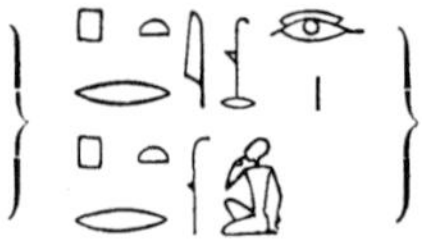 to see, look at, observe.

Petrȧ 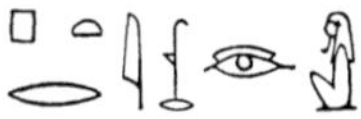 the name of a god.

Petrȧ-sen  the name of a river.

Ptaḥ  Ptaḥ, the blacksmith-god of Memphis. 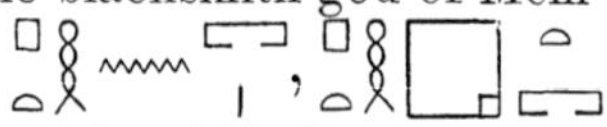 the temple of Ptaḥ.

Ptaḥ-ḥet-ka  or Ḥet-ka-Ptaḥ, "House of the double of Ptaḥ", a name of Memphis. The common name of Egypt, Αἰγύπτος, appears to be derived from these words.

 Memphis of the Other World.

Ptaḥ res ȧneb-f 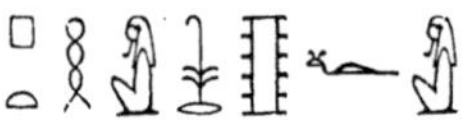 "Ptaḥ [to the] south [of] his Wall", Ptaḥ of Memphis.

Ptaḥ-Seker

Ptaḥ-Sekri 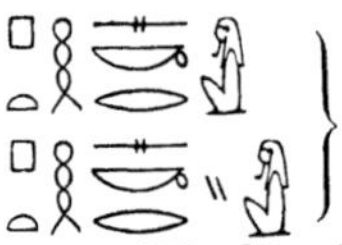 a dual god formed of Ptaḥ of Memphis and Seker, the old god of the Other World of the region of Memphis and Ṣaḳḳârah.

Ptaḥ-Sekri-Tem  a triad formed formed of Ptaḥ of Memphis, Seker, and Temu, an old god of Ȧnu, or Heliopolis.

Ptaḥ-Tanen 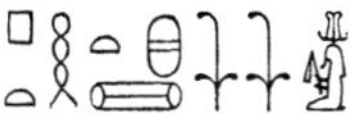 a dual god formed of Ptaḥ of Memphis and Tanen, an old cosmic god of the region.

Ptaḥ-mes  a proper name.

peṭ  to open out, to extend, to stretch out.

peṭ  a kind of unguent.

Peṭeṭ  name of a god and city.

peṭsu  to break open, opener.

Peṭ-mer 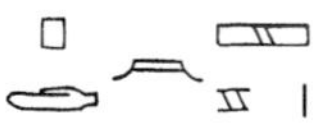 "Broad Lake", the name of a shrine.

 F.

f  he, him, it, its, his.

fa, ***fat***  to bear, to carry, be carried, to lift up, to diminish through decay.

bearers, carriers.

Fa-ā to raise the hand.

the god of the lifted hand.

Fa-ākhu a proper name.

Fa-pet "Supporter of the sky"; the name of the god of the Seventh Ȧat.

Fa-Ḥeru "bearer of Horus"; a name of Osiris.

Fat-Ḥeru "the city of the bearer of Horus".

Fau-ḥeru-sen "those who lift up their faces"; a class of divine beings.

fau riches, wealth, abundance.

fenkhu offerings.

Fenkhu the name of certain dwellers in Syria.

fent worm, serpent, reptile; plur.

fenṭ 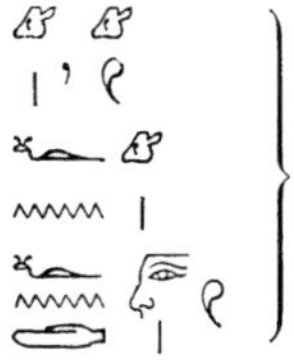 nose; plur. 

Fenṭi  a form of the god Thoth; the name of one of the Forty-two Judges in the Hall of Osiris.

fekh 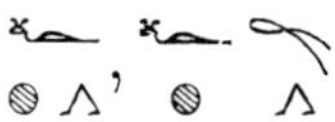 to untie, unloose, destroy.

fekhekh 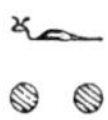 to burst through.

feqat  a bread-cake, food in general.

feḳa  to make water.

fetu 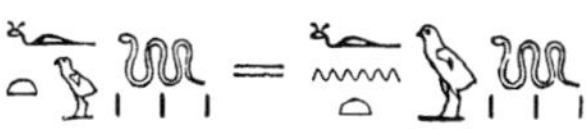 worms.

fettu  fish.

feṭ-àb 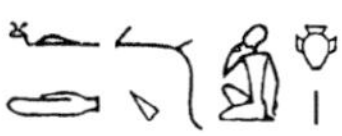 languor, disgust, weariness.

fṭu  four; 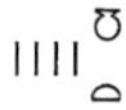 fourth.

feṭqu  destruction, damage.

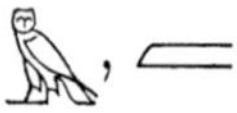 M.

em  sign of the present participle.

em  particle of negation, no, not; 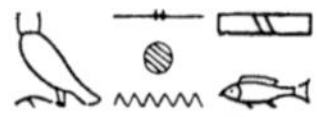 let not make to stink (my name).

em 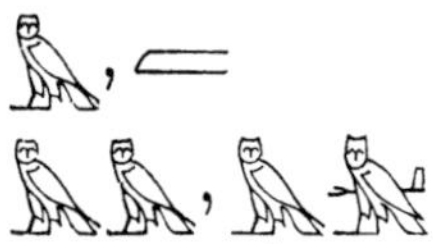 in, into, from, on, at, with, out from, of, upon, as, like, according to, in the manner of, among.

em āb 

 opposite, in front of, confronting.

em ābu 

em āb sa 

em baḥ  before, in the presence of; the old form is  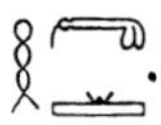.

em baḥ ā  before, in the presence of.

em paitu  before, when not yet.

em nem (*uhem*) 
em nem (*uhem*) *ā* 
} a second time.

em ruti  outside.

em ḥāt 
em ḥāti ā 
} before.

em ḥer  upon.

em khen 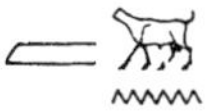
em khennu  
em khennu ā 
} inside, within.

em khert 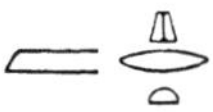 on behalf of.

em khet  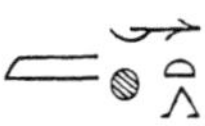
} behind, after, in the train of.

em sa  at the back of, behind, after.

em qeṭ round about, throughout.

ma part of a boat.

ma to be new, to renew,
maui made new,
mat new.

maa to see, to look upon, to behold, observe, perceive;
maau
maat
seen, observed; plur. part.

maa sight, view, glance.

maat (or ***ȧrit***?) eye; eye to eye; an eye.

maati (or ***àriui***?)  the two eyes.

maat  eyes.

maat nebt  every eye, *i. e.*, every body, all people, folk, mankind.

maat Rā 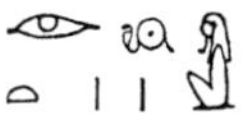 eye of Rā.

 right eye of Rā.

maat Ḥeru  eye of Horus, the name of offerings.

maat Shu  eye of Shu, *i. e.*, the sun.

maat Tem 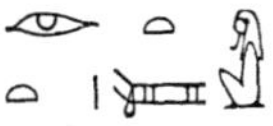 eye of Tem, *i. e.*, the sun.

maa-ànt-f  the name of a plank, or peg, in the magic boat (Chap. XCIX).

maa-ànuf  the name of one of the Forty-two Judges in the Hall of Osiris.

Maa-àtef-f-kheri-beq-f  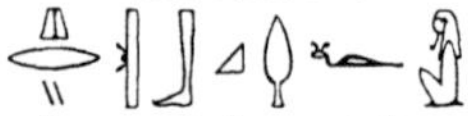 the name of one of the spirits who guard the bier of Osiris.

Maati-f-em-khet  "he whose two eyes are of fire"; the name of one of the Forty-two Judges in the Hall of Osiris.

Maati-f-em-ṭes  "he whose two eyes are like knives"; the name of one of the Forty-two Judges in the Hall of Osiris.

Maa-em-ḳerḥ-ànnef-em-hru  "he who seeth in the night what is brought to him in the day"; a proper name.

Maa-ḥa-f 

Maa-ḥa 

"seeing what is behind him"; a proper name.

Maa-ḥeḥ-en-renput  "seeing millions of years"; a proper name.

Maatuf-ḥer-ā a proper name.

Maaiu-su (?) a proper name.

Maa-thet-f a proper name.

maar, ***maȧr*** restraint, misery, affliction, wretched one, oppressed one.

maȧ lion.

maȧuti the lion-lioness god, *i. e.*, Shu and Tefnut.

maā, ***maāu*** to be right, straight, just, true, to pay which is legally due, or what it is right to pay, to give a statutory offering.

maā-kheru, ***maāt-kheru*** "true word", or "true of word", or "true voice", or "true of voice", he whose word when spoken is followed unfailingly by the effect desired. These words are placed after the names of the dead, and appear to mean something like "triumphant", a crown of triumph; to be right.

maāt — truth, what is right, true, straightness, law, order; doubly true: the scales balance exactly. "[with] the cord of maāt", *i. e*, uniformly and regularly; beautiful truth.

a righteous judge.

true, right of heart.

real lapis-lazuli.

thy genuine friend.

real royal scribe.

in very truth.

really true.

 most truly a mystery.

Maāt 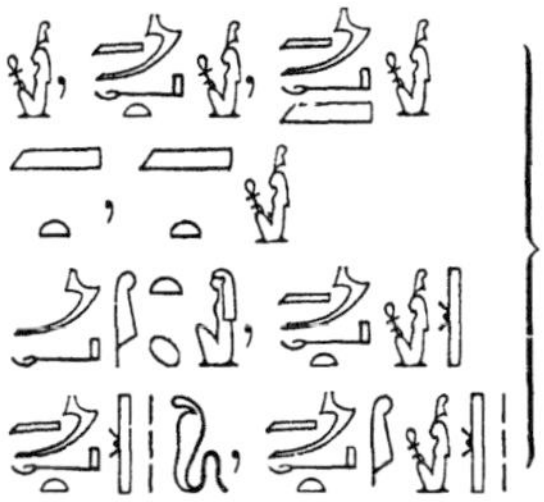 the goddess of truth, law, order, etc.

Maāti  the two goddesses of truth, law, order, etc.

maāti  truth, right.

Maātiu  the gods of truth, law, order, etc.

maāt 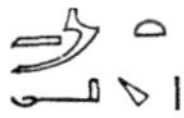 a district, or region.

Maāti 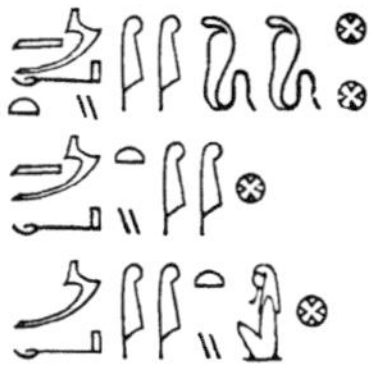 the cities or districts of the two Maāti goddesses.

maā  limb.

maā 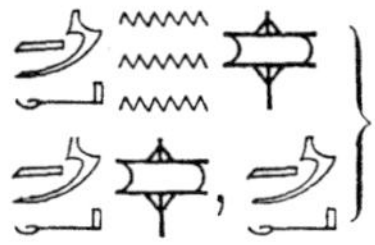 windsail, wind, breeze; plur. 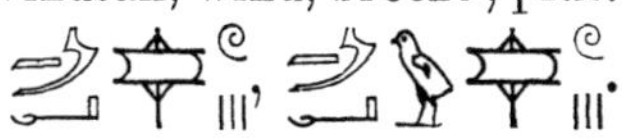

maā to stretch out (?).

maā to journey.

maautu stalk.

mafṭet lynx.

mama palm (?) tree.

Manu the Mountain of Sunset.

maḥa a part of the head.

maḥu part of a boat.

maḥu a crown, wreath.

mast leg; dual .

Mastiu a group of star-gods.

maqet ladder; plur. .

maḳ a precious stone.

maut }
matu } incense.

Matchat the name of a city.

mȧ as, like, concerning, even as.

like that same one.

inasmuch as, even as.

like that which.

after the manner of.

mȧti a person or thing resembling another person or thing, type, copy.

divine image; his divine images.

mȧtet picture, likeness, similitude, like unto, copy of; likewise.

mȧn to-day.

mȧnt , , , with , daily.

mȧu to be like

mȧu , cat, cat's skin.

mȧu lion ; lions.

mȧu to knead, to mould, to fashion.

mā , give, grant, let there be! who? what? behold! be-hold thou! behold ye!

mā
māȧ
māȧi come! give! bring!

Māau-taui name of a god.

māāt place.

māāat name of a place.

māb thirty.

mābiu the thirty great gods.

mābit 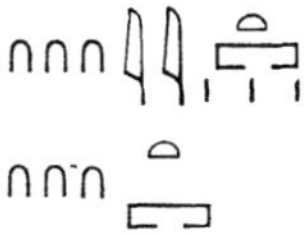 name of a place or building.

māfket 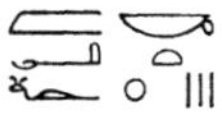 turquoise.

Mānāat 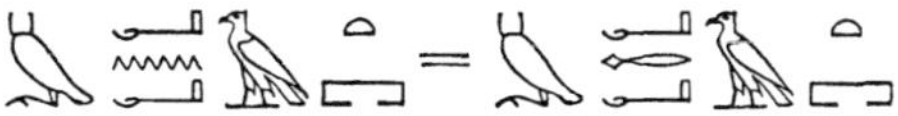 ?

Mārqathȧ  the name of a god.

māhaiu  people, tribe, generations (?).

māhaṭṭi  fire.

māhui  milk vessels, udders (?).

māhenȧ 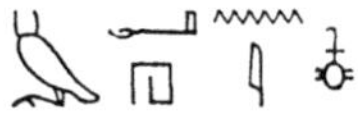 milk vessel.

māḥā  standard.

Māḥu 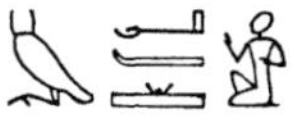 the name of a man.

mākha 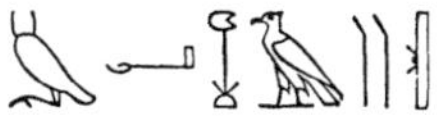 to weigh.

mākha 

mākhat 

mākhaȧt 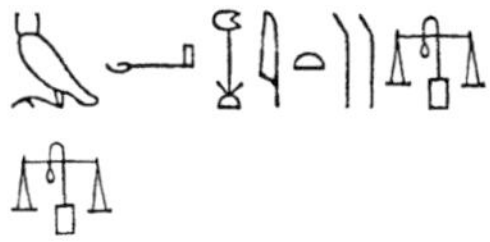

a pair of scales, a balance; 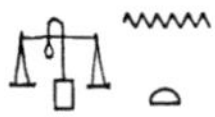  the balance of the earth.

mākhatu  intestines.

mākhait  sledge for a sacred boat or god.

mākhiu  altars with incense burning on them.

mākhent  a boat.

māsheru  evening, eventide.

mākat  place.

māku 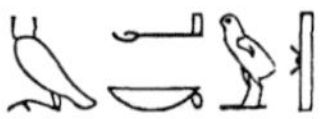 to protect, protection.

māki  protector.

māket  a thing which protects, amulet.

mākefitiu  objects made of turquoise.

mākḥa  to turn round, or behind, back of the head.

māket  station, place.

māqet  ladder.

mātau  weapons, short spears, harpoons.

mātenu  ways, roads, paths.

Māṭes 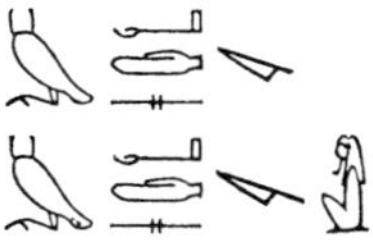 a proper name.

Māṭes-ȧrui (?)  the gods with knife-like eyes.

māṭet (***māntchet***) 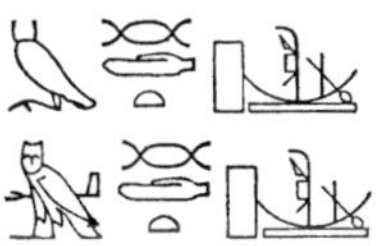 the boat in which the sun sailed from sunrise to noon.

māthennu  ways, roads, paths.

mātcha  phallus.

mātchabu 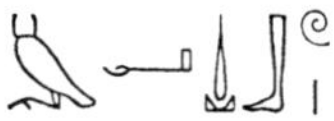

mātchabet  chain, fetter.

mātchabet  part of a ship.

Mātcheṭ 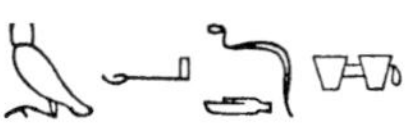 a proper name.

mātcheṭ — to use force, to compel, to constrain.

Mi-sheps — a proper name.

mu — water, essence.

pool; the pool of the well of Ȧmenti; the pool of Kher-āḥa.

the god of the water, or divine essence; essence of Rā.

brow (surface?) of the water.

what is in the water.

m[u]it — water.

mu — a decoction, as in:—

ānkham flower water.

myrrh water.

saltpetre water.

incense water.

incense water.

dirty water.

mut mother.

muti parents.

Mut the Mother-goddess *par excellence* of Egypt; "Mut in the horizon of heaven". mother-deities.

mut weights for scales.

Mut-restȧ a proper name.

Mut-ḥetepth a proper name.

mut to die, death, the dead, the damned; plur. .

Menu name of a god of generation and fertility.

Menu-Ḥeru Menu + Horus.

Menu-suten-Ḥeru-nekht a name of Osiris.

Menu-qeṭ a proper name.

men, *ment* to be permanent, stable, firm, to be fixed, to remain; abiding, fixed.

menu possessions, things which abide.

menu chamber.

menu bases, pedestals.

Ment name of a god.

menti, *mentiu* the two thighs.

men to be in pain, sick.

ment, *menut* pain, sickness, disease.

men — such and such an one.

Menȧ — name of a god or city.

menȧ — to tie up a boat to the mooring post, to come into port, to land, to die; arriving.

menȧ, *menȧt* — post to which boats are tied up or moored.

menȧu — mooring posts, stakes of death.

menȧ, *menȧt* — end, ending; a happy ending, or death.

menȧ, *menȧ-tu* — the dead.

menȧt — funerary bed, bier, death.

meni — to slay, put to death.

menȧt a musical instrument.

menāt breast.

menu ministrants.

menmen to go about.

menment cattle, farm stock.

menḥ wax.

menḥu to offer up.

Menḥu name of a god.

menkhu to work, wrought, well finished, excellent, worked or inlaid, perfect, well disposed, well-doing; [hieroglyphs] perfected; [hieroglyphs] valuable things.

Menkh the beneficent god (?).

menkhet apparel, clothes, garments.

Menqet		the name of a goddess.
Ment		a proper name.
ment		swallow.
menṭ-t	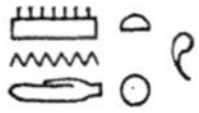	apple of the eye.
menṭi	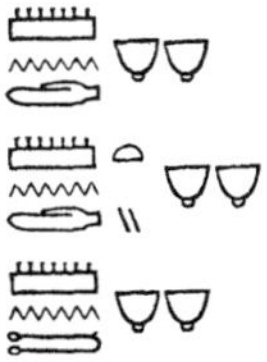	the two breasts.
Menthu	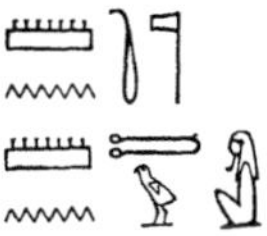	the War-god of Hermonthis, who was at a later period identified with Rā.
Mentchat		the name of a city.
mer		overseer, superintendent.
	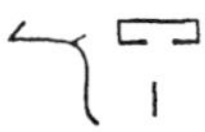	major-domo, steward.
		officer of soldiers.
		overseer of the granaries.
mer		a water-course, canal.

mer  pool, tank, cistern; plur. 

 swamps, lakes.

 Lake of Maāt.

 Lake of the Maāti gods.

 Lake of the geese.

 Lake of the horizon-gods.

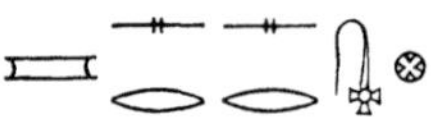 Lake of Fire.

 name of a mythological Lake.

meru  peasants, agricultural labourers.

mer  to be sick, ill;  sick;  diseased, or perhaps =  the dead.

meru  }
merȧu  } pain, sickness, disease, decay.

Mer  a proper name.

mer, *meru*, *merr*, *merru* — to love, to desire, to wish for, to will. loving, lover, beloved; lover, beloved; lovers.

mertu, *mert*, *merit*, *merrt* — love, desire, wish, will.

Mer — a proper name.

Mert — name of a goddess.

Meritti — a group of gods.

Merti — two goddesses.

mer — to bind, to tie.

meru		swathing, bandage.
Mer-ur		the Mnevis Bull.
merāḥāt	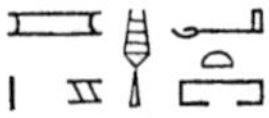	tomb, sepulchre.
meruḥ		oar, paddle.
meriut		a kind of tree.
Meres		a proper name (?).
Meri-s	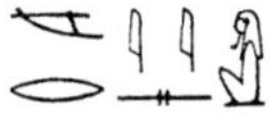	
merḥ		wax.
merḥet	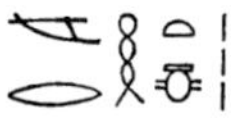	
mert	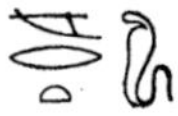	the name of a part of a boat.
Mert		name of a city.
Mert		a proper name.
mehait		roof.
meḥ		cubit, 

meḥ to fill, be full; , full; filling, filler; the filling of the Utchat, *i. e.*, full moon; the filling of the Eye of Horus; a stream filled with flowers.

meḥ sa to be complete.

meḥ to be inundated, submerged, drowned.

meḥit flood.

Meḥ-urt
Meḥt-urt a very ancient sky goddess, afterwards identified with Nut.

meḥ unguent (?).

meḥ	wing, pinion.
meḥ	garland.
Meḥānuti-Rā	a proper name (?).
meḥut	offerings.
meḥuti	oil.
Meḥi	a proper name.
Meḥiu	a proper name.
meḥit	fish.
meḥef	a kind of stone.
Meḥen	name of a god and goddess.
Meḥent	name of a god and goddess.
Meḥenit	name of a god and goddess.
Meḥenet	name of a city.
meḥenet	the north wind.
meḥt	placed before numbers;

meḥt vessel, plaque (?).

meḥt, *meḥti* the north in general, the north of Egypt, *i. e.*, the Delta; north-west.

meḥtiu northern beings, men or gods, lords of the north, *i. e.*, in late times, the Greeks; nest of the northerners.

Meḥt the goddess of the North.

meḥt, *meḥit*, *meḥuiu*(?), *meḥu* the north wind.

meḥti oil.

Meḥti (?)***-sāḥ-neter*** the name of one of the Seven Cows.

meḥṭet to bathe.

Em-khent-maati (?) (?).

em khennu within.

mekhsef name of a wooden instrument.

mes, ***mesu*** to bring; bringer, bringing.

mest to walk, approach.

to give birth to, to bring forth, to produce, to fashion; , born of; born; giving birth a second time to mortals; ; .

mest , genetrix.

mest  birth; plur.  birthday.

mestu

mes  child, offspring.

mesu  children.

mesesiu

mesu nebu  all who are born, *i. e.*, the human race.

mesu beṭesh 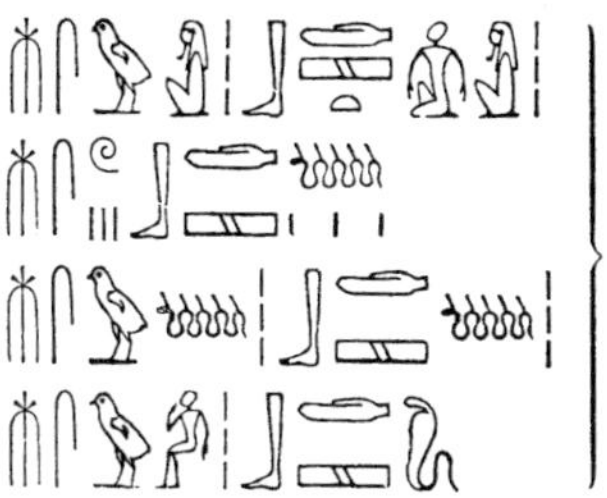 malicious but powerless fiends.

mesu ent Nu  children of the divine water, *i. e.*, plants.

mesu Nut children of the Sky-goddess.

mesu Ḥeru children of Horus (Kesthȧ, Ḥāpi, Ṭuamut-f, Qebḥsennuf).

mesu Serȧt beqet . . . .

mesit cakes eaten in the evening.

mesbeb (?) banded (?).

Mes-peḥ a proper name.

Mes-Ptaḥ a proper name.

Mes-em-neter a proper name.

mesmes to count (?).

mesmes Vol. II, p. 251, l. 2.

mesnekht birthplace.

emseḥ, ***emseḥu*** crocodile; plur. , eight crocodiles .

emseḥu — to slay.

meskhen

meskhent — the birth-place of a god or goddess; a region in the Sekhet-Ȧaru where the gods were produced; the four birth-places of Abydos.

Meskhen-āat — the name of a goddess of birth, or of a birth-place.

Meskhen-ment — the name of a goddess of birth, or of a birth-place.

Meskhen-nefert — the name of a goddess of birth, or of a birth-place.

Meskhen-Seqebet — the name of a goddess of birth, or of a birth-place.

Mesespekh — a proper name.

Messhenu — = Meskhenu.

meska skin.

Mesqen, ***Mesqet*** a region of the Other World through which the deceased must pass before he could reach the Sekhet-Ȧaru.

mesqet weapons.

mesṭemu to paint the eyes with *koḥl.*

mesṭemet eye-paint, stibium, *koḥl.*

mesṭet leg.

mesṭ, ***mesṭeṭ*** to dislike, to hate.

mesthȧ palette. The true reading is Ḳesthȧ, *q. v.*

Mesthȧ one of the four sons of Horus. The true reading is Ḳesthȧ, *q. v.*

mestcher ear.

the two ears.

mestchetch to hate.

meshā bowmen, soldiers.

meshen Chap. CX. B. 16.

Em-qeṭqeṭ the name of a spirit, or god.

met (*mut*) the dead, the damned.

met ten.

tenth.

metu venom, poison.

metut seed, progeny;

metmet to eavesdrop (?).

met, *meti* to be right, what is right, the mean; the exact truth (?).

meter, *metru* to bear witness, to testify, to give evidence.

meṭu — to speak, to talk, tell, declare.

meṭ, meṭu, *meṭet* — word, speech, talk, declaration; pronouncement.

meṭut — words, speech, things (like the Hebrew דָּבָר); word of wisdom; words of the gods; words of truth; words of evil, blasphemy.

Meṭu-ta-f — a proper name.

Meṭes-ḥer-àri-mer — "Knife-face, guardian of the Lake"; the name of the doorkeeper of the Sixth Ārit.

Meṭes-sen — the name of the door-keeper of the Seventh Ārit.

metch — to be deep; deep; very deep.

metchtu — abyss.

deeps, depths.

metchaub — to fetter.

metchet — salve, ointment, oil.

N.

n — a preposition, in, to, for, because. With additions :—

n — of; with plural following,

n  we, us.

n  no, not =  invisible.

na  those, the;  those who are after.

naiu  those of;  those of thine;  those belonging to.

na
nai
nȧu

air, wind.

Naȧrik 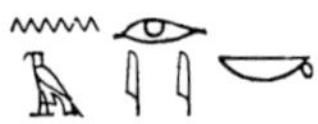 a proper name (?).

Naȧrruṭ
Naȧrruṭf
Nanȧaruṭf
Nȧareruṭ

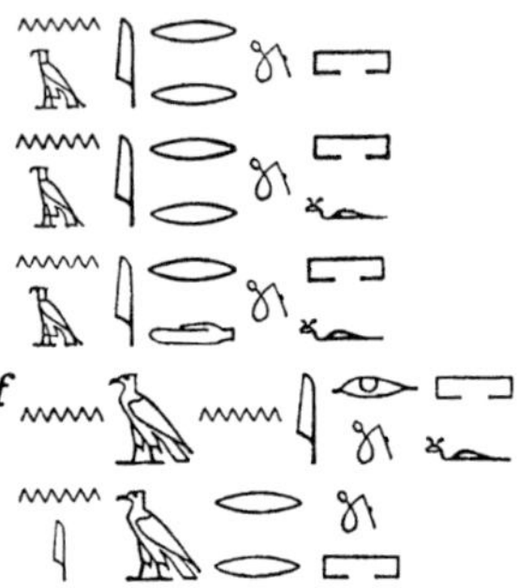

"the place where nothing grows", a name for a region of the Other World. See Ȧn-ruṭ-f.

Nasaqbubu name of a god.

Nak (?) = en Aker (?).

Nathkerthi name of a god.

n-à , , I, me, my.

nàh injury.

nàs , , to call, cry out, invoke; , invoked.

nàsu

Nàk the name of a fiend and enemy of Rā.

fiends, enemies.

nā

nāai to journey, to travel, to come, to arrive, to advance.

nāt

Nāàu name of a god or devil.

nāu fiend, devil; plur. .

nāā a decree (?), a design, picture.

nār a reed pen, painting reed.

Nārt a proper name.

Nārtiānkhemsenf name of a fiend.

nāsh mighty one.

nāḳ to break open, to split.

nāḳeḳa to cackle.

ni (?) in and .

nimā who?

nini to salute, to acclaim.

nu of. , , , , , .

Nu name of a scribe.

nu the watery abyss of the sky.

Nu the Sky-god.

nu these; these very ones; these; these who.

nu season, period, time.

nu to see, to watch, to observe

nu to go away, go about.

nu to be strong, to strengthen.

nu hours.

nu (?) adorations, praise, worship.

nuit weapon, knife, short dagger.

nub gold; fine gold; golden light.

Nub-ḥeḥ "Eternal gold"; a name of Osiris.

nub
nubȧu — to mould, to shape, to fashion, to form; fashioned, inlaid.

nubḥeḥ — blossom, flower.

Nubti — name of the god of Ombos, *i. e.*, Set.

nun — to pay homage.

nur — a kind of bird.

nuḥ — to masturbate.

nuḥ — to bind, to tie, to fetter.

cords, cordage, rigging, tackle.

nuḥu — flower, blossom.

nuḥti — pair of horns.

nukh — to be burnt.

nuk — I. I, even I.

nut  the sky, heaven.

Nut 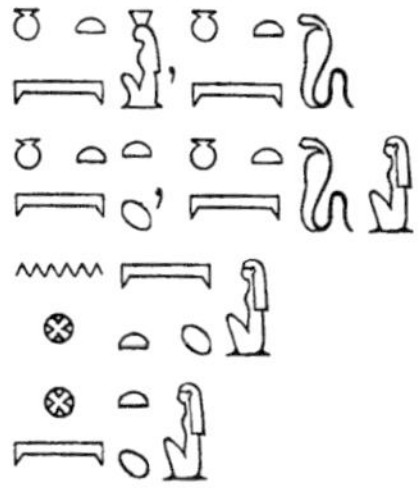 the Sky-goddess, the wife of Seb, or Ḳeb; the name of a sail in the magic boat.

Nut 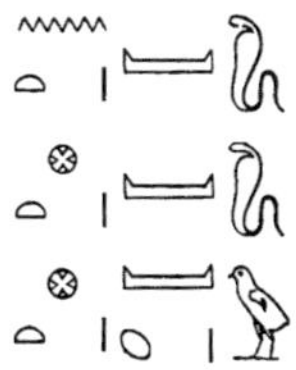 the night sky.

nut  cords, ropes.

nut  city; plur. ;  city of god.

nuti  citizens.

nui

nut  canal, stream, river, flood, any large collection of water.

Nut-urt "great city"; the name of a lake in Sekhet-Ȧaru.

Nutu-ḥru a proper name.

nuti sweet air (?).

nuṭ to bear, to carry, to journey.

Nuṭiu a class of divine beings.

neb, ***nebt*** (in late times or), each, every, any, all; plur. , , ; every kind of evil thing.

neb with *bu*, , every-where. See also under .

neb , , , lord, master, sovereign; plur. , , .

nebt lady, mistress; in late times "lord".

neb lord of, possessor of, owner of, *e. g.*, , , ; compare the use of בַּעַל.

neb åbu "lord of hearts"; a name of Åḥi.

neb Åbti "lord of the East"; a title of Rā.

neb åmakh "lord of veneration", *i.e.*, one to whom service is rendered and homage paid ; .

neb Åmenti "lord of Åmenti"; a name of Osiris ; the lords of the Other World ; "lady of Åmenti", a title of Hathor.

neb āāui "lord of the two hands".

neb ābui "lord of the two horns"; a title of Åmen ; the name of one of the Forty-two Judges in the Hall of Osiris.

neb ānkh "lord of life"; a title of Osiris.

the title of the sarcophagus and the bier; late form .

nebt ānkh "lady of life"; a title of Isis.

nebt unnut "lady of the hour"; a proper name.

neb urert "lord of the *urert* crown"; a title of Osiris and of Horus.

neb useru "lord of strength, or powers"; a title of the Sun-god.

neb baiu "lord of souls"; a title of several gods.

neb pāt "lord of mankind"; a title of Horus.

nebt per "lady of the house", *i. e.*, a married woman, house-wife. It is possible that is not intended to be read, and is only a determinative. The Egyptian to-day speaks of his "house", meaning his wife, or his wife and family.

neb mau possessor of many eyes, or good sight.

neb maāt possessor of truth or law, , .

neb Maāti lord of the double City of Truth.

nebt māket

nebu en meḥt "lords of the north"; the peoples of the Delta; in late times the Greeks.

Neb nebu "Lord of lords"; the name of one of the Forty-two Judges in the Hall of Osiris.

neb nefu "lord of winds"; a title of Osiris.

neb nemt "lord of steps", *i. e.*, one who has the power to walk.

neb neru "lord of victories"; a title of the heart of Osiris.

neb neter meṭut "lord of the words of the god", *i. e.*, one who understands the hieroglyphic language.

neb renput "lord of years", *i. e.*, aged one.

neb rekhit "lord of the *rekhit*", a class of men.

neb Re-stau "lord of Re-stau", *q. v.*, a title of Osiris.

neb henu "lord of praises", *i. e.*, he who is praised.

neb ḥeru "lord of faces"; the name of one of the Forty-two Judges in the Hall of Osiris.

neb ḥeḥ "lord of eternity"; a title of Osiris; plur.

Neb khat the goddess Nephthys (?)

nebu khaut "lords of altars", *i. e.*, gods to whom altars have been dedicated.

neb khāu "lord of crowns, or risings"; a title of Rā.

neb khut "lord of the horizon"; a title of Rā.

neb kheperu "lord of transformations", *i. e.*, he of many changes.

neb khet "lord of things", *i. e.*, lord of creation; plur.

nebu Kher-Āḥa "lords of Kher-āḥa", *i. e.*, Temu and his fellow deities.

nebt Sau the "lady of Saïs", *i. e.*, Neith.

neb setut "lord of light", *i. e.*, giver of light.

neb senṭ "lord of fear", *i. e.*, he who inspires fear.

neb sekhti "lord of the field", *i. e.*, master of the field, a title of the Bull-god.

nebt Seḳer "lady of silence"; a name of the Other World.

nebu kau "lords of food", *i. e.*, gods to whom food offerings are given.

neb kesu "lord of bowings", *i. e.*, he to whom homage is paid.

neb qerset "lord of the bier"; a title of Osiris.

neb taui "lord of the Two Lands", *i. e.*, of Upper and Lower Egypt.

neb taiu "lord of the lands", *i. e.*, of the world, a title of Osiris. "lords of lands".

Nebt-taui the name of a lake in the Sekhet Ȧaru.

Nebt-taui em karȧ the name of the mooring post for the magic boat.

Neb ta ānkhtet "lord of the Land of Life", *i. e.*, the Other World.

Neb ta tchesert "lord of the Holy Land"; a title of Osiris.

neb tau 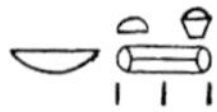 "lord of cakes".

neb temu  "lord of mankind".

nebu ṭuat  "lords of the Other World".

neb ṭeshert 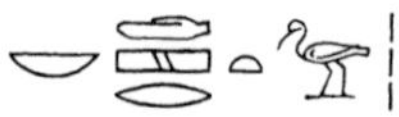 "lord of the red things", red clouds, or desert (?).

neb tchefau  "lord of divine food".

neb tchetta  "lord of eternity", *i. e.*, Osiris.

Neb-peḥti-petpet-sebȧu 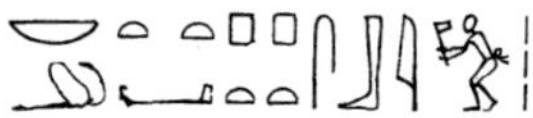 "lord of might, crusher of fiends"; a proper name.

Neb-peḥti-thes-menment 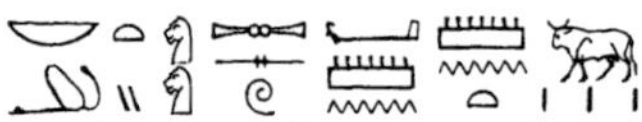 "lord of might, roper in of cattle"; a proper name.

Neb-maāt-ḥeri-reṭui-f  a proper name.

Neb-er-tcher  "lord to the boundary", *i. e.*, the Lord of the Universe, a title of Osiris.

Nebt-er-tchert 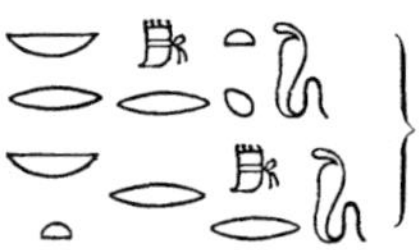 fem. of preceding.

Nebt-ḥet the goddess Nephthys, sister of Isis.

Neb-s a proper name.

Neb-seni the name of a famous scribe.

Neb-qeṭ the name of a scribe.

neba a weapon or tool, a pole.

Nebȧ the name of one of the Forty-two Judges in the Hall of Osiris.

nebȧu
nebȧnȧu flame, fire, a burning.
nebȧt

nebȧu fashioner, moulder.

nebeḥ a kind of bird.

nebti (=), the two goddesses Nekhebit and Uatchit.

nebṭ, ***nebṭet*** lock of hair, tress; the name of a storm cloud; the name of a fiend.

nepu a part of the body.

neper grain, wheat, barley, dhura.

Neprȧ the Grain-god.

nepert corn-land.

Nepert the name of a city.

nef he, him.

nefa a sign of the demonstrative, this, that; plur. .

nefu air, wind, breath; breath of life.

nefu sailor.

Nef-ur the name of a city or district.

nefer — to be good, to be happy, to be beautiful, good, pretty, gracious, well-doing; beautiful, good; twice good, very good; good one or thing; fine gold; gracious speech.

with , happiness, joy, gladness,

neferu / ***nefert*** — beauties, splendours, fair things, good things.

Nefer-ḥer — "fair face", a title of Rā and of Ptaḥ.

Nefer (?) — the name of a lake.

neferu — to be glad (?).

Nefert — girl, maiden; a proper name.

nefert name of a tree.

Nefer-uben-f , a proper name.

Nefer-sent name of a city.

Nefer-Tem , name of a god, the son of Ptaḥ and Sekhet.

nem to defraud = (?).

Nem a proper name.

nem , to walk, to stride, go about, wander about.

nemȧ

nemnem

nememti

nemt , step, stride; plur. , , ,

nemā who? who then? who then art thou?

nemm to lie dead.

nemmȧt bier.

nemmȧ pygmy, dwarf.

nemeḥ to understate the reading of the tongue of the balance, to be young, lowly, poor, humble.

nemes the name of a crown, tiara, or fillet for the head.

nemt block for slaughter, the chamber in which the damned suffered decapitation and mutilation; plur.

nemtchet a place of slaughter.

nen a sign of the demonstrative; this is he who; these who;

nen 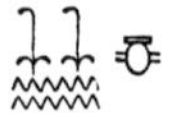 unguent.

nen  a kind of stuff, linen.

nen 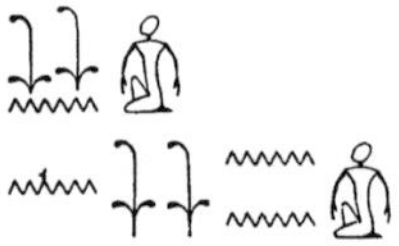 to be weak, helpless, exhausted.

neni, ***neniu***  weak or helpless folk, fiends, etc.

nenaiu  winds.

Nin-årruṭ-f (?), ***Nen-aårruṭ-f***  see Ȧn-ruṭ-f.

Nenunser  name of a Cow-goddess.

nenmet  (a late form) bier.

Nentchā 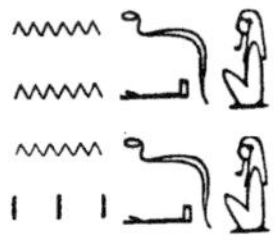 the name of a god.

Ner  name of the Herd-god; a proper name.

Nerȧu  name of the Herd-god; a proper name.

ner, nert  men and women, mankind.

neru, ***nerȧu***, ***nerr***  to be strong, to strike fear into any one.

nerȧut, ***nert***  victory, conquest; plur. 

Neri  "mighty one"; name of a god.

Nerȧu-ta  a proper name.

nerȧut  vulture.

neh  to conquer.

neha  to alight.

neha  to advance.

nehaȧs to awake.

nehapu to shine, give light.

nehat sycamore, fig-tree; the two sycamores, fig-trees.

Nehatu the name of a city.

nehep to copulate.

nehep to have power over.

nehpu strength.

nehpu light, fire, to shine.

nehem to rejoice.

rejoicings.

nehemnehem to destroy (?).

neheh fire.

nehhu needy one.

nehes  to wake up, rouse up.

Nehesu  a group of divine beings.

Nehes-ui 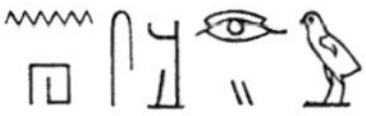 a proper name.

Neḥ  the name of a god.

neḥ  to beseech, pray, entreat.

neḥa  to be bad, stinking.

Neḥa-ḥāu  "stinking limbs"; a proper name.

Neḥa-ḥer  the name of one of the Forty-two Judges in the Hall of Osiris.

neḥait 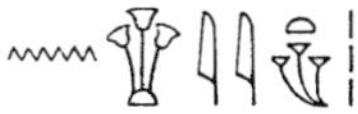 flowers.

neḥit  time, eternity (?).

neḥeb  to coerce, put the yoke on some one.

neḥebet 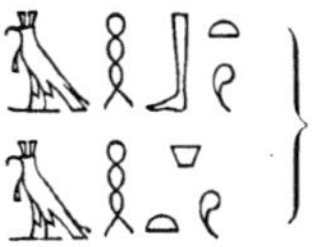 neck; plur. 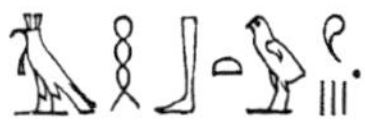.

Neḥeb-nefert 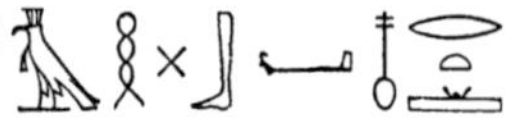 the name of one of the Forty-two Judges in the Hall of Osiris.

Neḥeb-ka / ***Neḥeb-kau***  "he who yokes together the Kau"; a proper name.

neḥep 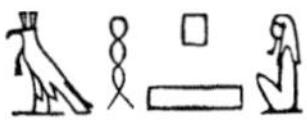 the divine potter's table.

neḥem  to carry off, to plunder, to deliver, release;  deliverers;   delivered.

neḥeḥ 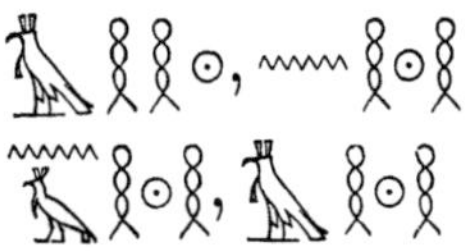 eternity, for ever; with  time without beginning or end.

neḥeḥ  to invoke, entreat.

neḥes 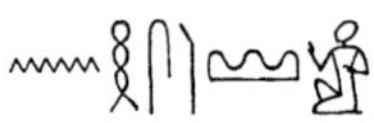 negro, a Sûdânî man in general.

neḥṭ-t  jaw teeth (?).

neḥṭ-ui	the two jaws (?).
	. . . .
nekh	to cry out, complain.
nekha	a sharp knife.
nekhakhat	, humours (?), variant … .
nekhȧu	protector.
Nekhebet	the goddess of the city of Nekheb (Al-Kâb).
nekhebet	flowers.
Nekhen	a city of Upper Egypt, … the god of Nekhen.
nekhen	babe, child.
nekhenu	children.
Nekhenu	the name of one of the Forty-two Judges in the Hall of Osiris.
nekhenit	girls (?).
nekhekh	old man.

nekhekh 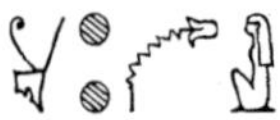 Vol. II, p. 251, l. 10.

nekhekh  whip, flail.

nekht 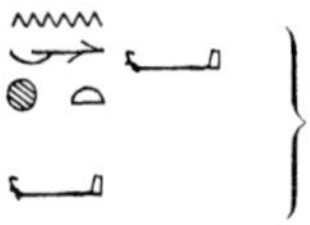 to be strong, strength, powerful.

nekhtu  valour, bravery, conquest.

Nekht  a proper name.

nekht  strong (in a bad sense).

Nekhtu-Åmen 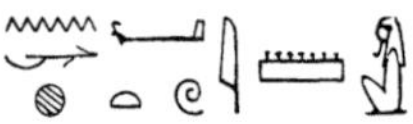 a proper name.

nes 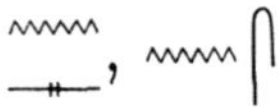 she, her, it.

nes 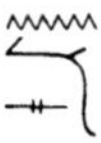 to belong to.

 belonging to him.

nesu 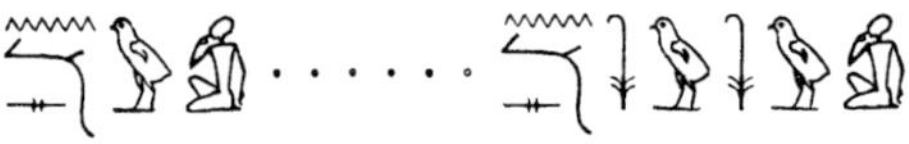

nes *nesau*		tongue; ; plur. .
nes		to eat, devour, consume.
nes	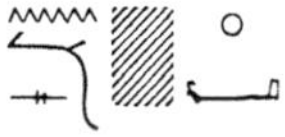	to arrange (?), order (?).
nes *nesnes*	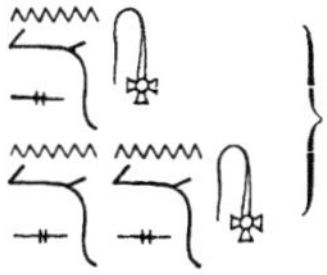	flame.
nes	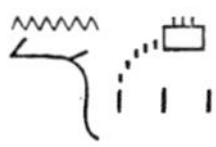	grain (?).
nesut		weapons of war.
nesb	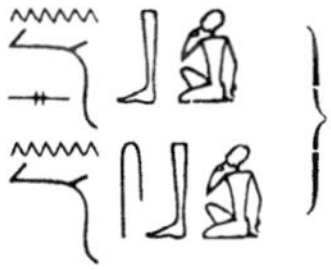	to eat; .
nesbit		to eat, devour.
Nesbu		devouring gods.
nespu		slaughter, wound, knives.
nesert		flame, fire.

Nesert a fire-goddess.

Nesersert the Fire-city.

nest throne; plur.

Throne.

nesti a class of divine beings.

nest cakes (?).

ṅesh to walk (?).

neshau plates of metal.

neshu a weapon (?).

neshi — to make the hair bristle.

neshep to snuff the air.

neshem, ***neshmet*** } a precious stone.

neshmet the name of a sacred boat.

neshni, *neshen*, *neshenu* 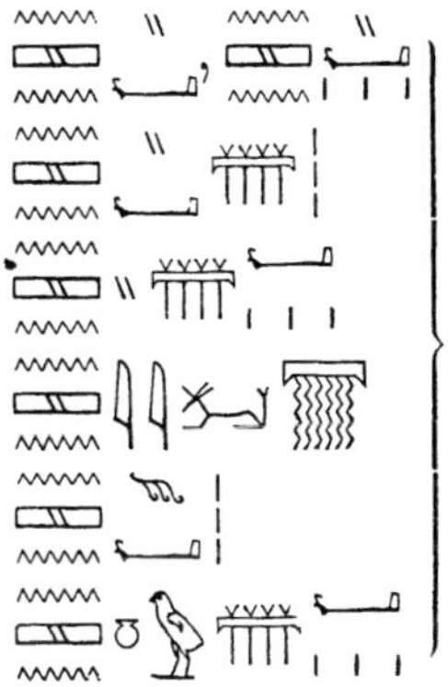 to be stormy, to revolt, a thunder-storm, destructive winds, whirlwind, tempest in general, revolt; 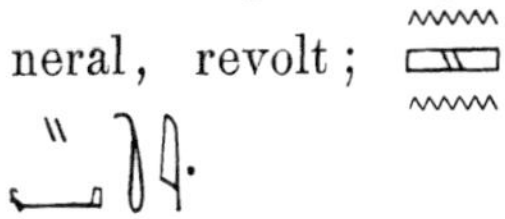.

nek  thou, thy.

nek  to copulate;  to have union with himself.

nekek 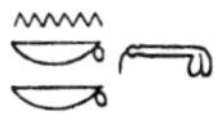 to commit sodomy.

nek nekek  to have union with a sodomite.

nekau  . . . . . .

nekai  injury.

 ill-doing fiends.

Nekȧ 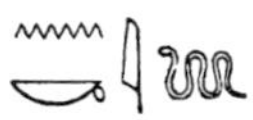

Nekȧu  the name of a fiend.

neken 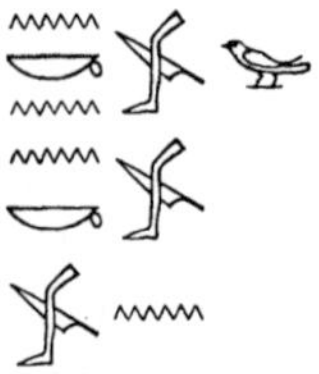 to do harm or injury to anyone.

nekent  injury; plur. , .

nekenu  injury, evil, harm.

neqāut  shackles.

neqāiut  those who steal away.

neḳa  to chew.

Neḳau  a Bull-god.

neḳeḳ  to cackle.

Neḳeḳ-ur  "Great Cackler"; name of the Goose-god.

Net  Neith, the great goddess of Saïs.

ent  of.

net  water, stream.

ent-ā — to ordain, order, ordinance, decree, customary rite;

enti — who, which, that which; plur.

entiu, *entet* — things which exist, persons or beings who are.

enti — sign of the negative, no, not, without.

neti — to vanquish, conquer.

Enti-mer-f — a proper name.

Enti-ḥer-f-emm-mast-f — a proper name.

entu —

netu — fastenings, cords.

entuten — ye, you.

entef — he.

netnet — that which flows.

neter god, Copt. ⲛⲟⲩⲧⲉ great god; self-created, great god; god One; the City-god; god with a dog's face.

neteru gods, all the gods of the Three Companies, *i.e.*, Heaven, Earth, and the Ṭuat; all the gods.

the father-gods.

the mother-goddesses.

the Four gods.

the Forty-two gods.

gods celestial and gods terrestrial.

gods of heaven and gods of earth.

gods of the Ṭuat.

gods of the Qerti.

gods guides of the Ṭuat.

gods of the East.

gods of the North.

gods of the West.

gods of the South.

neter-ui the two gods Horus and Set; the two divine eyes, *i. e.*, Sun and Moon.

netert goddess, late form ; plur. , , .

netri to be a god or like unto a god, divine , , , divine.

he who is divine; , "divine god".

neter åtfui the two divine fathers.

neter meṭu "the words of the god", *i.e.*, hieroglyphic writing.

neter nemt the block or execution chamber of the god (Osiris).

neter ḥāu the body, or limbs, of the god.

neter ḥet "god-house", *i. e.*, temple.

neter ḥetepu "god-offerings", holy offerings, sepulchral meals.

neter khert "underworld of the god"; a name for the grave and for the place of departed spirits.

neter khet "god-property", *i. e.*, things dedicated to the service of the god.

neter shems "god-follower", a member of the god's "body-guard".

neter ṭuai "god-star", the morning star, Venus.

neter ṭuau — "god-adoration", to give thanks to God.

neter ṭepṭ — "god-boat", divine barque.

neter tcheṭ — "god-word", sacred speech.

Neter — name of a lake in the Other World.

Neteru, ***Netri*** — name of a town or city.

Netert-utchat — name of a place.

entes — she.

ent-sen — them, they.

entek — thou (masc.).

Netqa-ḥer-khesef-åtu — the name of the herald of the Fourth Ārit.

ent — thou (fem.).

netet — cattle for sacrifice.

entet — which, that which is.

neṭ — to bandage, to tie.

Neṭit — a proper name.

Neṭbit — name of a town or city.

Neṭet — name of a town or city.

netch, *netchet* — to protect, guard, avenge.

netch ḥer — "homage to thee", a form of salutation to gods.

netchti — protector, advocate, avenger.

netch meṭu, *netchtu re* — to discuss a matter with someone, to converse, to take counsel.

netchnetch — to take counsel with someone, to discuss a matter.

Netcheb-ȧb-f — a proper name.

Netchfet — name of a town and its god.

netchem, ***netchemu***, ***netchemet*** 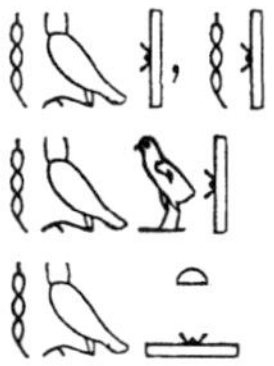 to be sweet, pleasant, to rejoice, be glad;  very pleasant;  pleasant things.

netchemmit  love-making, the delights of sexual love.

Netchem  the god of love.

netcher  to grasp, hold fast.

netcheriu, ***netcherit*** 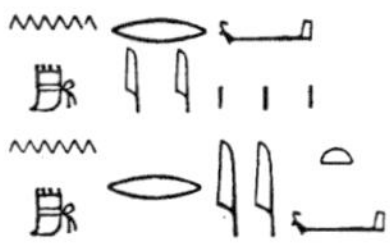 clinchers, grapplers.

netcherȧ  to hew, to carve.

netchḥet 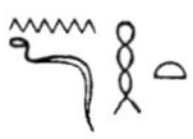 to strengthen.

Netcheḥ-netcheḥ, ***Netcheḥ-tcheḥ*** 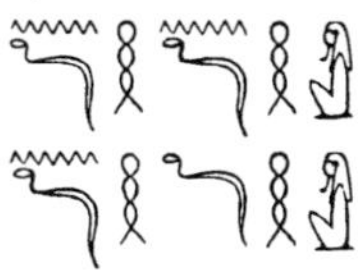 the name of one of the Seven Spirits who guard Osiris and his bier.

netches — to be little, little, weak.

netcheset — lesser gods, perhaps "false gods".

Netchesti — a name of Osiris.

Netchses — a name of a god.

Netchet — a name of a town or city.

R or L.

er — at, to, with, into, among, against, from, according to, near, by, towards, upon, concerning. With compounds :—

er åmi — among.

er åmi tu, *er åmi thu* — among, between.

er åsu — in return for, as reward or recompense for.

er mā — with, near.

er men	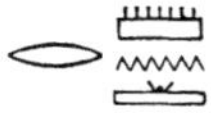	as far as.
er entet	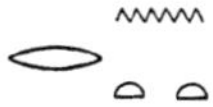	because.
er ruti		outside.
er ḥāt		before.
er ḥenā	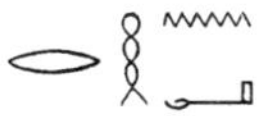	with.
er ḥer		away from.
er ḥeru		above.
er kheft ḥer		in the face of.
er kher		under.
er kherth	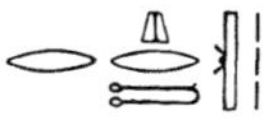	on behalf of.
er sa		by the back of.
er ḳes	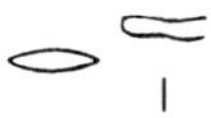	near, by the side of, in the track of.
er		sign of the comparative: more than, *e. g.*,

 glorious more than the gods.

 divine more than the gods.

 swift more than greyhounds.

 swift more than the shadow.

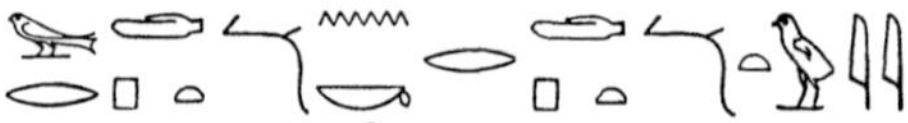 great is the taste to thee more than that taste.

 Horus is bolder than all the gods.

 provided more than the gods.

 a name greater than yours.

 stronger than the gods.

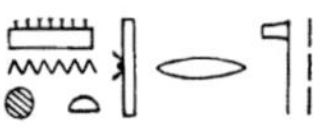 more gracious than the gods.

 brighter than the House of the Moon.

 thy speech is more piercing than the [cry of] the *tcheru* bird.

er 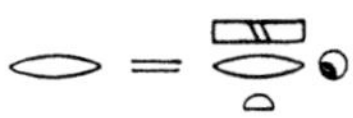 cake, offering.

re  goose.

re worms (?),

re door, opening, entrance, mouth, speech, chapter; plur. ; opening of the mouth, appearance; strong of mouth; doors of the Ṭuat; chapters of commemorations; a single chapter; a chapter of words; a chapter of mysteries; to set the mouth in motion against any one, *i. e.*, to slander.

re åpt (?) brow.

Re-āa-urt "opening of the great door"; the name of a town.

re-uat entrance to the roads.

re Ḥāp mouth of the Nile.

re Khemenu the entrance to the city of Hermopolis.

re Sekhait mouth of the goddess Sekhait.

Re-stau the "entrance to the corridors" in the Other World of Seker at Ṣaḳḳârah.

re-pu or.

re-per temple.

temples; temples of the South and North.

Re (***Maȧu***?) the Lion-god.

Re (?)-***Iukasa*** the name of a god.

Re (?)-***Rā*** the Lion-god Rā.

rā  work.

Rā  the Sun-god *par excellence*; 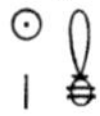 like Rā.

rā  day. 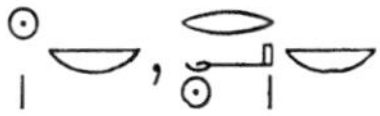 daily, every day.

Rā-Ȧsȧr  Rā-Osiris, the Sun-god of day and night.

Rā-Ḥeru-khuti  "Rā-Horus of the two horizons", Rā-Harmachis.

Rā-Tem  Rā-Tem, the Sun-god of day and night.

Rā-Maāt-men  the prenomen of Seti I.

Rā-men-kau 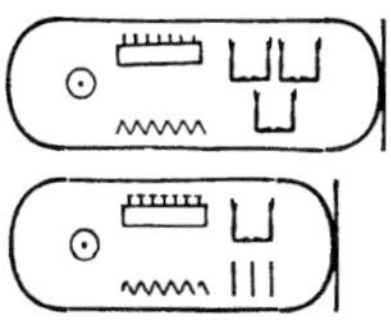 the Mykerinos of the Greeks.

Rā-mes-meri-Ȧmen-meri-Maāti  Rameses IV.

Rā-er-neḥeḥ 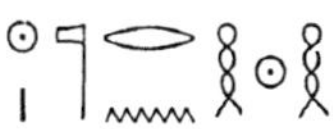 a proper name.

ri 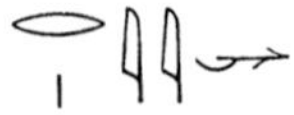 door.

ri  bandage, swathing.

riu  emanations.

ru  . . . . . .

ru  . . . . . .

ru  to fall, drop (of the wind).

ruȧ, *ruȧa*  to separate from, move away from, depart.

rui  journey, departure.

ruti 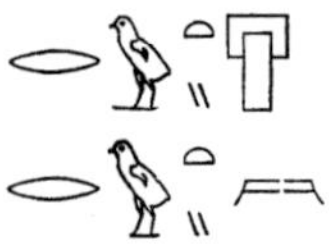 the two leaves of a door.

ruṭ 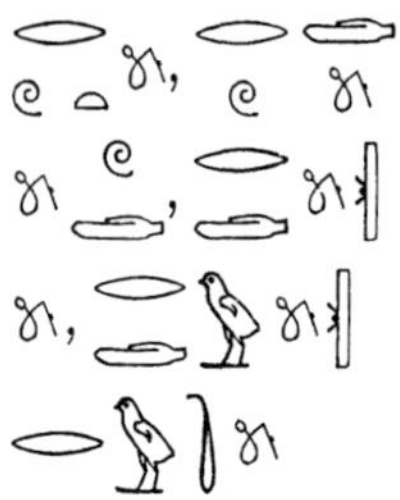 to grow, flourish, to be firm and healthy, to be taut (of ropes and sails); 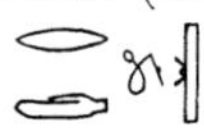 .

ruṭi  strong, vigorous.

ruṭ
ruṭu } plants, things which grow.

Ruṭ-en-Ȧst a proper name.

Ruṭu-nu-Tem a proper name.

Ruṭu-neb-rekhit a proper name.

ruṭu •superintendent, overseer.

ruṭ staircase.

eref an intensive particle, then, therefore.

erpā
erpāt } hereditary tribal chief.

erpit image, statue, august person.

erpti the two august goddesses, *i. e.*, Isis and Nephthys.

remu fish.

Remu the "town of fish"; a proper name.

Remi  the Fish-god.

rem 

remu  to weep.

remt  tear; plur. , .

rem-tȧ  studded (?).

ermen 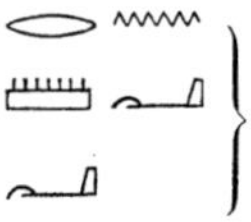 arm, shoulder, one side of the body.

ermenui  the two arms, shoulders.

 the two sides of a ladder.

ermenu 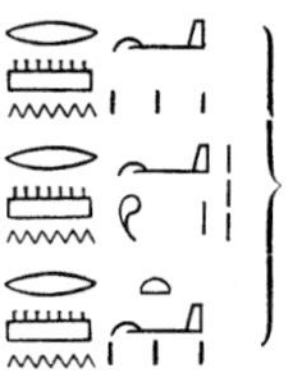 shoulders, arms, supporters, the branches of a tree.

ermen — to carry away, to bear, to remove something, to shoulder.

Remrem — the name of a god.

ren — name; plur.

ren — to nurse (see *renen*).

renp — to be young or youthful, renewal of youth, to become young; youthful one.

renp-tȧ — youthful, made young; very young.

renpit — year; plur. *renput*

renpit — plants, vegetables, fruits.

Renen the name of a god.

renen to nurse, to suckle.

Renenet
Renutet } the goddess of grain crops and the harvest.

rer (*peḥer*?) territory, a place for walking about.

rer
reru } to walk about, to go round about, to revolve, to encircle; *thes rer* again, repetition, conversely.

rertȧ encircled.

reri those who revolve, or go about.

rer khet going about retreating.

rert circle.

rert drugs, medicine.

rer pig.

reru . . . .

reru . . . .

rert mistake for or men.

Rertu-nefu a proper name.

Rerek name of a serpent fiend in the city of Åses.

Rerti (?) (***Maȧuti*** ?) the Lion-god and Lion-goddess, *i. e.*, Shu and Tefnut (?). The name of one of the Forty-two Judges in the Hall of Osiris.

rehebu flame, fire. Compare Heb. לָהַב.

rehen to rest upon, to support.

reḥ to enter.

reḥu a man deified, later a god.

reḥui  the two combatant gods, Horus and Set.

reḥti  the two combatant sister goddesses, Isis and Nephthys.

Reḥui 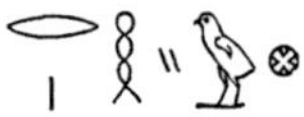 the town of the two combatant gods.

Re-ḥent  a proper name.

Re-ḥenent 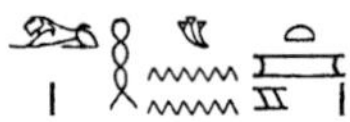 name of a lake or canal.

Re-ḥenent 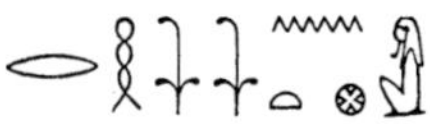 the name of a town or its god.

rekh 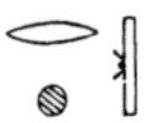 to be wise, to have knowledge; 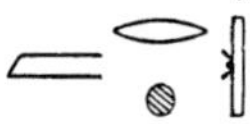 knowingly, with intent; 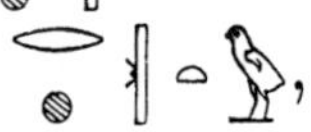,  known;  unknown.

rekht  knowledge, a list, inventory, total.

rekh ȧb to understand.

rekhu khet "knowers of things", *i. e.*, the wise gods.

rekhit beings of knowledge, rational beings, men and women, people, mankind.

rekhes to sacrifice, to slaughter.

Rekhti the two goddesses Isis and Nephthys.

Rekhti-Merti-neb[ti]-Maāti the two goddesses who were the ladies of the city of Maāt.

res to watch, be awake; awake; rouse up! wake up!

resu

resit the nine watchers.

restu night watchers.

Res-àb the warder of the Fourth Ārit.

Res-ḥer the warder of the Third Ārit.

res south, southern; South and North, all Egypt.

resiu southerners, southern gods.

Resu a proper name; fem.

resu south wind.

Resenet (?) a proper name.

resh to breathe with joy, to rejoice.

resht gladness, joy, to snuff, to inhale.

reshui the two nostrils.

rek then, an emphatic particle.

rek		time.
rekḥ	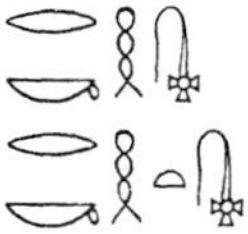	to burn, to be hot.
rekḥu		fire, flames.
Rekes	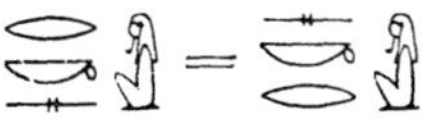	
req *reqa*		to incline away, fall away from; .
reqi		fiend, enemy.
reqau	 (or )	fiends, enemies.
ret	 = 	*i. e.*, *reret*, or *peḥrert*.
ret (*remt*)		men and women, people, mankind.
		everybody.
Retasashaka		a name of Ȧmen.

reti	the two leaves of a door.
reṭ	leg, foot.
reṭui, ***reṭi***	the two feet.
reṭȧu	feet.
reṭ (remt)	men and women, people, folk, mankind.
reṭ	steps, staircase.
erṭā, ***erṭāt***	to give, to set, to place, to put, to cause or make to happen; … As an auxiliary verb: … and see *passim*.

Erṭā-nefu  a proper name.

Erṭā-ḥen-er-reqa  a proper name.

reṭut  places, abodes.

reṭu  . . . .

reṭu 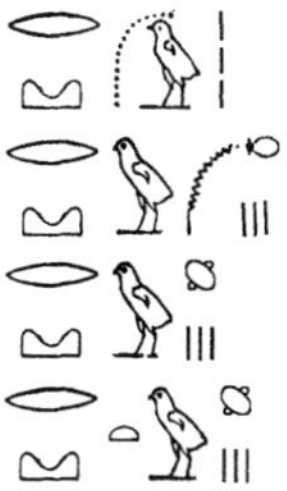 emanations, effluxes, droppings.

reth  men and women, people, folk, mankind.

 everybody.

 H.

ha  interjection, O! Hail!

ha  to be strong;  strength.

ha, *hai*, *hait* — to descend, to go down into a place, to embark on a ship, to fall, to go in, enter, advance into; those who enter.

hau — time, period, reign.

Haȧker — name of a festival.

Hai — "phallus"; the name of one of the Forty-two Judges in the Hall of Osiris.

hai — interjection, O! Hail!

hai — to shout with joy, rejoice.

haiu — the gods who rejoice.

hait — a large chamber, heaven (?).

hab — to send, to send forth, to go forward.

habu — those who fall down.

Hab-em-atu — "advancing at the moment"; a proper name.

habeq — to fail.

hamu — blemish, defect, sin.

Hart-àb — to please.

Hahuti-àm- ..... — the name of a fiend.

Haḥetep — a proper name.

Hakheru — a proper name.

Hasert — a city in the Seventh Àat.

haker — the name of a god and of a festival.

haq — =

Haqahakaḥer — a proper name.

hat  interjection, O!

hat  descent, entrance, embarcation.

hatu  brow (?).

haṭ  to suppress, to beat down, subdue.

hi  to rejoice.

hu  to enter, descend, fall.

Hunefer  the name of a scribe.

Hu-kheru  the name of the herald of the first Ȧat.

heb  ibis, the bird sacred to Thoth.

heb, ***hebt***  to send out, to go forward.

hepu 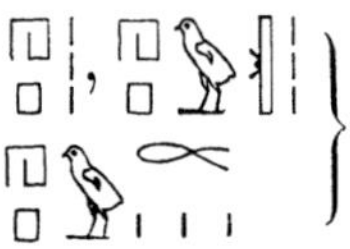 laws, ordinances, regulations.

hem  fire.

hemu		men and women, folk, people: see also *ḥenmemet*.
hemhem		to roar, cry out, bellow (of a bull).
hemhemet		outcries, roarings.
Hemti		runner.
hen	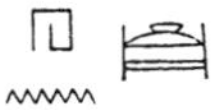	funeral chest, coffin.
Henȧ		the name of a city.
henȧnȧu	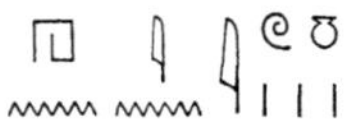	pleasant things.
henu		to sing songs of joy, to praise.
henu		praises, shouts of joy, singers.
henhenu		the watery abyss of heaven, flood.
henhenit		the watery abyss of heaven, flood.
hensheses	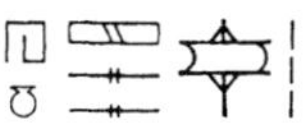	the east wind.
her		to be content, pleased.

her-àb / ***hert-àb***	pleased in heart, content, pleasure.
herà	a vessel.
heru	day; plur.
	this day, to-day.
	judgment day.
	birthday.
	birthday of Osiris.
	day of the funeral.
	every day, daily.
	a happy day.
	daily, course of each day.
heriu	those who are content (?).
herret	things which please.
heh	flame.

heker 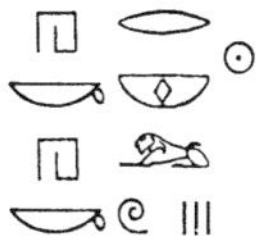 ***hekeru*** } name of a festival.

heq 

hetu  to be addressed.

hethet  to go round about.

heṭ 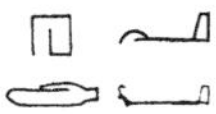 to subdue. 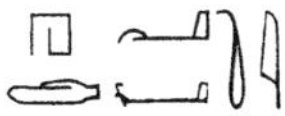 subdued.

 Ḥ.

. . . . . . 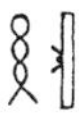 with 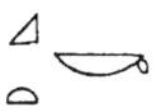 . . . . . .

ḥa  behind, get back! back thou! (in addresses to fiends).

ḥa  back of the head and neck.

ḥa  a cry, a precative particle.

Ḥaȧs  a proper name.

ḥaȧu  the dwellers in the Delta and in the marshes near the sea-coast.

ḥai  to be bright, to shine.

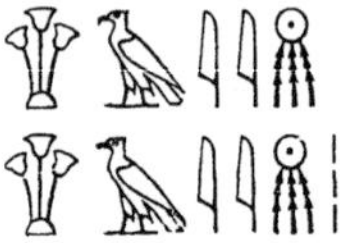 light.

Ḥai, *Ḥait*  a proper name.

ḥait  to grasp.

ḥau, *ḥauu* 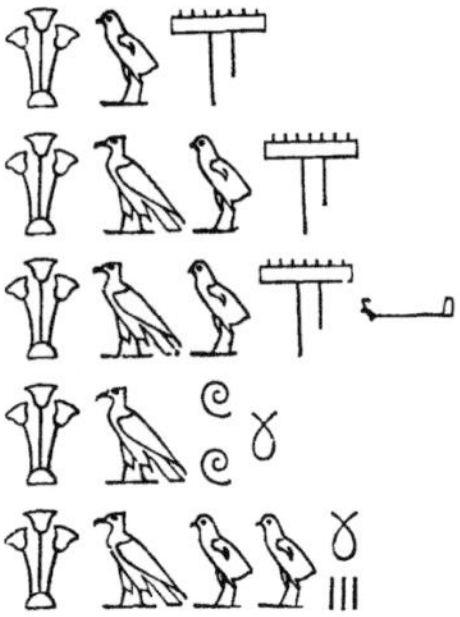 to be unclothed, to strip off apparel.

ḥaui  naked man.

ḥau  addition, increase, things added.

ḥauatu filth, dung.

ḥan-re to have a care for, assuredly.

Ḥa-ḥer a proper name.

ḥap
ḥapu
ḥapt } to enshroud, to hide, to cover over.

ḥap to advance, move forward.

ḥaputi runner (?).

Ḥap the Bull Apis;

Ḥap
Ḥapi } one of the four sons of Horus who protected one quarter of the body of the deceased.

ḥapu oar, steering pole, rudder.

ḥaptu } oars, paddles.

Ḥapu-en-neb-sett a name for the cemetery.

Ḥapṭ-re a proper name.

ḥam
ḥamt } to net birds and fish.

ḥamiu fishermen, fowlers.

Ḥarpuḳakashareshabaiu a proper name.

Ḥareti a proper name.

ḥaqet to capture, make prisoners, captives.

ḥaqet fetters.

ḥaqu name of a plank or peg in the magic boat.

ḥat pit.

ḥaṭ tomb.

ḥaṭ
ḥaṭu } net.

ḥatȧ, *ḥatȧtu*, *ḥattui* — storm, whirlwind.

ḥā, *ḥāa* — to rejoice, be glad; rejoicing; glad.

ḥāiu — rejoicings.

ḥāā — to rejoice.

ḥāāiu, *ḥāātu* — rejoicings, those who rejoice.

[*ḥā* — limb, member of the body, the body itself.]

ḥāu, ***ḥāt*** — limbs, members of the body; one body; thy own self.

Ḥāp, ***Ḥāpi*** — the Nile.

Ḥāp-ur — the Great Nile.

ḥā[t]-ā — the beginning or front of anything; the opening words of a book.

ḥāt — the beginning or front of anything, bows of a boat, the breast; before.

[***ḥāt-ā*** — prince, chief] the two divine princes.

ḥāti — the heart; plur.

ḥātet — a rope in the bows of a boat.

ḥāti — unguent of the best kind.

Ḥi-mu (?) — the name of one of the Forty-two Judges in the Hall of Osiris.

Ḥit — a proper name.

ḥu — a mistake for .

ḥu — hair, tresses.

Ḥu, ***Ḥui*** — the god of food, divine food.

ḥu — to smite, to strike; smiting (*i.e.*, clapping) their hands; smiting.

ḥut — a smiting.

ḥuit-Rā — smiters of Rā.

Ḥu-tepa  a proper name.

ḥua  to be filthy, in a stinking, corrupt, or rotten state.

ḥuaat  filth, dung, offal;  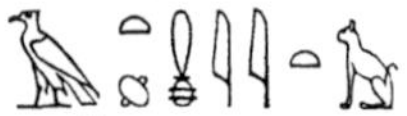 "filthy cat".

ḥui 

ḥuia  to decree, issue a command.

ḥun  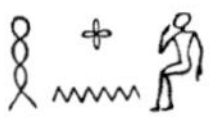

ḥunu 

ḥunen 

to be in the state of a child; boy, child, young man; plur.  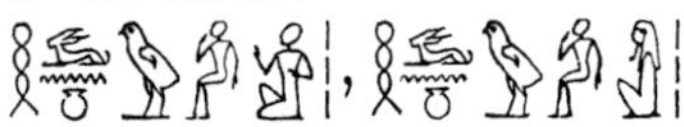 

ḥunt  maiden, girl.

Ḥunt-Pe-...  . . . .

ḥuḥu  waterflood, a large mass of water.

ḥeb — festival.

ḥebu, *ḥebit* — festivals.

ḥebt — the book containing the words of the festival service.

ḥeb — fowls and fish for the festival.

ḥebā — to play (at draughts).

ḥebt, *ḥebbet* — stream, flood.

ḥebenut — a cake, confectionery.

ḥebs — to be clothed; clothed, a garment.

ḥebs — garment, clothing, a swathing; plur.

Ḥebṭ-re-f a proper name.

ḥept for *q. v.*

ḥept to embrace, embrace ; ,
.

ḥept breast (?), embrace.

Ḥept-ur a proper name.

Ḥept-shet the name of one of the Forty-two Judges in the Hall of Osiris.

ḥeptu oars of a boat, doorposts.

ḥept , to move forward, advance; see advancing.

ḥeptet a course, a place for walking.

Ḥepṭ-ur a proper name.

Ḥepṭ-re a proper name.

ḥepṭ-re to shut the mouth, to gnaw (?).

ḥefau  serpent, snake.

ḥefi  a serpent with two legs.

ḥefait 

ḥefiu  . . . .

ḥefen 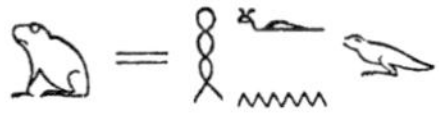 one hundred thousand.

ḥefṭ  to sit down, to rest.

ḥem  a particle.

ḥem  to retreat, make to go back.

ḥem  to steer, or paddle a boat.

ḥemu 

ḥemi 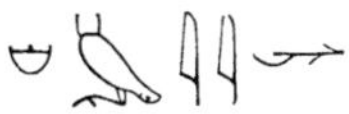 paddle, oar, rudder, steering pole.

ḥemu 

ḥemit  paddles.

ḥemaḳa  to grasp.

Ḥemaḳa  the name of a town and of a god.

ḥematet — name of a chamber.

ḥemu — artificer, workman.

ḥemt — work, handicraft.

ḥemt — a mineral.

ḥemt — copper, bronze.

ḥemen — slaughter.

Ḥemen — the name of a god.

ḥement — forty.

ḥems — to sit, be seated, to dwell; , sitting, sitting ones; seated.

ḥemset — a sitting, seat.

ḥemt — woman, wife; plur. , .

woman belonging to a man, wife.

king's woman, *i. e.*, queen.

god's woman, *i. e.*, priestess.

Asiatic woman.

women goddesses.

a proper name (?).

ḥemt cow, cow-goddess; plur.

ḥen servant, slave; plur.

ḥent servant (fem.), slave.

ḥen neter god's servant, *i. e.*, priest.

ḥen ka priest of the *Ka*, or double.

ḥen majesty;

ḥen, **ḥenen**, **ḥenḥen** to go forward, to run.

ḥen, **ḥenu** to bestow, to be given or provided with, ordered, arranged.

ḥen, ḥeni 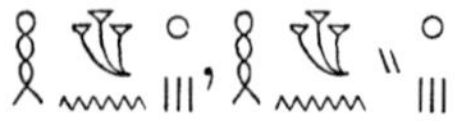 flowers, plants, blossoms.

ḥen  to praise; .

ḥenā 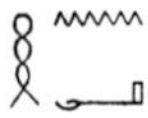 with, along with, and; 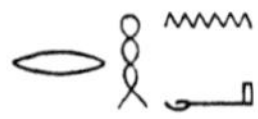 with; 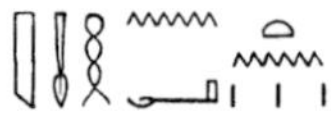 triumphant with you;  god spake with god.

ḥenu  offerings, gifts.

ḥeniu  offerings, gifts.

ḥenu  pillars.

ḥenu 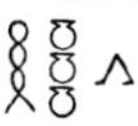 to draw to oneself.

ḥenbet  corn-land.

ḥeneb  offerings of grain produce.

Ḥenbi 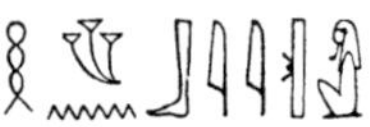 the god of the cultivated lands.

ḥenmemet  also  men and women, folk, people, mankind.

ḥenemnemu devourers (?).

ḥenen to labour, toil.

ḥenen

ḥenu (or *ḥennu*) phallus; phallus of Rā.

Ḥenu, *Ḥennu* name of a sacred boat which was drawn round the sanctuary at dawn at Memphis.

ḥennui to go about, to wander, move forward.

ḥennui the beginning and end of time or of eternity.

ḥennuti crocodiles.

ḥennuit, *ḥennut* fraud, deceit.

ḥennuti two horns, a pair of horns.

ḥens to block the way.

ḥenseki
ḥensekit
ḥensekt
ḥensekti
ḥenkesti (sic)
} hair, lock of hair, tress.

Ḥensek a god with much hair.

Ḥensektiu the gods with much hair, *i. e.*, the gods with long hair and beards.

Ḥenseket-menȧt-Ȧnpu-em-kat-en-utu name of a rope.

ḥenk } to give, present, offer; offered, given.

ḥenket offerings.

Ḥenku-en-Ȧrp a proper name.

Ḥenku-en-fat-Maāt a proper name.

ḥenku  balance.

ḥenket 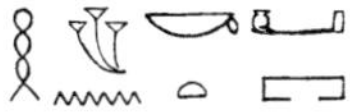

ḥenkit 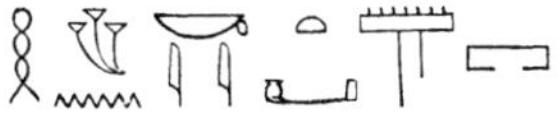 } the funerary bed, or chamber.

Ḥenket  the name of a town.

ḥent 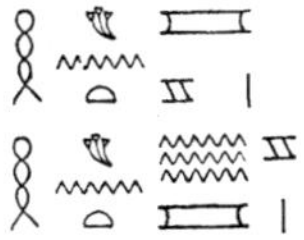 lake, canal, stream, pool.

ḥent 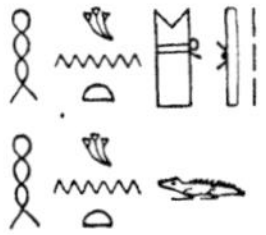 to be hostile.

ḥent 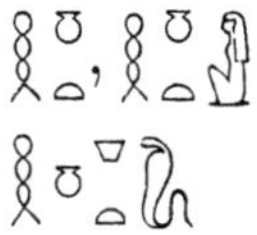 mistress, lady, sovereign, queen.

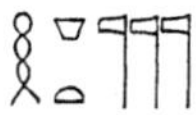 queen of the gods.

 lady of the crowns of the South and North.

 mistress of the pylons.

 queen of the Two Lands.

Ḥent  crocodile.

ḥenta  to fall into oblivion, or decay.

Ḥenti  god of the two crocodiles, a name of Osiris.

ḥenti  crocodile.

ḥenti  a pair of horns.

 the two-horned gods, or the two two-horned gods.

ḥenti 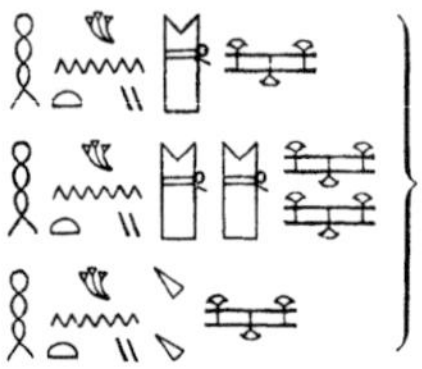 the beginning and end of time, or of eternity.

ḥenti pet  the two ends of heaven.

Ḥenti-requ  a proper name.

Ḥent-khent-ta-meru 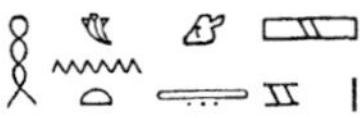 a proper name.

ḥer 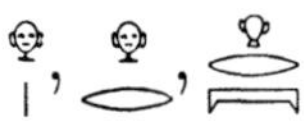 in, at, upon, on, by, etc.; 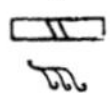 *en ḥer* upon.

ḥer-ā  on the hand, *i. e.*, straightway, immediately.

ḥer-ȧb 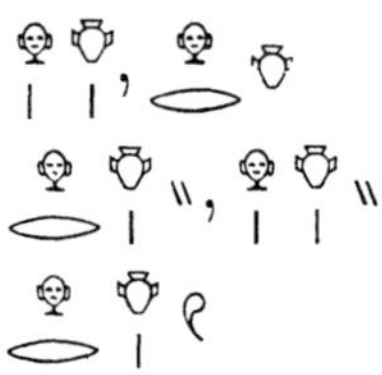

ḥer-ȧbt  in the middle of, dweller in; plur. .

Ḥer-àb-uàa-f "within his boat"; a proper name.

Ḥer-àb-àrit-f "within his eye; a proper name.

Ḥer-àb-karà-f "within his shrine"; a proper name.

ḥer mā straightway, forthwith.

ḥer entet
ḥer enti sa } because.

ḥer sa besides, in addition to.

ḥeri } he who is above, or over, chief of, principal of.

chief scribe; chief of the writings; chief of the altar; chief of the altars.

ḥeriu } those who are over, those who are above, celestial beings; chiefs.

ḥeriu
ḥertu  those who are over, those who are above, celestial beings; chiefs.

ḥeru  the upper regions, what is above;  heaven, .

ḥeri tchatcha  chief, governor, pre-sident.

 chieftainess, goddess.

ḥert  the upper regions, the sky, heaven.

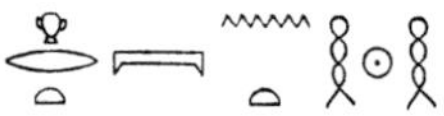 the heaven of eternity, *i. e.*, the everlasting heaven.

Ḥeri-aḳebȧ-f  "chief of his ocean"; a proper name.

Ḥeri-uatch-f 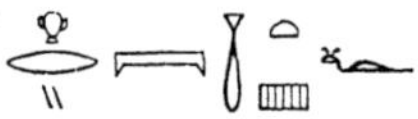 "chief of his sceptre"; a name of Horus.

Ḥeri-uru  "chief of the great ones"; the name of one of the Forty-two Judges in the Hall of Osiris.

Ḥeri-sesh "chief of the writings"; a proper name.

Ḥeri-sep-f "chief of his time"; a proper name.

Ḥeri-sesh[eta] "he who is over the secrets"; *i. e.*, secretary.

Ḥeri-shā-f "he who is on his sand"; a title of Osiris.

"those who are on [their] sand"; a name of the dwellers in the desert.

Ḥeri-ta "governor of the land".

Ḥeri-tchatcha-taui "governor of the Two Lands"; *i. e.*, Egypt.

ḥer and.

ḥer face; plur. , ; two faces; the divine face.

ḥer em ḥer face to face.

ḥer neb every one.

ḥeru nebu , folk, all men, mankind, all the people.

Ḥerui  the god of the two faces.

Ḥerui-f  he of the two faces.

Ḥer-uā  a proper name.

Ḥer-f-em-qeb 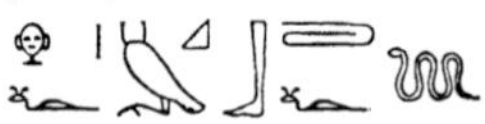 the name of a fiend.

Ḥer-nefer 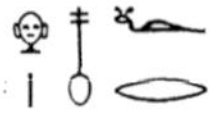 "beautiful Face"; a name of Rā and Ptaḥ;  

Ḥer-f-ḥa-f  "he with his face behind him"; the name of one of the Forty-two Judges in the Hall of Osiris.

Ḥer-k-en-Maāt  a proper name.

ḥer 

ḥeru   to terrify, be frightened.

ḥerit  terror, fright.

ḥeri 

ḥeru  to go away, depart, be away, be afar off; 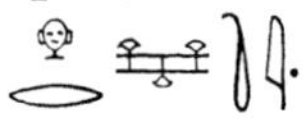.

Ḥer  the ancient name of the Sun-god; applied to the king as the representative of the Sun-god on earth.

Ḥerui  the pair of Horus gods, *i. e.*, Horus and Set.

Ḥerui-senui  the two Horus brethren.

Ḥeru-āa-àbu  "Horus, great one of hearts".

Ḥeru-àmi-àbu-ḥer-àb-àmi-khat   "Horus, dweller in hearts, he who is in the intestines".

Ḥeru-àmi-àthen  "Horus, dweller in the Disk".

Ḥeru-àrit (?)  the "Eye of Horus".

Ḥeru-āḥāi  Horus the Fighter (?).

Ḥeru-Un-nefer  "King of the South and North, Horus Un-nefer".

Ḥeru-ur  The elder Horus as opposed to Horus the son of Isis.

Ḥeru-merti  Horus of the two Eyes, *i. e.*, Sun and Moon.

Ḥeru-em-khebit  Horus of the North.

Ḥeru-em-khent-en-merti .

Ḥeru-neb-urert  "Horus, lord of the Urert-crown".

Ḥeru-netch-ḥer-åtef-f  "Horus, the advocate of his father".

Ḥeru-ḥer-neferu  "Horus on the pilot's place [in the Boat of Rā]".

Ḥeru-khuti  Horus of the horizons of sunrise and sunset.

Ḥeru-Khuti-Kheperå 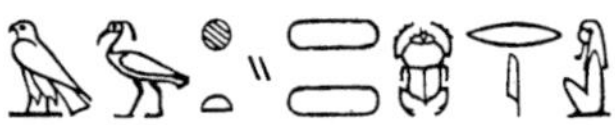 Harmachis Kheperå.

Ḥeru-khenti-ȧn-Merti (?) 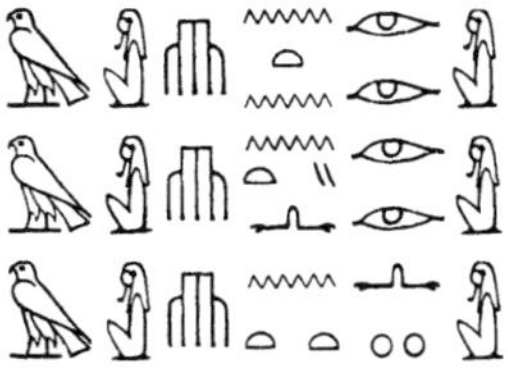 "Horus dwelling in blindness", *i. e.*, Horus (the sky) when neither the sun nor moon is visible.

Ḥeru-khent-Ḳhaṭti .

Ḥeru-khenti-ḥeḥ  "Horus, governor of eternity".

Ḥeru-khenṭ-ḥeḥ  "Horus, traveller of eternity".

Ḥeru-khenti-Sekhem 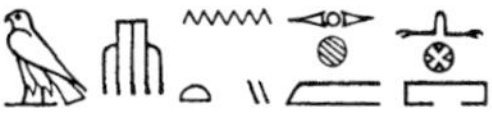 "Horus, governor of Sekhem" (Letopolis).

Ḥeru-khesbeṭ-merti  "Horus with eyes of lapis-lazuli", *i. e.*, blue-eyed Horus.

Ḥeru-sa-Ȧst  "Horus, son of Isis".

Ḥeru-sa-Ȧsȧr  "Horus, son of Osiris".

Ḥeru-sa-Ḥet-Ḥeru  "Horus, son of Hathor".

Ḥeru-sekhai 

Ḥeru-sheṭ-ḥer an obscure form of Horus.

Ḥeru-Ṭeḥuti "Horus-Thoth".

Ḥeru-ṭesher-merti "Red-eyed Horus".

Ḥeru-shemsu "followers of Horus", or "body-guard of Horus"; a class of mythical beings.

Ḥeru ṭāṭāf a son of King Khufu who "found" certain Chapters of the Book of the Dead.

ḥerset crystal.

ḥeḥ million, a number past counting; plur. , . Two millions (?) .

ḥeḥui . . . .

ḥeḥ en sep a million times, millions of times.

millions of festivals.

ḥeḥ . . . .  the land of millions of years.

ḥeḥ 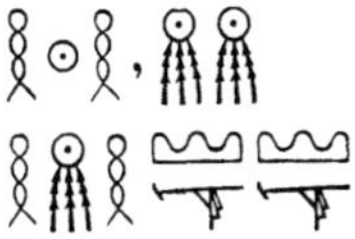 eternity, everlastingness.

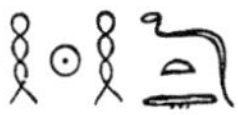 for ever and ever.

Ḥeḥi 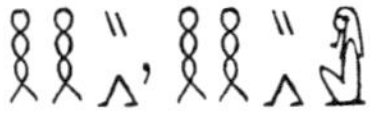 the name of a god.

ḥeḥi 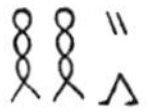 to hasten after, search for; .

ḥes 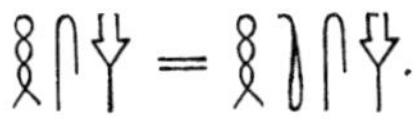

ḥes 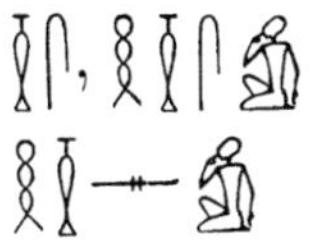 to praise, be praised, to give a reward as a sign of praise;  praised.

ḥesu, *ḥeset*  favour, act of grace, the gift of praise.

 favours, praises.

ḥesi 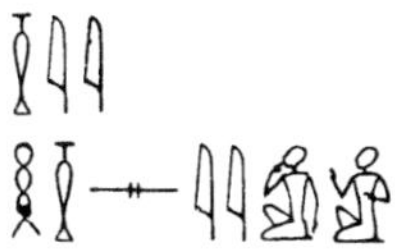 he to whom favour has been shewn by the king or god.

ḥesiu — plur. of preceding.

ḥesuiu

ḥesu — a hymn of praise; the 70 hymns of praise of Rā.

Ḥest — name of a very ancient goddess.

Ḥes-ḥer, *Ḥesi-ḥer* — "savage face"; a proper name.

Ḥes-tchefetch — "savage eye"; a proper name.

ḥesu — dirt, filth.

ḥeseb — faïence (?).

. . . .

ḥeseb — to count up, reckon, estimate, calculate; , , reckoned up.

ḥesbet — a reckoning, an account.

• — computer of holy offerings.

ḥeseb qeṭu — he who estimates characters or dispositions.

ḥeseb ..... — accountant of the linen cloths.

ḥesbet — knife (in the passage).

ḥesepu, *ḥespu* — nomes.

ḥespet — gardens.

Ḥesepti — a king of the 1st dynasty. The true reading of this name is Semti, *q. v.*

ḥesmen 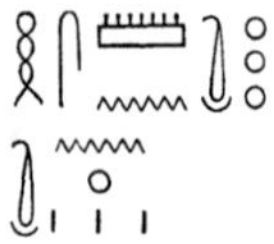 natron.

Ḥesert  the name of a town sacred to Thoth.

ḥesq  to cut, be cut, cut off, to wound, to mow.  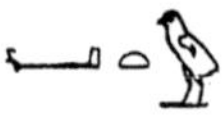 cut.

ḥesqet 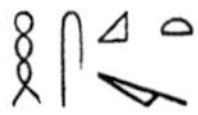 knife.

Ḥest  the name of a city.

ḥest  libation vase.

ḥekau 

ḥekat  incantations, enchantments, magical formulae, charms, amulets.

[**ḥeken** 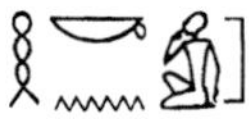 to praise.

ḥekennu  a hymn of praise, praise.

 praises, songs of praise.

those who praise, singers.

ḥekennu an unguent or salve.

Ḥekennut the name of a city.

ḥeq to rule, give commands.

ḥeq ruler, governor; plur.

ḥeqet rule, sovereignty, dominion.

ḥeq sceptre, emblem of rule.

ruler of Åmenti.

governor of towns.

governor of the Two Lands.

governor of the world.

governor of eternity.

Ḥeq-ānṭ 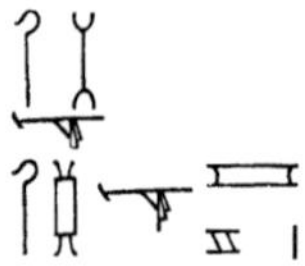 the XIIIth nome of Lower Egypt (capital Heliopolis).

Ḥeq-Maāt-Rā setep-en-Ȧmen  prenomen of Rameses IV.

ḥeq, *ḥeqt*  ale, beer.

ḥeqr 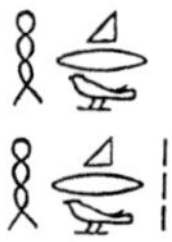 to be hungry.

ḥeqr  hunger.

ḥeqr, *ḥeqrȧu*  hungry man.

Ḥeqtit 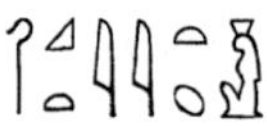 a goddess.

ḥet  to rejoice.

ḥet 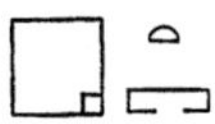 house, section of a book, chapter. Compare the Arabic بيت *bêt*, couplet, stanza, portion of a poem. 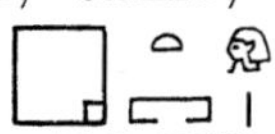 first section, 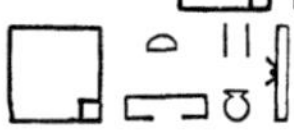, 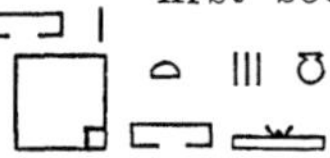, etc.

ḥet 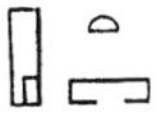  house, temple; plur. 

Ḥet-àāḥ 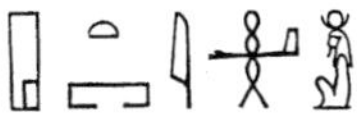 House of the Moon-god.

Ḥet-Àsàr 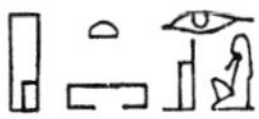 House of Osiris.

Ḥet-Àmen 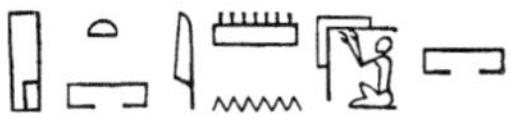 the Hidden House.

Ḥet-Ànes  House of the Ànes garment.

Ḥet-āshemu  House of the statues of the gods.

Ḥet-ur  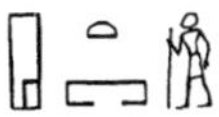 House of the Prince.

 city of the Prince.

Ḥet-uhem-ḥer  House of the Face Renewer.

Ḥet-Usekh-ḥer 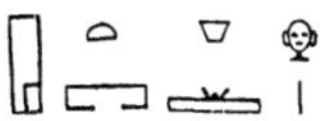 House of Broad-face, *i. e.*, Rā.

Ḥet-Ba  House of the Soul.

Ḥet-Bàti  House of the king of the North.

Ḥet-Benbent 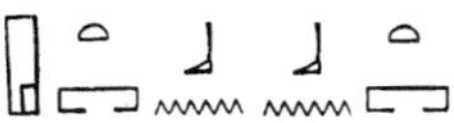 House of the Obelisk.

Ḥet-ka-Ptaḥ 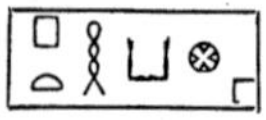 House of the Ka of Ptaḥ, *i. e.*, Memphis.

Ḥet-nemt 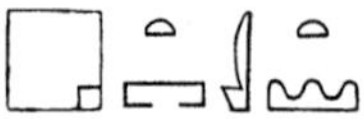 House of the . . . . .

Ḥet ent Ȧnpu  House of Ȧnpu.

Ḥet ent ḳem-ḥeru  House of the gods who have . . . . their faces.

Ḥet-nub 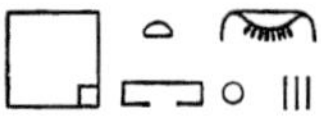 House of gold, *i. e.*, sarcophagus.

Ḥet-nemes 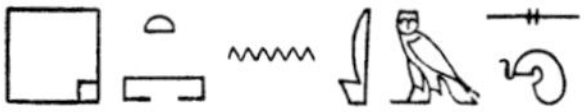 House of the Nemes tiara, or headcloth.

Ḥet-Ḥeru  House of Horus, *i. e.*, the goddess Hathor.

Ḥet-Kheperȧ 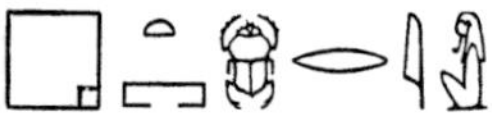 House of Kheperȧ.

Ḥet-seru  House of the Ram-gods.

Ḥet-kau-Nebt-er-tcher  House of the Kau of the Universal Lady.

Ḥet-ṭesheru 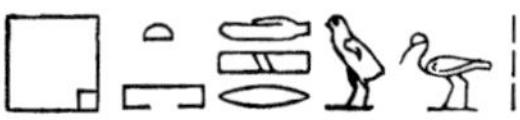 House of the red-gods.

ḥeti smoke.

ḥeti a wooden pole.

ḥeti heart.

ḥeti = strength.

ḥeti, *ḥetit* throat, gorge.

ḥetep , to be at peace, to rest, be satisfied or content, to be at peace with anyone, to remain in one place, to set (of the sun); , sa-tisfied, content; setting in life, *i. e.*, alive when setting; "I make Rā to set like Osiris, and Osiris to set as Rā sets".

ḥetep, *ḥetepu* peace, content; peace of heart; at peace on truth, or resting on truth.

 in peace; 

ḥetep  a table of offerings.

ḥetep, *ḥetepet* 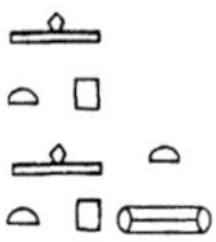 food which is offered to the gods and the dead.

ḥetep neter 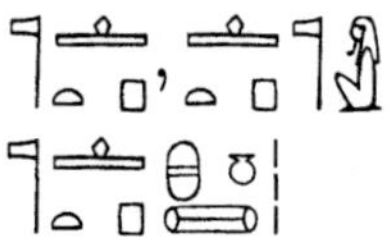 offerings, sacrifices, temple property in general.

ḥetep, *ḥetepet* 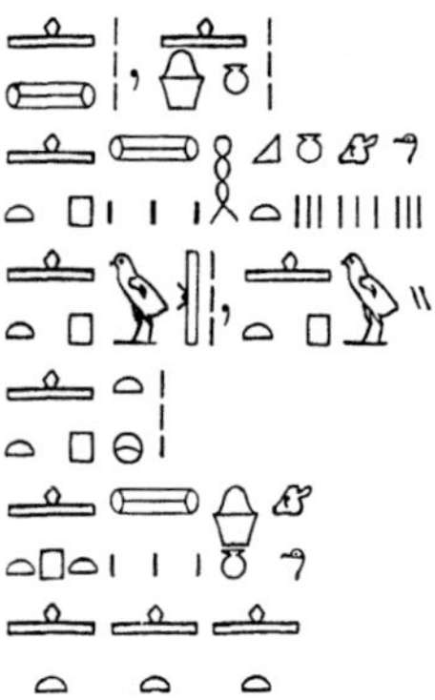 offerings of cakes, ale, oxen, fowl, etc., offerings of propitiation.

Ḥetep  the god of offerings; plur. .

Ḥeteptiu  gods who are regularly provided with offerings.

Ḥetep 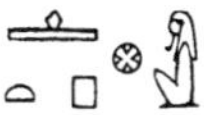 the town of the god Ḥetep.

ḥetepu  geese.

Ḥetep-mes  a proper name.

Ḥetep-Ḥeru-ḥems-uāu  a proper name.

Ḥetep-sekhus 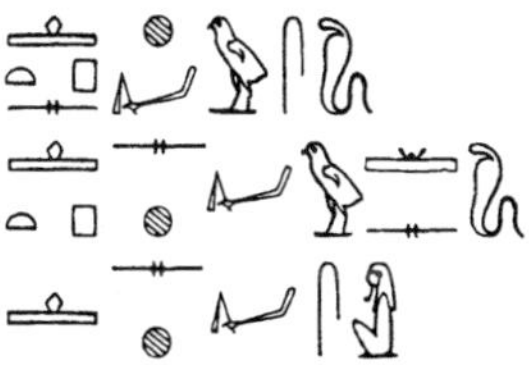 the name of a goddess.

Ḥetep-ka 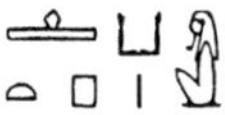 a proper name.

Ḥetep-taui  a proper name.

ḥetem  to destroy, be destroyed.

ḥetemu  destroyers.

ḥetem — to be filled with, provided with; provided.

Ḥetem-ur — "great destroyer"; name of a god.

Ḥetemt-ḥer — "destroying face"; name of a god.

ḥeter — to pay something which is obligatory, legal due, something like tithe.

ḥetru — impost, tax.

ḥetes — to be lord of.

ḥeṭeṭ — scorpion.

Ḥeṭeṭ-t — Scorpion-god.

ḥetch — to do evil, to plunder, steal, waste, destroy, filch away.

ḥetchet — theft, wickedness.

ḥetch — white metal, silver.

ḥetch — to be bright, to shine.

ḥetch ta  dawn, daybreak.

ḥetchu  light.

Ḥetch-åbeḥu 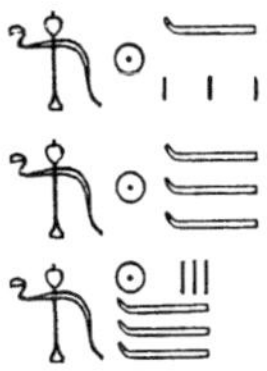 "White teeth"; the name of one of the Forty-two Judges in the Hall of Osiris.

Ḥetch-re 

Ḥetch-re-pesṭ-tchatcha  a proper name.

ḥetch-ḥetch  light.

ḥetchet 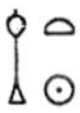 white.

ḥetchet  the White Crown, or Crown of the South.

ḥetchti 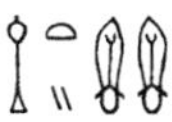 white sandals.

ḥeṭṭ  light.

ḥetchu  loaves.

ḥetchas 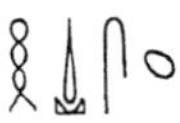 . . . .

KH.

kha 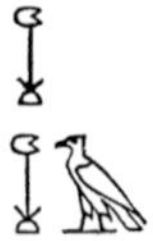 one thousand; 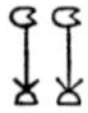 two thousand; plur. 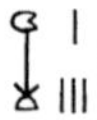; .

kha 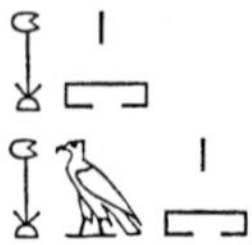 chamber.

kha
khat  the material body, dead body;  divine corpse; plur. .

khaā  to set aside, cast away, to throw.

khāā 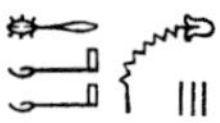 emissions.

khaām  to hasten.

khaāmt  throat.

khaibit  shade, shadow; plur. 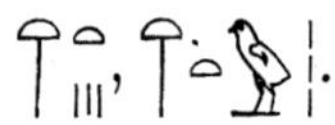.

khaitiu  slaughterers.

khau  fire.

khaut  fire-altar, altars for burnt offerings.

khaut  festival of burnt offerings.

khau  evil, sin.

khau  basins, bowls.

khau  to be plentiful, abundant.

khaui  darkness, night.

khaut  fiends, the dead.

Khau-tchet-f  a proper name.

khabesu 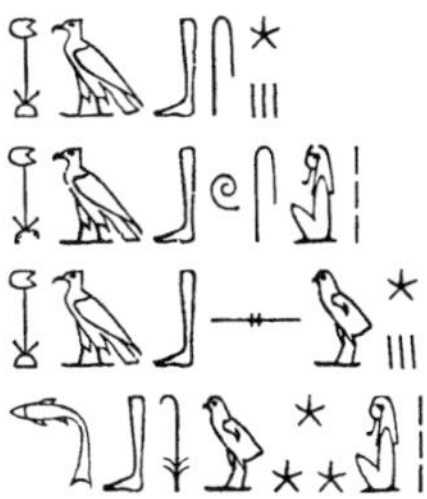 the stars, the thirty-six dekans; the sing. is .

khabet fraud, deceit.

khapa a portion of the body, the navel; plur. buttocks (?) *pudenda muliebris* (?) thighs (?).

Khap-khap a part of the sky, the god of the Ecliptic (?).

kham to subdue, be submissive.

khamesu ears of corn.

khart, ***kharu*** a kind of bird with a piercing cry.

Kharsatȧ a proper name.

khakh to seek, run after.

swift.

khasu the lower eyelids.

khasi bad, evil, wicked, cowardly.

khast territory, country. Perhaps the reading of .

khak-àbu the timid-hearted, enemies.

khaker to be decorated, pretty.

ornaments, decorations.

Khatiu a class of divine beings.

khat fire altar.

khat body, belly, womb; core of the sycamore; plur. , , .

khat the XVIth nome of Lower Egypt (?).

khat a kind of ground.

khatu dead body.

dead bodies.

khatememti nostrils.

khā, ***khāu*** — to rise like the sun, to ascend the throne, to be crowned, to appear (of the king or god). he who rises; one who rises; rising; risen, crowned; beautiful appearance.

khāu — risings, splendours, coronations.

khāu — crowns, diadems.

khāi — crown.

khi — babe, child.

Khiu — the name of a god.

khiuaut — perfume.

khu — to dress.

khu, *khui*, *khaui*  to protect, strengthen, to do good to.

khu, *khut*  protection.

khu  the spirit soul of man which was immortal, as opposed to the  or heart soul which fed upon offerings and lived with the Ka.

 the equipped soul.

 the perfect soul.

khu  plur. of preceding. Four Khu and Seven Khu are mentioned, and certain of the Khu were nine cubits high.

khu  the spirit soul of Osiris, or Rā.   is a title of Osiris.

khu  to shine, be glorious.

khu, ***khut***  glory, splendour, radiance, brilliant things, light.

khu  words of power.

khut  the name of a light-goddess.

Khu-kheper-ur  a proper name.

Khu-tchet-f  a proper name.

khunt  drink offerings.

khus  to construct a building, make a cistern.

khut  fire.

khut  the place in the sky where the sun appears on the horizon in rising or setting, the horizon.

 northern horizon.

 western horizon.

 eastern horizon.

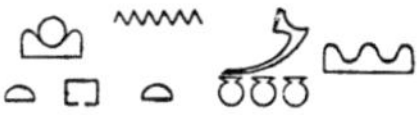 the horizon of the mountain of sunset.

 the hidden horizon.

khuti  the gods or beings of the horizon.

khui  words of power.

kheb to defraud, pilfer, steal.

kheb slaughter.

kheb
khebȧ to be defeated, overthrown.

khebu defeat, defeated ones.

kheba to destroy.

khebu to be dipped into some liquid, steeped.

Khebent a proper name.

khebent evil, wickedness.

khebenti evil doers.

khebkheb to destroy.

khebkhebt destruction.

khebkheb torture chamber.

khebs 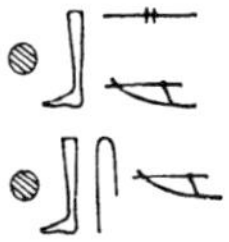 to plough;  plougher.

khebs ta 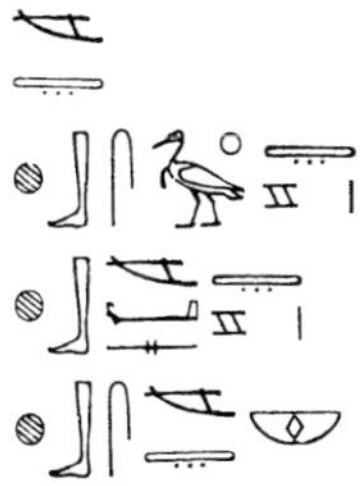 the ceremony or festival of ploughing the earth.

khebsu  devourer (?).

khebs  star, lamp.

 stars, the Thirty-six dekans.

khebt  loss, injury, damage;  destroyer.

khebt  dance.

khebt 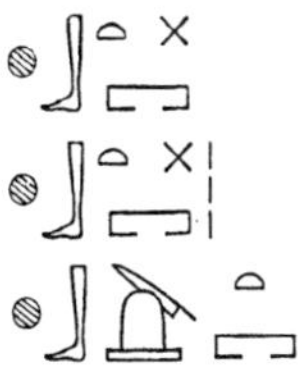 torture chamber, slaughter house.

khep to travel, journey.

khept journey.

khep a part of the body, navel (?).

khepu = .

Khepiu = the gods who are.

kheper, ***kheperu*** to come into being, become, exist, subsist, to turn into something, to create, to form, fashion; , non-existent; when takes place, when it happens; to be or become satisfied; is thy name what? , those who become.

self-created.

khepert that which is, what exists, thing.

kheperu — form, phase of being, something evolved, transformation, change.

kheperu — forms, transformations.

kheperut

kheper — scarab, beetle.

khepreṛ

Kheperȧ, *Kheperrȧ* (?) — the Beetle-god, a form of the Sun-god.

khepesh — thigh; plur.

Khepesh — the constellation of the Thigh.

khept

kheptet — buttock; plur.

khept

khefa — food.

khefā — to grasp, to seize with the hand;

khefā — fist, grasp.

khefāt

khefit — quay, river bank.

kheft — in front of, according to, conformably to, when.

kheft ḥer — opposite to, before the face of.

khefti — enemy, fiend.

kheftiu — enemies.

khem to burn.

khem shrine.

khem to be ignorant, to put an end to (?); ignorant, helpless; unknown is his name.

khem an ignorant man.

khem to overthrow, destroy.

khemiu overthrower, those who overthrow, destructions.

khemit

Khemi the name of one of the Forty-two Judges in the Hall of Osiris.

khemā to lay hold of, to seize and carry off.

khemāu snatchers, seizers.

khemu wind, air.

khemenu eight; eighth.

Khemenu the eight gods of the Company of Thoth who dwelt at Hermopolis.

Khemenu the city of the Eight gods, Hermopolis.

khemt three; third.

khemt to think, to know, to intend. is sometimes written by mistake for .

khemt the god of thought.

khen, *khenn*, *khennu* to hover over, to flutter like a bird when alighting on a tree, to perch on something.

Khenit the goddesses who fly or dance.

khen 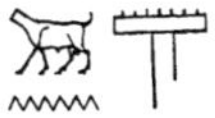 to be dressed, garment.

khen 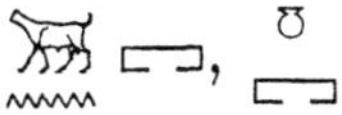 the inner part of a house, house.

 within.

Khennu  the name of a city in the Sekhet-ḥetep.

khen 
khenn  to decay, to rot, to wither.

khen  to break, smash, destroy, stir up strife, disturb, trouble.

khennu 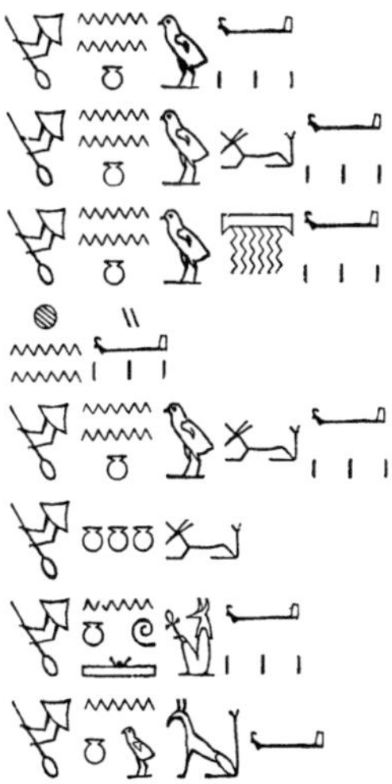 trouble, revolt, destruction, storm, opposition.

khenui  rebels.

khen 

khenen 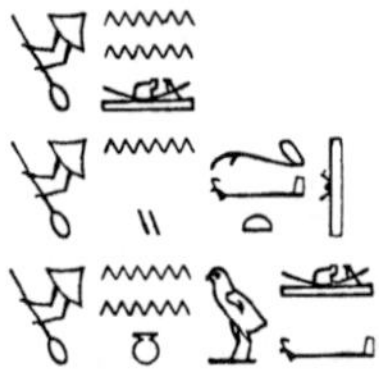 to ferry across a stream, to transport by water, to row, to paddle.

khent  a passage, a journey.

khenen  sailor.

khenȧ 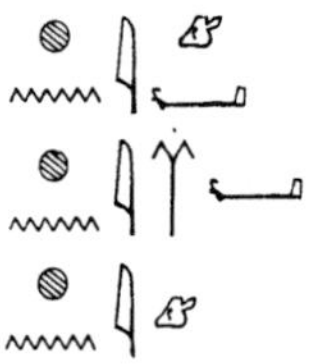 to lock up, shut up, keep in captivity.

khenp 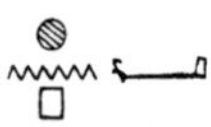 to draw out, pluck out.

 a tearing; 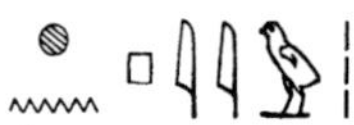 tearers, renders.

khenf  a bread-cake.

khenem  jasper, carnelian.

khnem  to form, join up or together.

Khnem  the god Khnemu, the Potter-god.

Khnemu-Ḥeru-Ḥetep  the name of a god.

khnem  well;  a proper name (?).

Khnemet-urt  a proper name.

Khemet-em-ānkh-ȧnnuit 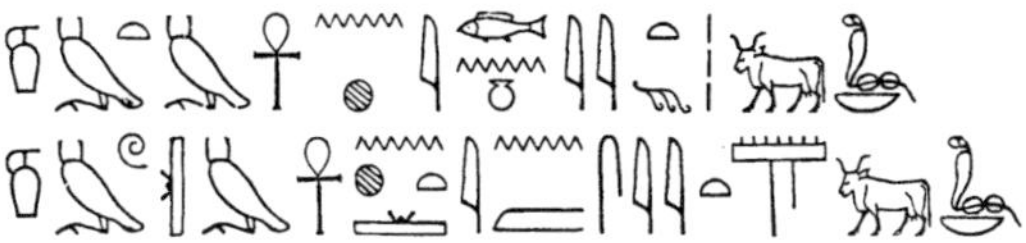 the name of one of the Seven Cows.

khenem 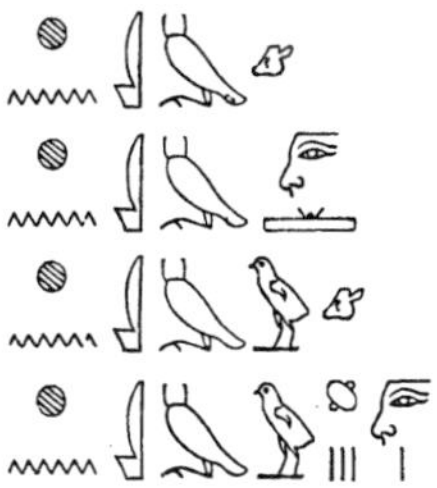 to snuff the air, to smell, scent out.

khenemti  nurse, servant, companion.

khenemu  . . . .

Khenem-nefer  a proper name?

khenemem  to smell, feed upon (?).

Khenememti 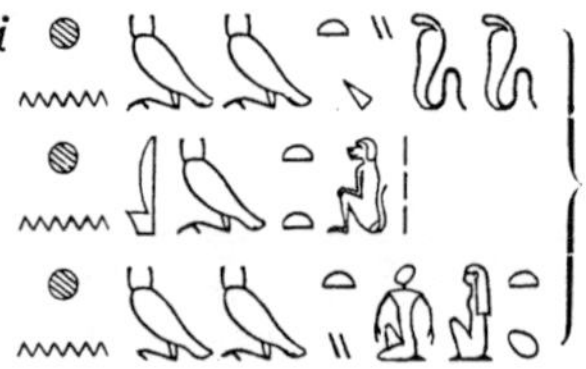 the two ministering goddesses, Isis and Nephthys.

khenemes 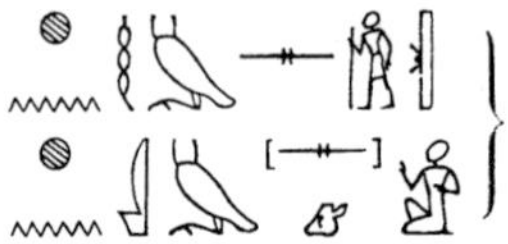 protector, friend.

khennu  those who cry out.

khennu 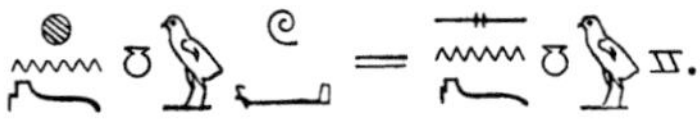

khennu  injury, evil hap.

khenrȧ 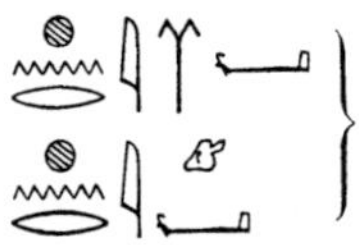 to shut in, imprison.

khenrȧ 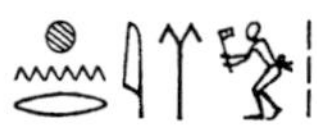 fiends.

khenrit 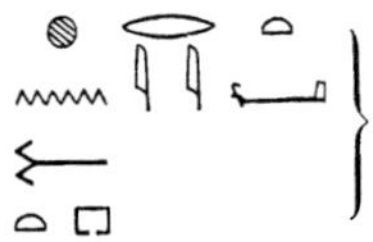 prison.

khens  to stride about, to journey, travel.

Khensu  "traveller", a name of the Moon-god.

Khensu-p-åru-sekheru em Uast 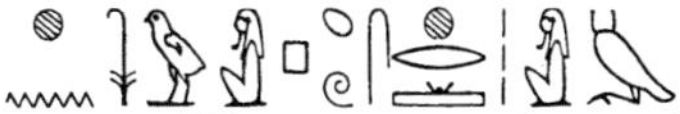  Khensu, worker of destinies in Thebes.

Khensu em Uast Nefer-ḥetepi  Khensu in Thebes, Nefer-ḥetep.

khent 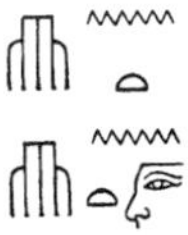 the nose.

khent  the fore part of anything, the front, in front of, before.

khenti  he who is in front, or at the head, chief, governor.

Khenti Åmenti  He who is at the head of Åmenti and of those who are therein; a title of Osiris.

Khenti Āḥa  he who is chief of the fighting.

Khenti-aḥāt 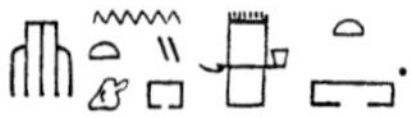

Khenti-āt-ȧment 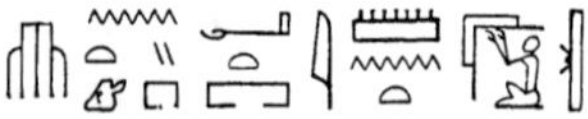 a title of Osiris.

Khenti-Un  a title of Osiris.

Khenti-Peḳu  a title of Osiris.

Khenti-menȧtuf  a title of Osiris.

Khenti-Naȧreṭ-f  a title of Osiris.

Khenti-nut-f  a title of Osiris.

Khenti-nep  a title of Osiris.

Khenti-n-merti (?)  a title of Horus.

Khenti neter ḥet  "Chief of the god-house".

Khenti neter seḥ  "Chief of the god-hall".

Khenti Re-stau  "Chief of the funerary corridors"; a title of Osiris.

Khenti-hetut-f 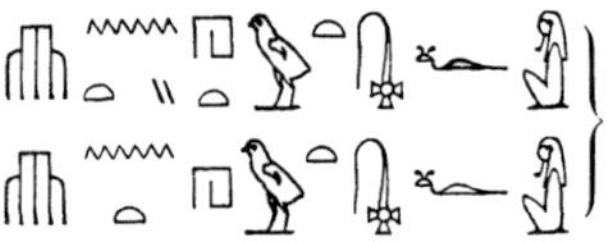 "Chief of his fire".

Khentiu ḥensekti  "Chiefs of long hair and beards".

Khent ḥeḥ  a title of Osiris.

Khenti Ḥeq-ȧnṭ  a title of Osiris.

Khenti ḥespu  the name of the bows of the magic boat.

Khenti-khas  a name of a god.

Khenti-Khati 

Khent-Khaṭti  "the dweller in the belly"; a title of Horus.

Khenti-Suten-ḥenen  a title of Osiris.

Khenti-Sekhem  a title of Horus of Letopolis.

Khenti-seḥ-ḥemt 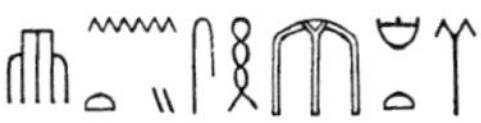 "chief of the house of the wife"; a title of Osiris.

Khenti-seḥt-kaut-f  "chief of the house of his cows"; a title of Osiris,

Khent-she (or ***mer***)-***Āa-perti*** "chief of the Lake of Pharaoh"; a title of Osiris.

Khenti-Tenent a title of Osiris.

khent abode, the private portion of a palace or temple; plur.

khent, ***khenti*** to sail upstream, usually to the south;

khentiu sailors.

khenti a mineral colour.

khenṭ to travel, journey.

khenṭi traveller.

khenṭi to ascend.

khenṭ 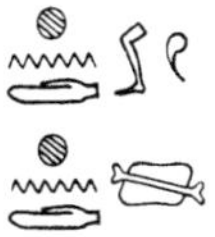 thigh, haunch.

Khenṭ-Ḥepiu  name of the steering pole.

khentch  to travel.

kher  a preposition, with, before, etc.;  under the Majesty of, in the reign of.

khert  the things of, the affairs of, property of; 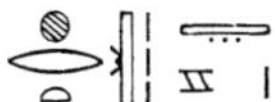 the affairs of the country;  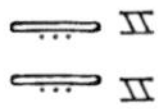 the business of the Two Lands.

kher  under, beneath;  things or beings who are below.

 under the favour of.

 before.

kheri  low-lying land, the earth as opposed to the sky; plur. .

kheru  men and women in subjection, serfs, vassals, or perhaps the tillers of low-lying lands.

kher  to have, hold, possess. 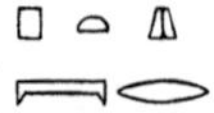

"heaven hath thy soul, earth hath thy form".

khert 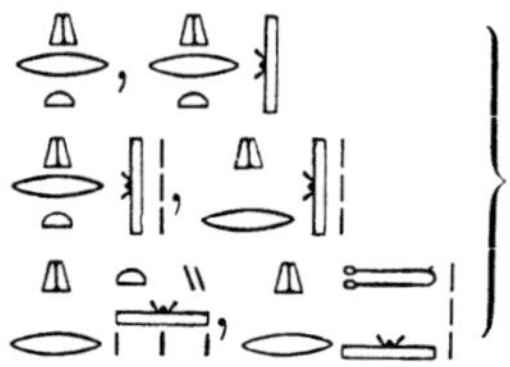 goods, possessions, share, portion, lot, what belongs to someone, property, wealth, products of.

khert hru  the things of the day, what belongs to the day, daily round or routine.

 every-day matters.

kher
kherui 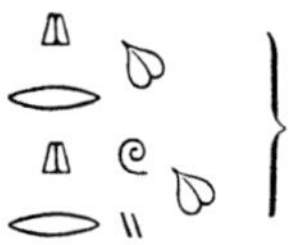 testicles.

kher — to fall down, to happen.

kheri — fallen one, foe.

kherit — the dead, the damned.

kherit — victims for sacrifice.

Kher — the name of a god.

Kherȧ — a proper name.

kheru — voice, word, speech, sound; plur. reading unknown.

loud-voiced.

a man's voice.

multiplying the sound of words, *i. e.*, talking overmuch.

kheriu 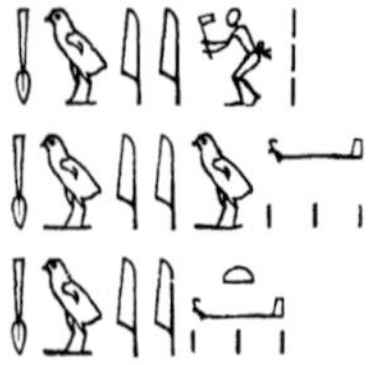 enemies, hostile attacks.

Kher-āḥa  a city near the site of the modern Fusṭâṭ, or Old Cairo.

kherp 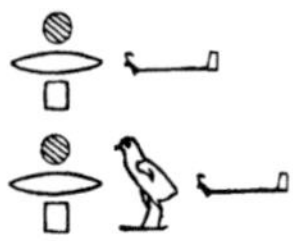 to be chief or master, to direct, be in command, to present an offering.

Kherp  Prince, Chief; plur. .

Kherp-nest  title of a priest.

kherpu  steering pole.

kherefu  two Lion-gods.

kher ḥeb  the priest who recited religious compositions and the Liturgy.

Kherserȧu  a proper name.

khersek to destroy;

Khersek-Shu a proper name.

khert course.

khertu it is said, speech.

kherṭ child; plur.

a title of the scribe Nebseni.

khekh to run.

khekh, ***khekhi*** throat.

khekhu darkness.

khes to slay.

khesu ritual, a book.

khesbeṭ blue stone, lapis-lazuli;

real lapis-lazuli as opposed to blue paste.

blue-eyed.

khesef to meet, to oppose, to drive back, repulse; repulse; irresistible.

khesef-ā

kheseft repulse.

khesefu adversaries, foes; hostile faces.

bowings down before.

Khesef-aṭ a proper name.

Khesef-ḥer-āsh-kheru a proper name.

Khesef-ḥer-khemiu the name of the herald of the Seventh Ārit.

Khesem Letopolis.

khesṭeḥ to destroy.

khet steps, throne.

great stairs of Osiris.

khet fire, flame.

khet wood, tree, stick, staff, sceptre, board; planks of a ship; rod.

khet mast.

khet, ***khetkhet*** to retreat, go back.

khet back, behind.

behind, in the following of.

followers.

khet, ***khetu*** to write, to cut on wood or stone; , cut, engraved.

khet  things, affairs, cases, goods, property.

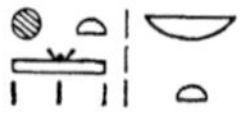 everything.

 all sorts of bad things.

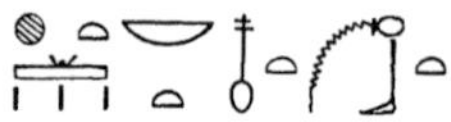 everything beautiful and pure.

 all most beautiful things.

 sweet things.

 everything bad and evil.

 weak things.

 things about Osiris.

 things on the altars.

 things of Horus (*i. e.*, offerings, property of).

 things (offerings) of the night.

 things of the festal altars.

 things of his father Osiris.

things of the Eye of Horus.

things of the Boat.

their personal things.

khetu . . . .

khetita fiends, devils.

khetem to shut in, to seal, close the door on;

khetemiu those shut in.

khetemit closed place, prison.

kheṭ to float down stream.

kheṭebet = .

S.

s , her, she, its;

= .

sa person, man, one.

everyone, everybody.

set woman.

sa son.

son of Rā.

firstborn son.

sat daughter.

daughter of Rā.

sati the two divine daughters, *i. e.*, Isis and Nephthys.

Sa-mer-f "Son loving him"; title of a priest.

Sa-pa-nemmȧ a proper name.

Sa-ta "son of the earth"; the name of a serpent.

sa side, back.

in the side.

afterwards.

behind.

after.

by the back.

sa chamber (?).

sa to protect, a thing which protects, amulet; plur. , as a protection. See .

sa to perceive, know, recognize.

knower of hearts, trier of reins.

sauu wise man.

Sa

Sau the god of knowledge.

Sa-Ȧmenti-Rā a proper name.

Saau-ur a proper name.

Saa "shepherd"; a name of Osiris.

21*

sau 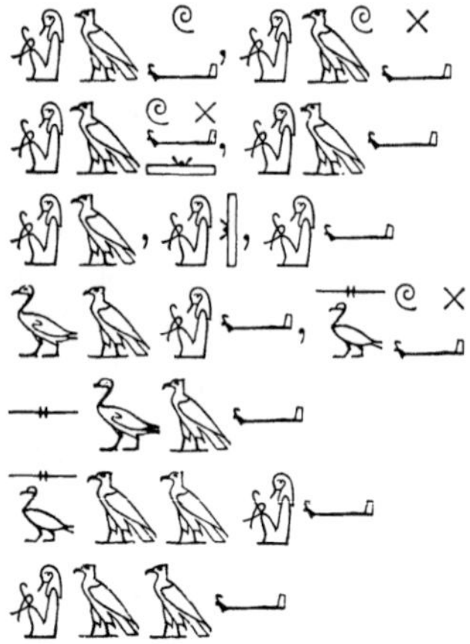 to watch, keep guard over, protect, keep in restraint; to tend sheep.

sau, sai  watcher, guardian, shepherd.

 plur. of preceding.

 people in fetters.

 watchers, warders, fetterers, fetters.

sait — restraint, ward.

sau — corruption.

Sau — the city of Saïs.

Upper Saïs.

Lower Saïs.

saāiu — evil ones (?).

s-au — to make glad, to provision.

wide goings, journeyings.

sauṭ — to transfer.

sab — making to cease.

sab — jackal; plur.

Sab (?)
Sabȧ — the name of a god.

Sabes — the herald of the Second Ārit.

sam — to consume, burn up.

Samiu		a group of gods or fiends.
samiu		the gods with hair.
samut		hair.
samit		tresses, hair.
Saneḥem		the city of grasshoppers.
saneḥemu		grasshoppers.
Sar	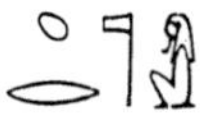	Osiris.
saru		order of dismissal (?).
sariu		evilly disposed persons.
saḥ	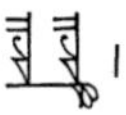 	to journey, to travel.
saḥt	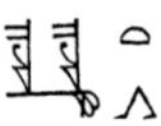	journey.
saḥ	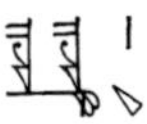	an estate, farm, homestead.
saḥ	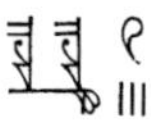  	fingers, toes, claws.

Saḥ  Orion.

Saḥ-en-mut-f 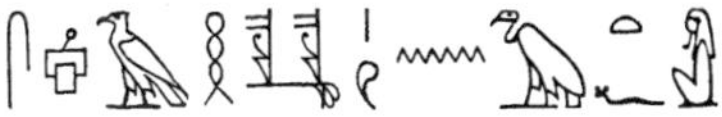 a proper name.

saq  to collect, gather together.

Saq-baiu  "collector of souls"; the name of a boat.

Saqnaqat  a proper name.

sat 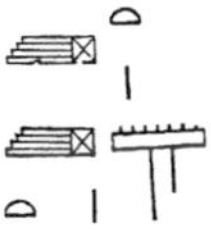 apparel, garment, robe, dress.

sat  to think scorn of the god.

sat  evil, evil one.

satu  wall, building.

sat  earth, ground, floor of a chamber.

sati  threshold.

Satiu the city of Siut, the modern Asyûṭ.

saṭu terrors.

Sȧ the name of a town and of a god.

Sȧa the god Sa.

Sȧa the name of a town and of a god.

Sȧu to cry out.

sȧat to encroach, attack.

Sȧatiu slaughterers.

; plur.

sȧu to drink water.

sȧbit animals for sacrifice.

sȧb-kui to make to weep.

sȧp to judge, decide, compute, reckon up, examine, inspect, inquire into; , judged, computed.

sȧpu judge, judgment; plur.

sȧp, **sȧpti** account, reckoning, a list of goods, property.

Sȧp the name of a god.

sȧpt abode of the god Sȧp.

sȧm (**sȧam**) to shew kindness.

sȧn length, extent.

sȧn to be kind, do good to, benefit, nourish; things which benefit.

sȧn clay.

sȧn to walk, march, pass along.

sȧn to pull, draw.

sȧn to be in good case.

sȧs six; sixth; = 1/6; the festival held on the sixth day of each month.

Sȧsȧ  the name of a city =  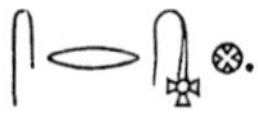.

sȧka 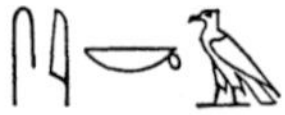 to afford relief.

sȧqer  to make strong, or perfect.

Sȧti  the name of a city.

sȧtti (?)  executioners.

sȧṭi  headsman, executioner.

sȧṭen  to transfer.

sāa 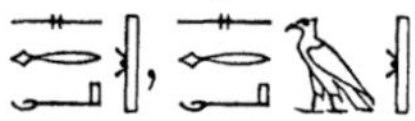 to magnify.

sāam  to slay.

sāb (***suāb***) 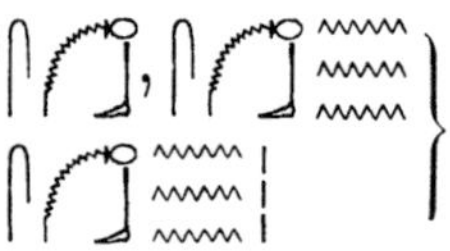 to wash, purify, cleanse.

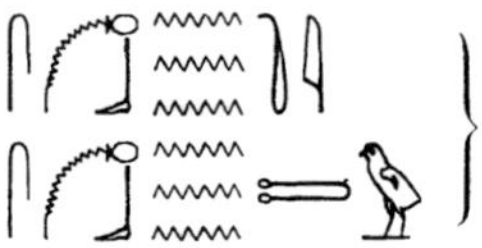 washed, plated.

sāba  to make to enter, force an entrance.

sām — to make to eat or drink, to swallow.

sāmiu — eaters, devourers.

Sām-em-senf — "drinker of blood"; a proper name.

Sām-em-ḳesu — "eater of bones"; a proper name.

sām — flowers, plants.

sāma — . . . .

sānkh — to vivify, keep alive. to support life, to feed, give sustenance to, "vivifier of hearts"; a title of Osiris.

sānṭ — to make strong.

sār — to make to come, to introduce.

sārt approach, introduction.

sāriu introducers.

sāḥ

sāḥu the spiritual body of a man, later the mummy; plur. Mentioned with the and the .

sāḥ to become a *sāḥ*, endowed with a *sāḥ*.

sāḥ honour.

sāḥā to set up, make to stand up.

set up a pillar.

set up the Ṭeṭ.

su  he, him; 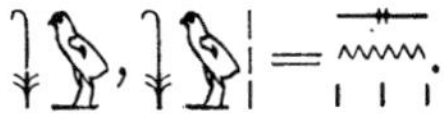.

su tchesef  he himself.

sua 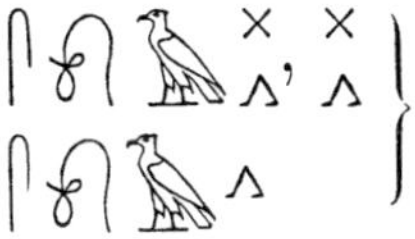 to pass by.

suash 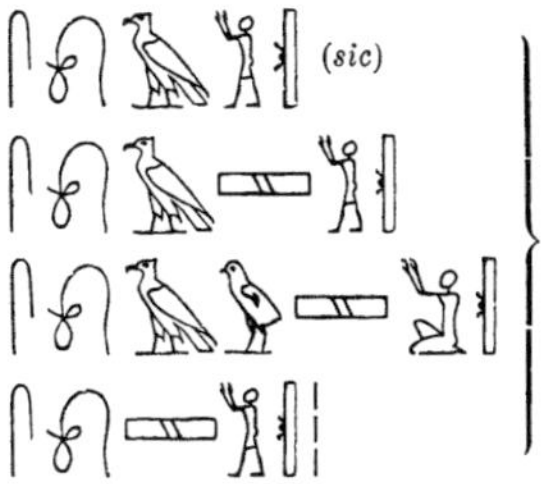

suatch 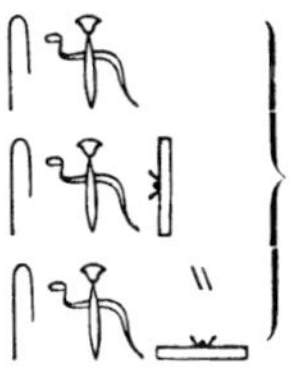 to be green, vigorous, flourishing.

suȧs  decay.

sui  crocodile.

sun  to open.

sun  to be destroyed.

sun, *sunen* 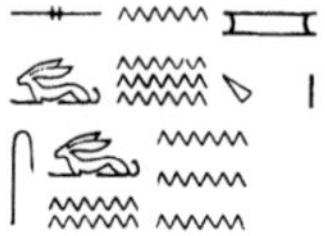 pool, lake, any large collection of water.

sunȧt  unguent.

Sunnu  the city called by the Greek Syene. Heb. סְוֵנֵה.

surȧ  to give to drink, to drink.

suriu  drinkers.

surṭ 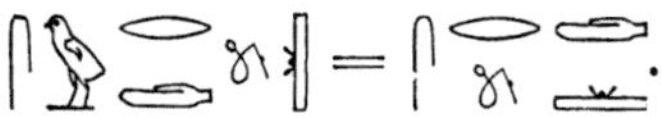.

suha  to supplicate.

suḥ  a garment.

suḥt  egg;  testicles (?).

sukha  evil recollection.

sukheṭ  to embalm, mummify.

suser 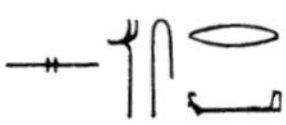 to strengthen.

susekh  to make broad, to make wide (*i. e.*, long) the steps.

Suḳaṭi the name of a god.

sut he, it, himself, they, them.

sut hair.

Sut, *Suti* the god of darkness and night, and of physical and moral evil.

Suti-mes a proper name.

suten king; king of the gods.

the reigning king.

kings.

sovereignty, kingship, reign.

sutenit to reign, sovereignty.

suten bȧti King of the South and North.

suteniu bȧtiu plur. of preceding.

suten båt Åsår — Osiris, king of the Two Egypts.

suten ḥeḥ — "king of eternity"; a title of Osiris.

suten Ṭuat — "king of the Ṭuat"; a title of Osiris.

suten ḥemt — "king's woman", *i. e.*, queen.

suten sesh — "king's scribe", *i. e.*, royal scribe.

suten . . . . — byssus; plur.

suten ṭā ḥetep — an ancient formula meaning "may the king give an offering", dating from the time when the king sent gifts for the funeral feasts of his loyal servants. At a later period its use was purely conventional in funerary texts.

Suten-ḥenen (or ***Ḥenensu***) — Herakleopolis, the חָנֵס of Isaiah XXX. 4. The Copts called it ϩⲛⲉⲥ, or ϩⲛⲏⲥ, or ⲉϩⲛⲏⲥ, and its Arabic name is اهناس.

sutennu to extend, walk with long strides.

suṭekh to treat with medicaments, to embalm.

sutcha
setcha } to set out on a journey, to go, travel.

sutcha
setcha } to be strong, sound, well, to make strong and happy.

si it, its, them.

si fulness, satiety.

sia = to cut, engrave.

Seb (***Ḳeb***?)
Sebu (***Ḳebu***) } the Earth-god.

the abode of Seb (or Ḳeb).

seb
sebbi } to guide, to lead, to pass by or through a place; , .

passage.

sba  star, Star-god; plur. 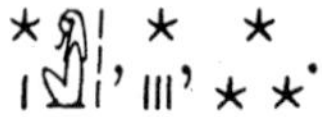.

sbaiu  stars.

sba 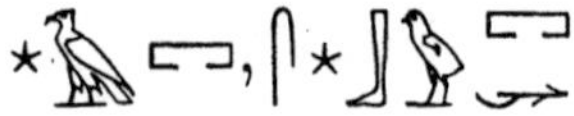

sbau  door, gate, pylon; the forms ,  also occur.

sbau  plur. of preceding.

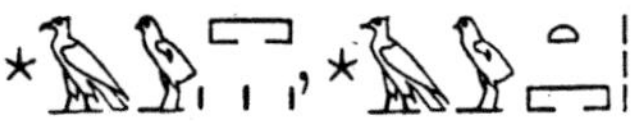 doors of the Other World.

sba  to instruct.

sbaut  to rebel.

sebaḳi  helpless one, inert, weak.

Sebȧ  the name of a goddess.

sebȧ  to be an enemy of some one.

sebȧ 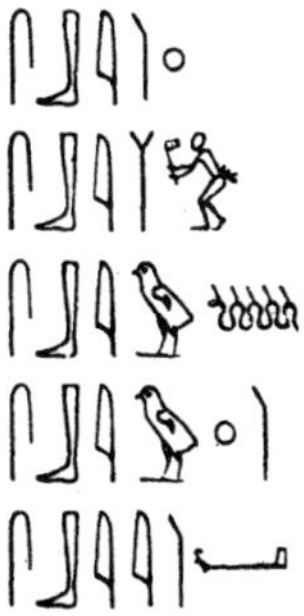 enemy, fiend.

sebȧu  plur. of preceding.

seben  to retreat, depart.

sebeḥ 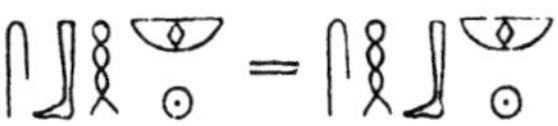 to keep a festival.

sebeḥ  to call upon someone, to invoke.

sebḥet 

sebḥit 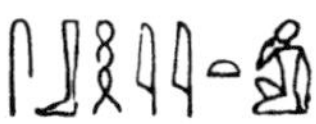 invocation, praise.

sebekh be master of, have power over (?).

sebkhet gate, pylon.

plur. of preceding.

sebekhbekht to scatter (?).

Sebek the Crocodile-god, who was a form of the Sun-god.

Sebeku the Crocodile-gods.

sebeq leg, thigh.

Sebeq-en-Shesmu a proper name.

Sebeq-en-Tem a proper name.

Sebeḳ

Sebḳa the name of a god.

Sebaḳu

sebt — to be pleased (?), laugh, laughter.

sebt — walls.

sep — season, luck, fate, occasion, opportunity, circumstance, case, etc.; plur.

a right case, a just trial.

ill luck, a bad time.

I am Fate and Osiris.

a prosperous time.

the occasion of the night.

likewise, at the same time.

another time or opportunity.

at no time, never.

primeval time, when the world began.

sep — time; twice; four times; millions of times.

sep sen duplicity.

sep to pass sentence.

sep crown (?).

Sep the name of a god.

Sepa the name of a god.

seppi, ***sepi*** remainder.

seppu omission.

sper to come to a place, to arrive at; comers.

sper to speak to, address.

speh to make to arrive at.

sepeh to tie with a rope, to fetter.

sepḥer to design, make a plan, draw, write.

sepḥer to make to revolve.

Sepes a proper name.

sept lip; edge of the water.

the two lips.

sept nome; plur. .

the nome of Maāti.

Septu a god of the Eastern Delta; a form of Horus.

Sepṭ the star Sirius.

sepṭ to be ready to do or use something, prepared; to be provided with. provided.

prepared for the moment.

having horns ready to strike.

ready of face, keen, alert (?).

sepṭ a kind of wood.

sepṭ leg.

Sepṭ-kheri-neḥait-ȧmi-beq a proper name.

Sepṭ-mast-ent-Reruti a proper name.

sef yesterday; .

sef maāt . . . . . .

sef ḥer to be gracious, longsuffering.

sefi babe, child.

sefekh seven.

sefekh to untie, undress, set free; , .

Sefekh-neb-s a proper name.

seft to slay.

seft knife, sword.

seft pitch, unguent.

sem a priest (also setem).

sma loin.

sma to join together, to unite with.

union, assembly.

smat (?) a burial place.

sma.ta union with the earth, *i. e.*, burial.

day of burial.

to unite the Two Lands, *i. e.*, Egypt.

sma to kill, slaughter.

slaughterer, butcher.

sma  cow or bull bound for sacrifice.

smaui  to renew, remake.

smaȧr  to oppress.

smau  branches.

 poles of a bier.

smaiu  branches.

smaiu  slaughterers, fiends.

 plur. of preceding.

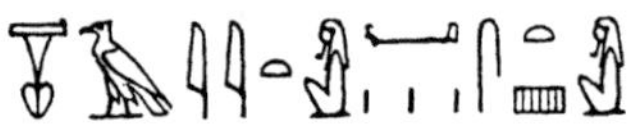 butchers of Set.

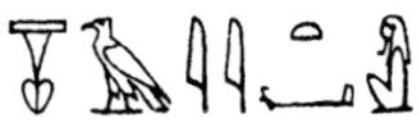 god of slaughter.

Smait 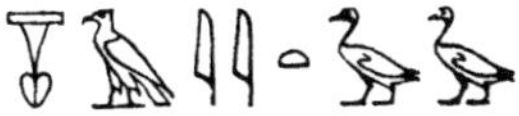 two goddesses of slaughter.

smaā  to pay what is due, make an offering.

smaāiu  slayers.

smaā-kheru  to justify, to make triumphant, to proclaim blessed.

smam  to slay, sacrifice.

smam  butcher.

smamiu  slaughterers, fiends.

smam  a bull for sacrifice.

smamu  cattle for sacrifice, victims.

Smam  the name of a god.

Smam-ur  the name of the Soul of Seb (Keb).

Smam  the name of a lake.

smamu  foliage or branches of a tree.

smamu clouds.

smat bows of a boat (?).

smatu torture chambers, shambles.

Smati a proper name.

Smamti a proper name.

smaṭ festival of the half month.

smȧ to report, announce, bear a message; reporting;

smȧ, ***smȧiu*** herald, announcer.

smȧ, ***smȧt*** report.

smȧ leather.

smȧu pieces of leather.

semu  herbs, pasturage.

semiu  devourers.

semi  to entreat.

smemā  to burn up.

smen 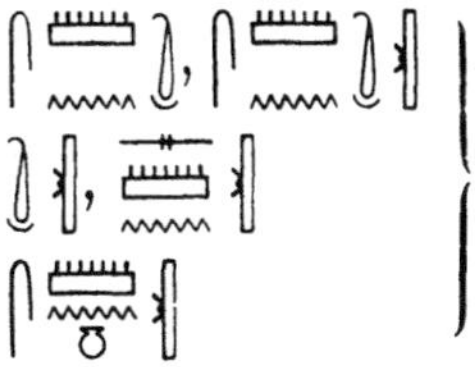 to stablish, be stablished, fixed, made firm.

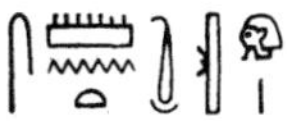 fixed head.

smen  a kind of goose.

smenkh  to repair, re-establish, beautify, make perfect.

smert 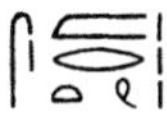 eyelids.

smer  to inflict or cause pain.

smeḥ 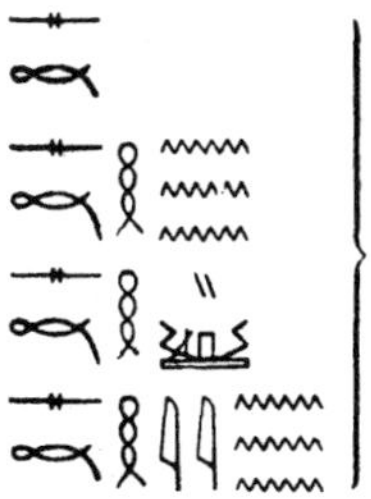 to flood, to submerge, water fields.

smeḥit 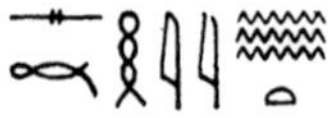 flood.

semkheṭ  . . . .

semes 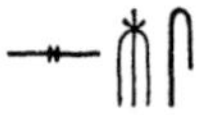 to make to be born, produce.

semsu  eldest, firstborn.

Semti (?)  a king of the 1st dynasty. This name was formerly read Ḥesepti.

smet 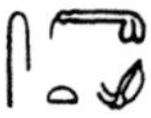 to listen.

smetmet (?) 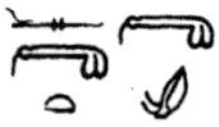 to pry into.

Smetu  the warder of the First Ārit.

smet 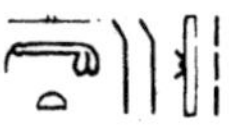 woven with, or shot with (of cloth).

Smet-āqa 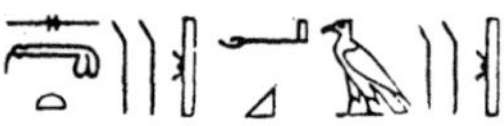 the name of a rudder.

Smeti-āqa  name of a part of the magic boat.

Smetti 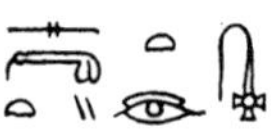 a proper name.

smetru to investigate, search out, find the truth.

semṭet servant, serf.

sen they, their, them.

sen two; second, fellow, equal, companion, like, equal; two breasts.

sen to smell, breathe.

sen ta to smell the earth, to pay homage.

sen house, abode (?).

sen brother; dual , ; plur. , , , .

sent sister.

two sisters, pair of sisters.

seni companion, fellow.

sen to pass away, depart, to walk.

sen to slit, to cut.

Senu a city near Panopolis.

senȧ adoration.

senȧha injury, misery.

senā restraint.

senāāt to beautify (?).

senb to be well, strong, healthy.

senbȧ health, soundness.

senb wall; plur.

senbet libation vessel.

senpu slaughterings.

senf — blood.

senfekhfekh — to be untied, set loose.

senem — abundance.

senem — to pray, to adore.

senemȧi — to make advance.

Senemti — a proper name.

senemem — hair.

senen — image, statue.

sennu — to cut, to sever; those who cut.

sennit — . . . .

sennu — to gather (?).

sennu — cakes, bread-offerings.

sennȧu  to fail.

sennuṭ  carrier.

ṣenni 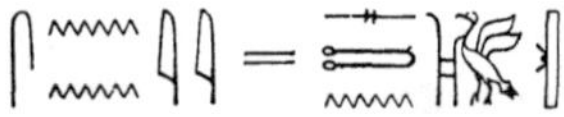

Sen-nefer  a proper name.

senneshni 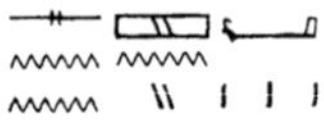 storm.

seneh  to be in servitude.

senehep  to be strong.

Seneh-paqarha 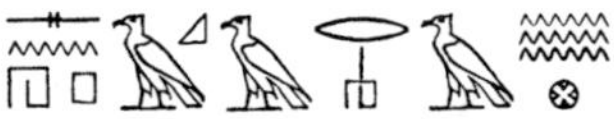 the name of a city.

Senehaparḳana 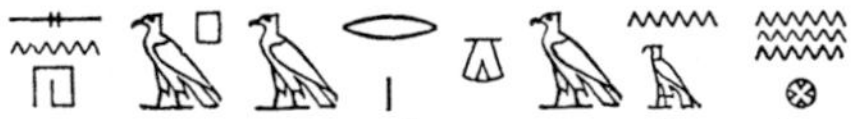 the name of a city.

seneḥem  to deliver.

senkha 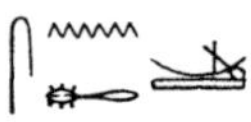 to disembark (?).

senekhekh 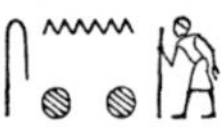 to grow old.

senes 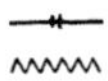 }
sensi 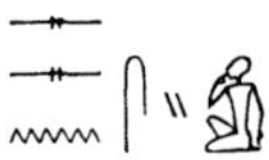 } to praise.

sensu  to cry out, invoke.

Senseneb  the name of the mother of Nu.

sensenni 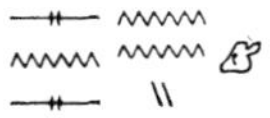 to breathe, snuff the air.

sensen 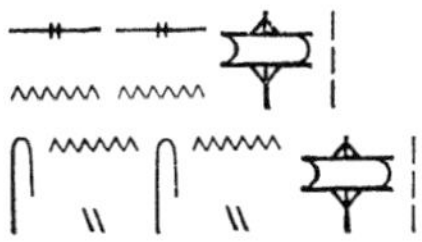 breathings, breaths.

sensen 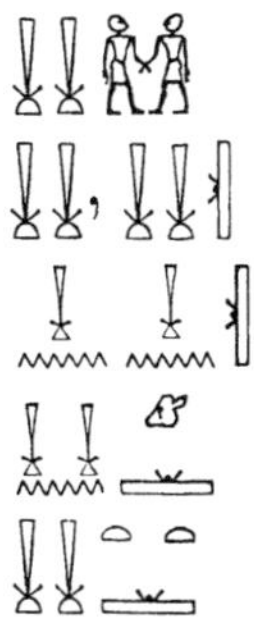 to become friendly with some one, to fraternize; to smell.

sensen 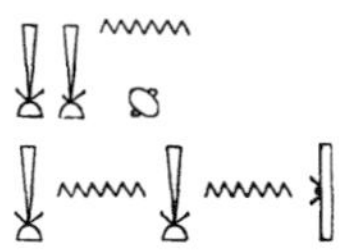 to have a bad smell, to become corrupt, to decay.

senesh 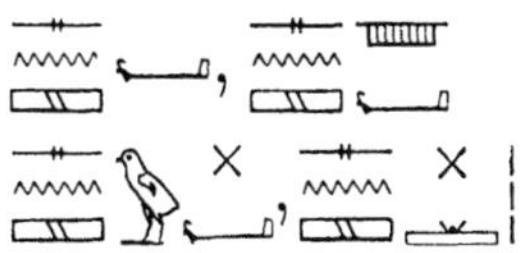 to unbolt, unbar, open.

senshu  bolts (?).

seneshni 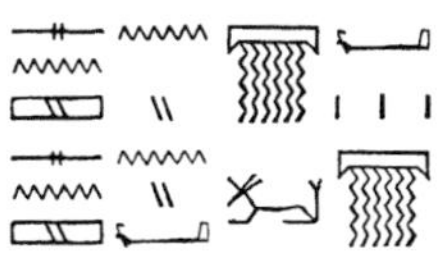 storm, hurricane.

Senk 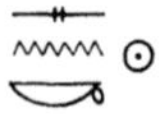 a proper name.

senket  light.

Senket 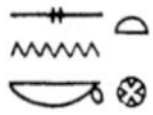 the name of a city.

senk-åb  strong-willed.

senq (?) 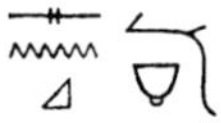
senqet  to suckle.

sent  labourers, builders.

sent 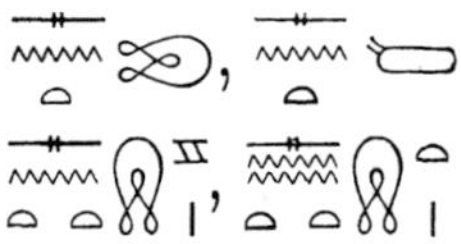 foundation.

sent 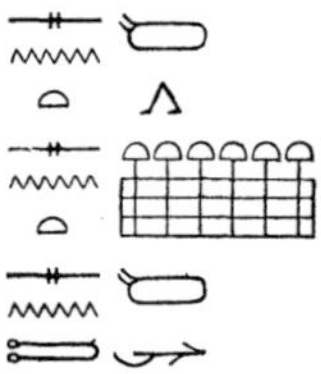 draughtboard, game of draughts.

sent  to pass away.

sent 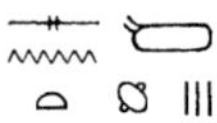 decay.

sentu  enemies.

Sent-Rā a proper name.

senter
senther incense offered to the god; censed; to cense the mouth.

senteḥ to have power over.

Sent..... the brother-gods Horus and Set.

senṭ to fear, be afraid.

senṭ ȧb timid.

senṭ fear.

senetchem to make glad or happy.

pleasure.

ease.

senetchem to sit.

sentchert restraint.

ser prince, chief; everlasting prince; a proper name.

plur. of preceding.

ser to give orders or directions, to announce, give tidings;

sert order, announcement.

Ser-kheru, ***Serȧ-kheru*** the name of one of the Forty-two Judges in the Hall of Osiris.

Serȧt-beqet the name of a sacred cow.

seru grain, barley.

seru		geese of a special kind.
serui (?)		flame.
serukheṭ		to treat with medicaments, embalm.
seruṭ	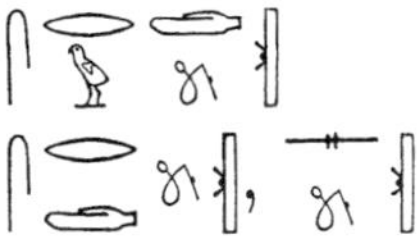	to make to grow, to flourish, to perpetuate.
seref	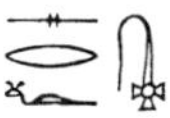	to be hot, flame, fire.
serem		to make to weep.
serenp		to make young.
serḥu (?)		to overthrow.
serekh	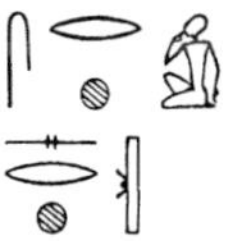	to make to know, to inform.
sẹrekh		a funerary building, a cognizance.
Serekhi	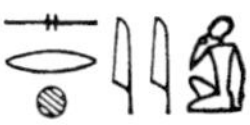	the name of one of the Forty-two Judges in the Hall of Osiris.
seres	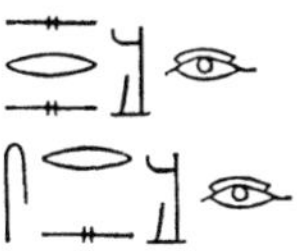	to be awake, to watch.
	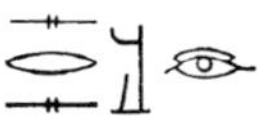	watch, watching, watcher.

Seres-ḥer  "watching face"; the name of a god.

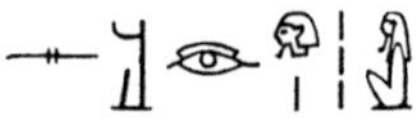 "watching faces"; a class of divine beings.

serqaȧu  to be refreshed, to breathe.

Serqet 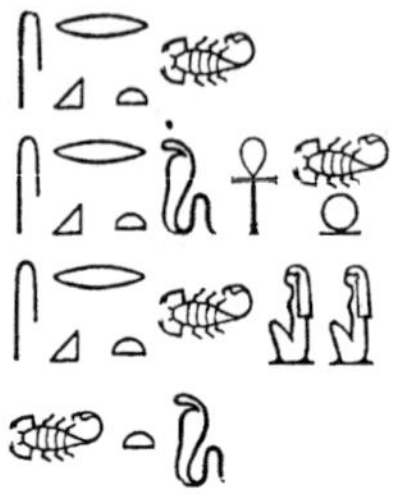 the goddess Serqet.

Sert  a city in the Seventh Ȧat.

sert  "goad"; the name of a part of the magic boat.

serṭ 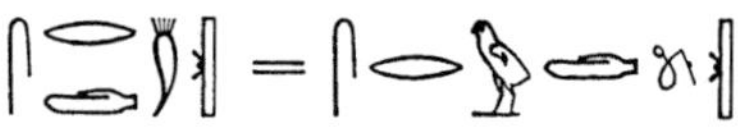

Serṭiu  the name of one of the Forty-two Judges in the Hall of Osiris.

sehep 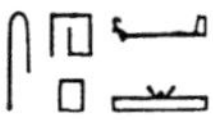 lawgiver.

seher 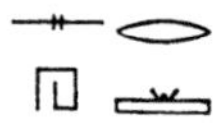
seherr 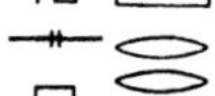 to make quiet, subdue.

sehert  carnelian.

seḥ — hall; the chamber of the embalmment of Osiris.

seḥap — to hide.

seḥuā — to confuse, disarrange.

seḥui — to gather together, collect.

seḥurȧ — to curse.

seḥeb — to keep a feast, to make festival.

seḥem — to turn back.

seḥeptet — name of a boat (?).

seḥen — to order, arrange (?).

seḥer — to drive away.

 driver away; plur. 

seḥes 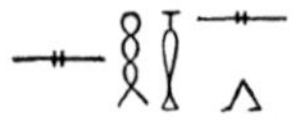 to make to meet.

seḥset 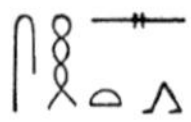 a meeting.

seḥeq  to cut off, hack in pieces.

seḥeq 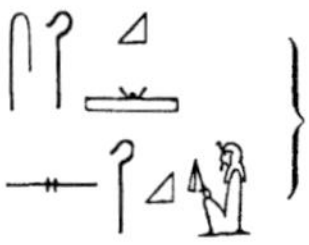 to appoint to some office.

seḥeqer  to cause to hunger, to keep hungry.

seḥetep 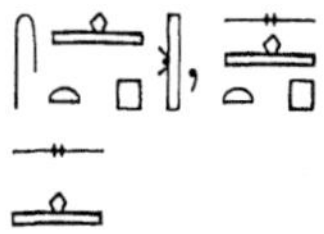 to make to be at peace, to propitiate, to pacify.

 to quiet the heart.

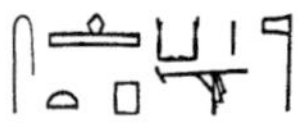 to propitiate the divine Ka.

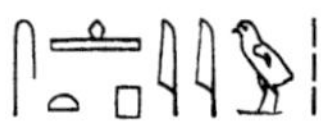 peacemakers.

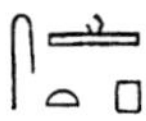 pacification.

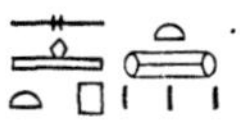 offerings which bring peace.

Seḥetep-taui 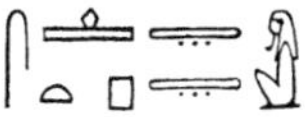 "pacifier of the Two Lands"; a proper name.

seḥetem  to destroy.

Seḥetemet-Au-ā-em-ābet   the name of the banks of a river.

Seḥtet  a proper name.

seḥetch  to emit light, illumine, to shine.

 light, radiance, brilliance.

Seḥetch-ur  "Great Light", *i. e.*, Rā.

sekh 

sekh 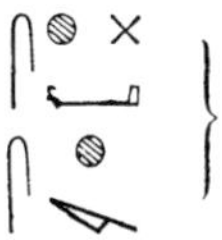 to break, strike, cut, wound.

sekha  to have in mind, to commemorate, to remember.

 remembrance for good.

memorial services.

remembrance of evil.

sekha to be deaf.

Sekhai a Cow-goddess.

sekhabui eaters (?).

sekhap to swallow.

sekhar to milk.

sekharu to plate, to mould.

sekhakeru to ornament.

Sekhat-Ḥeru a Cow-goddess.

Sekhāi to make to rise or appear, to crown.

Sekhiu the name of a double serpent god or fiend.

sekhu  to praise, glorify.

sekhu  praise.

sekhun 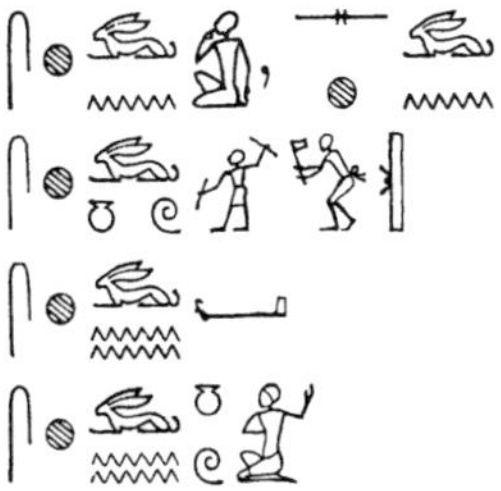 to revile, curse.

sekhuṭ  to fortify.

sekheb  see 

sekhep 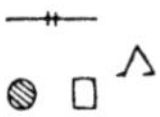 to make advance.

Sekhepti  a proper name.

sekheper 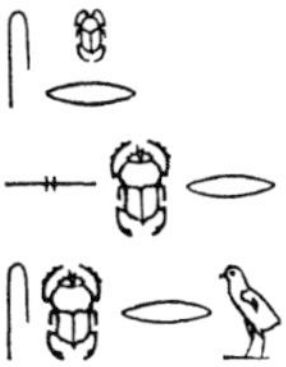 to make to become, to create, fashion, form.

sekheperu 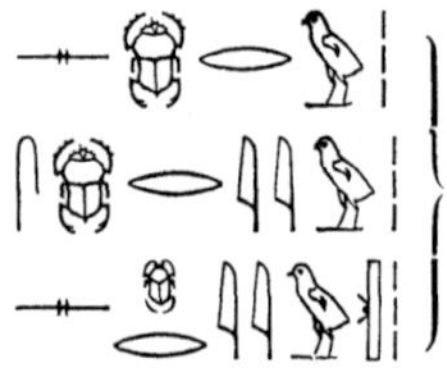 those who cause things to be.

sekhef  seven; 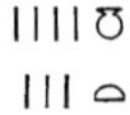 seventh.

sekhem 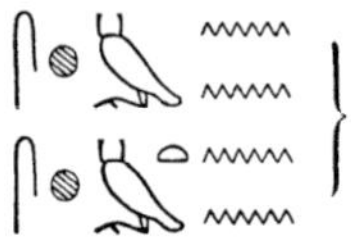 to forget, forgetfulness.

Sekhem 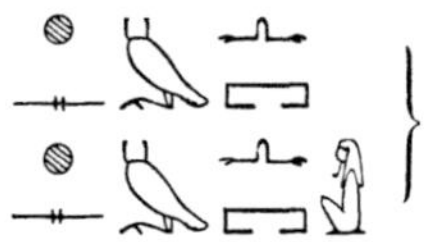 shrine, sanctuary.

 gods of the shrine.

 the city of Letopolis.

sekhem  to recite, to read.

sekhem — to be strong, mighty, to prevail over, to gain the mastery, show oneself strong, might, power.

bold man, victor.

brave in heart.

weak.

mighty one, strong.

Sekhem — the natural power, vital power of a man, any power spiritual or physical.

Sekhemu — the Powers; the Double Power.

Sekhem-ur — "great Power"; a proper name.

Sekhem-em-àb-f — "strong in his heart"; a proper name.

Sekhem-nefer  "good Power"; a proper name.

Sekhmet-ren-s-em-ḥemut-s  the name of a sacred cow.

Sekhmet (***Sekhet***)  name of a goddess.

Sekhmet-Bast-Rā 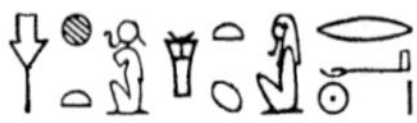 a solar triad.

sekhen  to direct (?).

sekhen 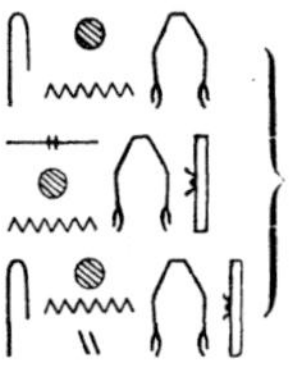 to embrace.

 "great embracer"; a proper name.

sekhni  to make to alight.

sekhenen  to become rotten, to decay.

sekhensh 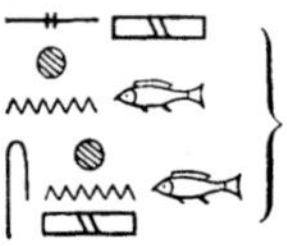 to make to stink, to calumniate.

sekhent  to make to advance.

sekhent pillars.

sekher to offend.

[***sekher*** plan, device, counsel, arrangement.]

plur. of preceding.

a plan of triumph, or blessedness.

celestial designs, ordinances of heaven.

sekher to overthrow.

fallen.

overthrow.

Sekher-āṭ the god of the Sixth Ārit.

Sekheriu the name of one of the Forty-two Judges in the Hall of Osiris.

Sekher-remu a proper name.

sekhekh to straighten.

sekhes to run.

sekhes, ***sekhsekh*** to fasten, make firm.

sekhesef to meet with hostility, to repulse, to contradict, give evidence against.

sekhet to net, to snare, spread out a net.

sekhtu, ***sekhtiu*** snarers, hunters, fowlers, fishermen.

sekhet , field, meadow; plur. .

sekhtiu the divine field labourers.

"Great Field", *i. e.*, heaven.

***Sekhet-Ȧanru* (or *Ȧaru*)** 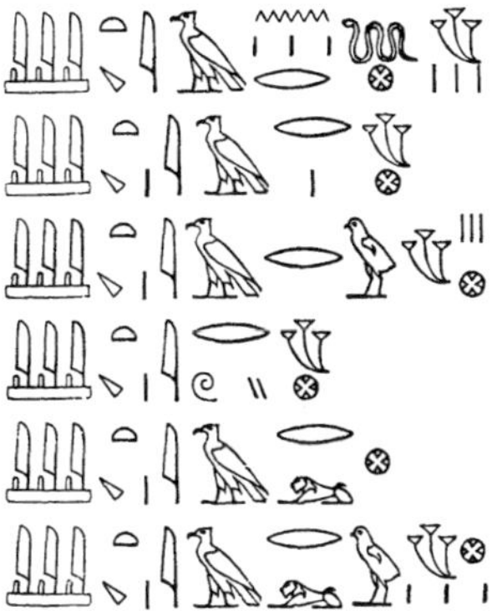 the "Field of reeds", *i. e.*, the Elysian Fields.

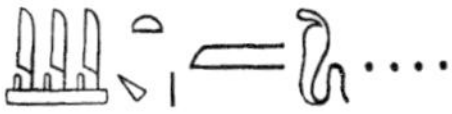 a proper name?

Sekhet-neḥeḥ 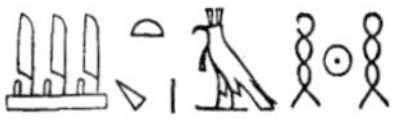 "Field of Eternity".

Sekhet-neteru  "Field of the gods".

Sekhet-Rā 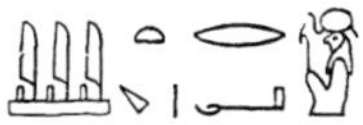 "Field of Rā".

Sekhet-ḥetep 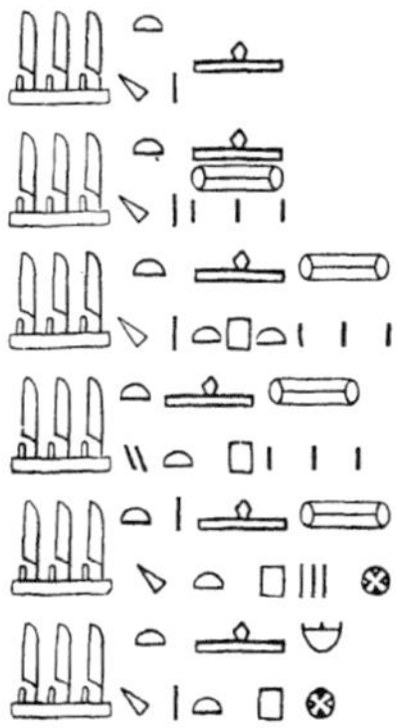 the "Field of Peace", or "Field of Offerings"; a name of the Elysian Fields.

Sekhti-ḥetep 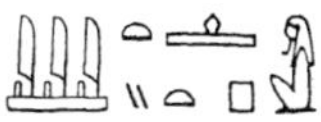 the god of the Field of Peace.

Sekhet-sanehemu  "Field of the Grasshoppers".

Sekhet-Sȧsȧ  "Field of Fire".

sekhettu  plants.

sekhet 

sekheṭ 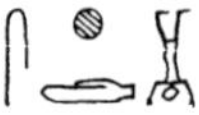   to turn upside down, invert, stand on the head; .

Sekheṭ-ḥer-āsh-ȧru  "inverted face, of many forms"; the name of the porter of the First Ārit.

sekhṭu  to hunger.

sesu  times, days.

sesun  to destroy.

sesunṭ  to destroy.

seseb  to slay.

sesen  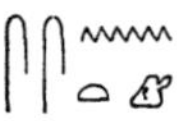 to snuff the air.

seska  body.

seset  legs.

seset 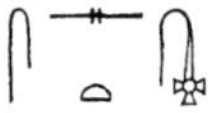 to burn up.

sesh 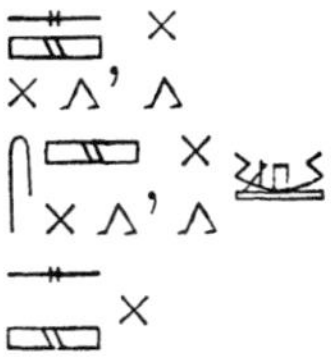 to pass, journey, travel.

 passage.

 impassable.

sesh 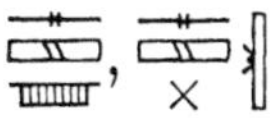 to open, unbolt.

sesh 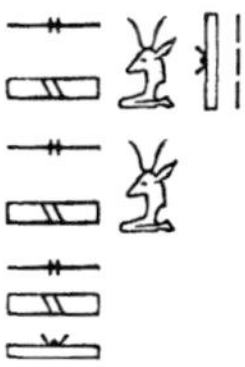 to be wise, skilful, knowledge.

sesh  nest; plur. .

 birth-place.

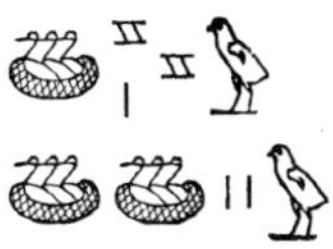 two nests.

Seshet  name of a town and its god.

sesh 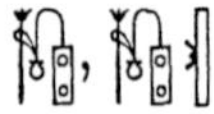 to write, draw, copy, make a plan.

seshu 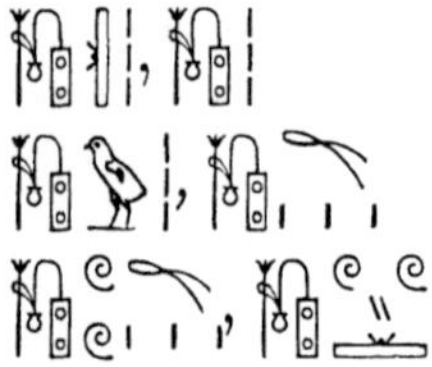 writings, decrees, documents, archives, books, copies of books, etc.

sesh 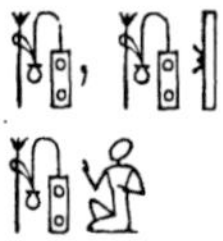 scribe, copyist.

 accomplished scribe.

 veritable scribe (as opposed to a titular scribe).

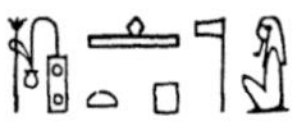 scribe of the temple property.

 scribe and draughtsman.

 scribe and draughtsman of the house of gold.

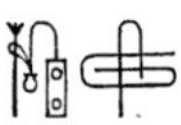 scribe and designer.

seshai  skilled, able, competent.

seshu  to be empty.

seshep 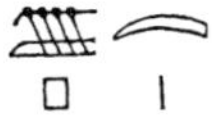 the measure of a palm.

seshepu 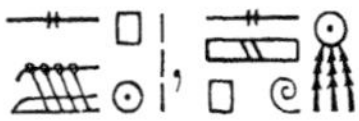 light, radiance; see SHESEP.

seshem  to lead, guide, conduct, guidance.

seshem  guide, leader.

 plur. of preceding.

seshmet  advance, guiding, guidance.

 gratification (?).

Seshemit  "conductress"; the name of a goddess.

Seshmu-ḥeḥ  "guide of eternity"; a proper name.

Seshmu-ta  "guide of the earth"; a proper name.

Seshmu-taui  "guide of the Two Lands"; a proper name.

Seshem  divine image, statue.

seshem  figure, design, image, form, similitude.

seshen 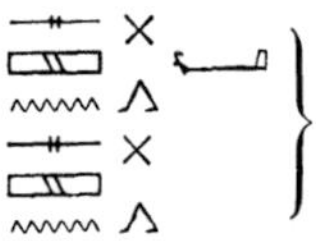 to scatter, destroy.

seshen  . . . . . .

seshen 

seshennu 

senshen 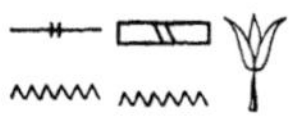

seshesh 

lily.

seshru  garments, apparel.

seshert a cake, loaf.

seshet (?) fire; plur. ; gods of fire .

Sesheta the goddess of architecture.

sesheta to be hidden, mysterious, incomprehensible.

sesheta hidden things, mysteries, secrets.

of invisible forms and shapes.

hidden of name.

very great mysteries indeed.

great secrets of Àmenti.

seshetu fiends (?).

seshet̤ bandage, bandlet, tiara, girdle, fillet for the head.

seshet-t 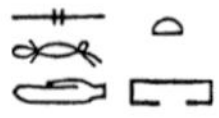 a chamber with a window or opening in it.

sek  to decay, perish; incorruptible. 

sek, *seksek* 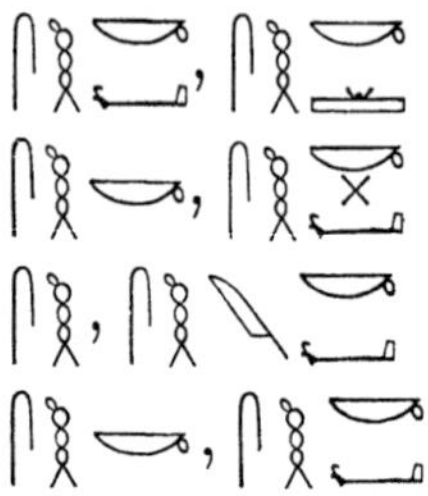 to break through, fight a way, to fight, destroy; to advance.

sek-re 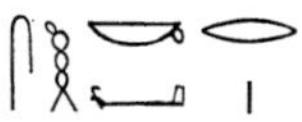 to direct.

Sek-ḥer  a proper name.

Seku 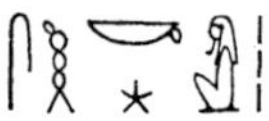 (with *àkhemu*) a class of gods.

seka  to plough.

sekemiu 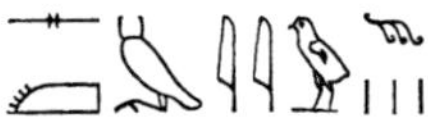 grey or white hair.

Seker, *Sekri* 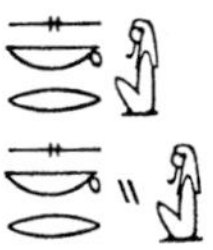 the ancient god of the Other World of Ṣaḳḳârah.

 Seker in his secret place.

Seker
Sekri 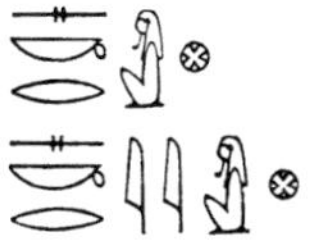 the town of Seker.

Sekri  the festival of Seker.

Seker 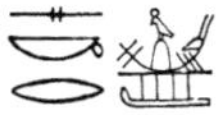 the sacred bark of Seker.

Seksek 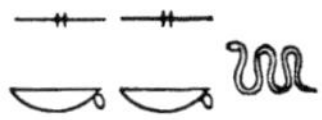 the name of a fiend.

sektiu  to fetter.

Sektet 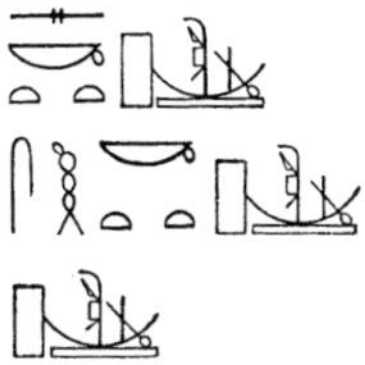 the boat in which the sun travelled from noon to midnight.

seq 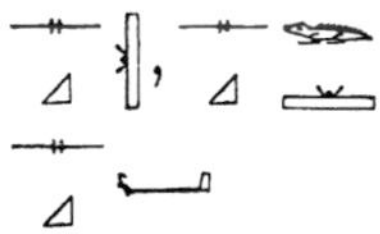 to collect, gather together.

seqa  to exalt, to lift up.

seqai  exalted one.

 plur. of preceding.

seqeb  image (?).

seqebb 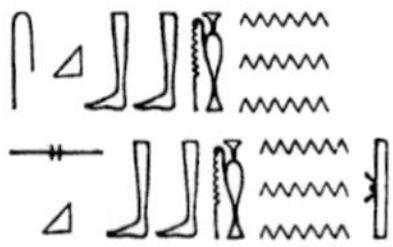 to cool, refresh oneself.

Seqebit  name of a goddess.

seqer  to smite, take prisoner.

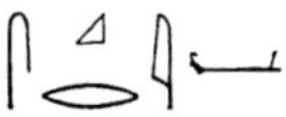 smiter.

seqeṭ 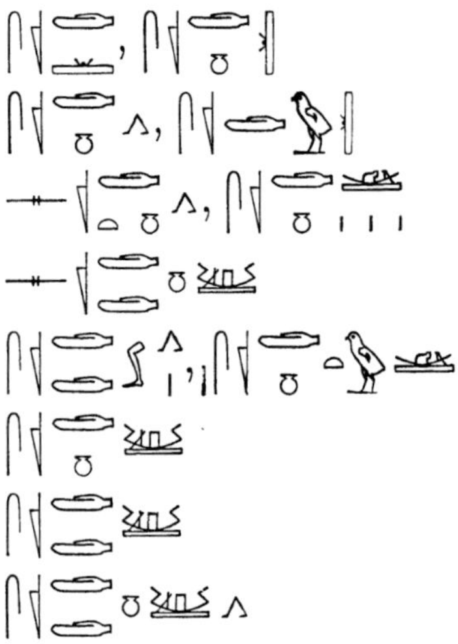 to sail in a boat, to journey, make a voyage; 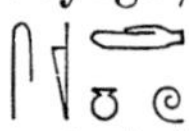 encircled.

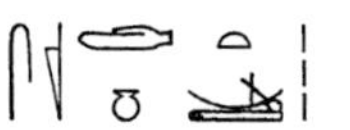 voyages, sailings.

 sailors, boatmen.

seqeṭ dispositions.

Seqeṭ-ḥer warder of the Second Ārit.

seḳenniu helpless ones, weak.

seḳer to put to silence, make quiet.

seḳert silence.

set she, it, its.

set they, them, their.

set (?) to break.

set ground.

Set the god of physical and moral evil; see Suti.

set (***semt***) mountain; plur.

set  to shoot arrows, to hurl stones.

set  to sow seed.

setit 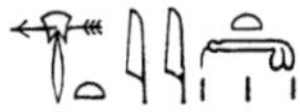 seed, progeny.

setut  arrows or beams of light, rays, radiance.

setau 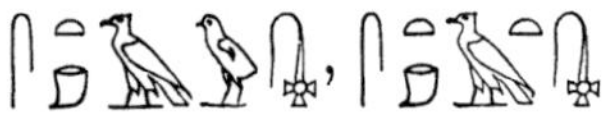 to light a fire, to burn, flame.

seti  burning, burner.

setit  adversaries (?).

Sett  the name of a goddess of the First Cataract.

Sett  an Asiatic woman.

Set-ṭemui  a proper name (var.  ).

Sta  a proper name.

sta, stat, ***stau*** 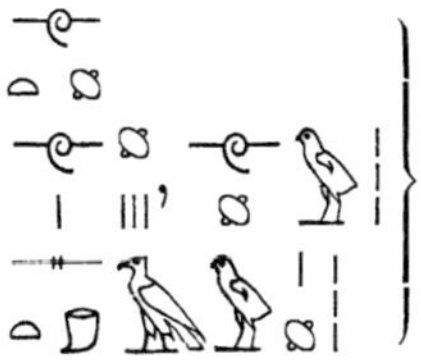 filth, dung.

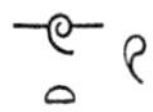 a portion of the body.

stat  filthy ones, fiends.

sta  to tow a boat, drag along, bring carry.

stau  those who tow, bearers, carriers.

stau 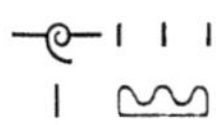 see 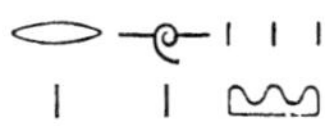 Re-stau.

stat 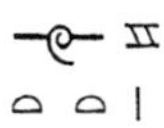 a measure of land.

sti  smell, odour.

sti festal perfume.

Sti "land of the bow"; a name of Nubia.

setua to make or ascribe praise.

setut (or *sutet*) to walk about.

setut to symbolize, typify.

seteb captives.

setep to cut.

setep to chose, chosen.

setepu choice cuts of meats.

setep sa to work protection on behalf of someone.

setem to hear; obey; hearer.

what is heard, listener.

setemiu  listeners.

Setem-ḥeri 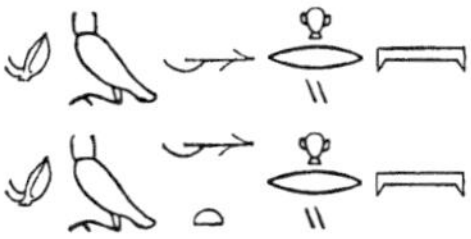 the name of the upper hinge.

Setem-kheri  the name of the lower hinge.

Setem-ȧnsi 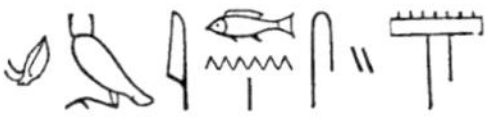 a proper name.

setennu  to be distinguished.

setentit 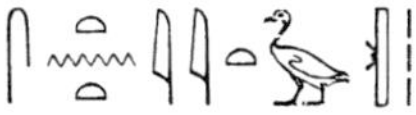 distinctions.

setenem 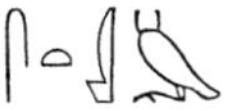 to make to walk.

seter  wooden tablet (?).

setḥu  to open.

set-ḥemt  woman, wife.

seteken 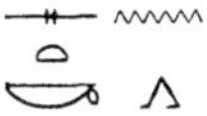 to make to enter.

 invaders, those who make to enter.

seṭ 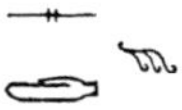 hair, foliage.

seṭ  to break, split.

Seṭ-qesu (or, *Seṭ-qersu*) 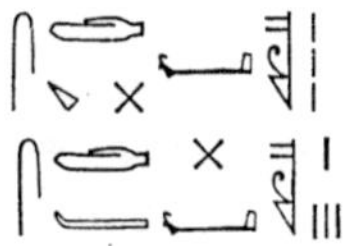 "bone-breaker"; the name of one of the Forty-two Judges in the Hall of Osiris.

seṭ  to clothe, to dress.

 a garment.

 those who clothe.

seṭa 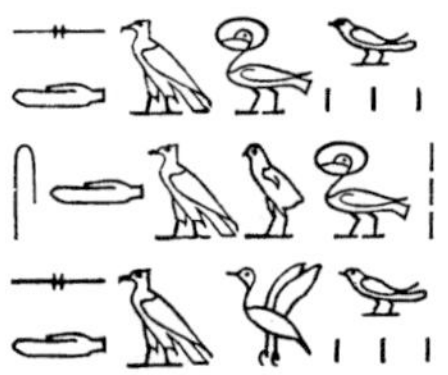 to tremble, quake, trembling, terror.

seṭui  to defame.

seṭu  . . . .

seṭeb  garment, hangings of a shrine.

seṭeb 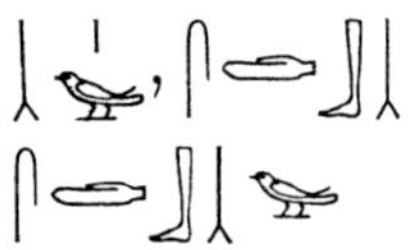 obstacle, disaster, calamity, misfortune.

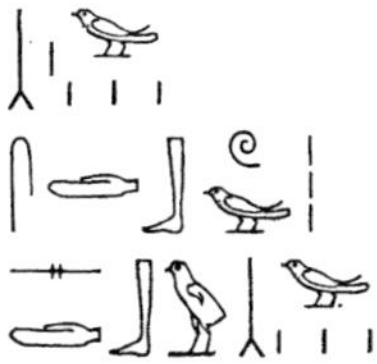 plur. of preceding.

seṭebḥ  to be ready, equipped.

seṭemu  edicts for slaughter.

seṭen  distinguished.

Seṭeḳ 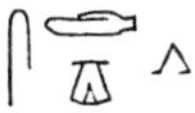 a proper name.

seṭeḳa  to cover.

seṭeḳaut  sleep.

seṭet 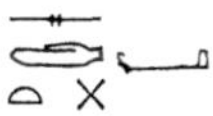 to break.

seṭeṭ 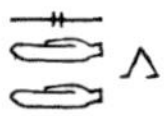 to travel.

seth 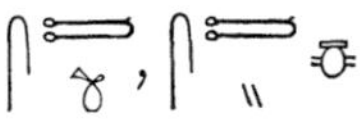 scent, unguent.

sethen  distinctions.

sethenem 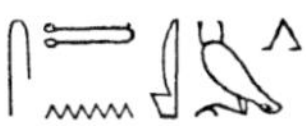 to make to walk.

sethes 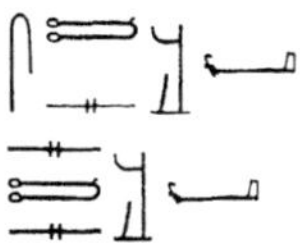 to raise up, lift up.

sethes — to praise, extol, "lift up", or "raise", a song or hymn, praisings.

sethesu — props, supports.

sethesu — supporters.

sethes Shu — what Shu raises up, *i. e.*, the sky.

sethesu Shu — the supports of Shu, *i. e.*, the four cardinal points.

sethes — to be laid out.

sethes — to knit together.

sethesu — libations.

setheken — to have sexual union.

setcha — to make to set out, travel.

setchami — to protect (?).

setchit seeds of a plant (?).

setcheb to oppose, be in the way of, obstruct.

setchefa to feed with food celestial or terrestrial.

setcher to lie down in sleep or death; dead, dead one; the dead.

bier.

setcheser to sanctify.

setcheṭfu to wound.

SH.

she pool, lake, laver; plur.

She asbiu Lake of flames.

She Aḳeb Lake of Aḳeb, *i. e.*, celestial ocean.

She Åqer Lake of Åqer, *i. e.*, the perfect lake (?).

She ur Great Lake.

She Maāti Lake of Maāti.

She em Māfket Lakes of Turquoise.

She Nu Lake of Nu.

She en Amu Lake of Fire.

She en Åsår Lake of Osiris.

She en Māat Lake of Māat.

She en Nesersert Lake of Fire.

	Lake of Fire.
She neter	Lake of the god, *i. e.*, Osiris.
She en Ḥeru	Lake of Horus.
She ḥeru	Lake of the celestial ones.
She ḥeḥ	Lake of Millions of years.
She en ḥesmen	Lake of Natron.
She Ḥetep	Lake of the god Ḥetep.
She ent ḥetch	Lake of Light.
She en khebentiu	Lake of the wicked.
She en kharu	Lake of the geese.
She en seḥetep	Lake of propitiation.
She en seshet	Lake of Fire.
Shet Ṭemui	Lake of the two knives.
She Tchesert	Lakes of the goddess Tchesert.
sha	field.

sha bread-cakes, food.

sha plants.

sha to destine, predestine, fore-ordain.

shaȧ pig.

shaȧs to travel, journey, go forward.

shaā one hundred.

shaā to begin, beginning.

unto, unto all eternity.

Shau the name of a city or town.

shauabti the name of the figure inscribed with the VIth Chapter of the Book of the Dead.

shauā book, writing.

Shai the god of Luck or Destiny.

Shabu the name of a god.

shabu water plants.

shabti See SHAUABTI.

shabu cakes, food.

Shapuneterårka name of an Utchat.

shamu damned (?).

Sharshar... a proper name.

Sharsharkhet name of an Utchat.

Sharshatåkatå a proper name.

shaheb south wind.

shas to journey, travel.

Shakanasa a proper name.

Shaka a name of Åmen.

shā sand.

shā (?) / ***shāt*** book, writing, document.

Book of praise.

		Books of holy words.
		Book of Thoth.
	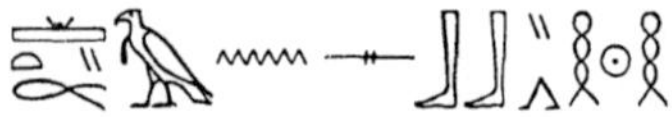	Book of traversing Eternity.
	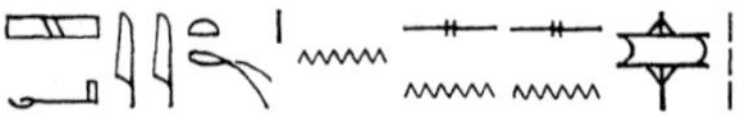	Book of Breathings.
shā		to cut, cut away, cut off.
shāit		knife.
shāmu		decorated (?).
shāt	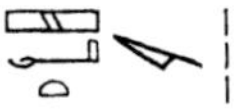	knife, knives.
shāṭ		to cut, to wound, hack off.
shāṭ ***shāṭet***	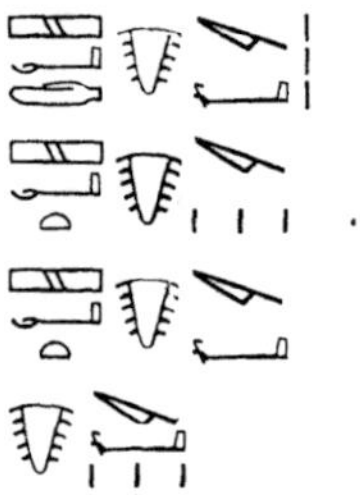	woundings, cuttings, slaughter, knives (?).
	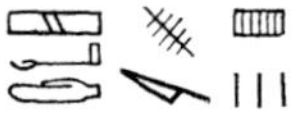	slaughter-blocks (?).
shu		to be dry, hot.

Shu		the god of the air, dryness, light, etc.; the counterpart of Tefnut.
Shut		fem. of preceding.
Shuu		the Sun-god.
shuit		light.
shuit		the abode of light (?) sky (?).
shu		to lack, be needy, in want of.
shu		plants, papyrus.
shut		feather.
shuti	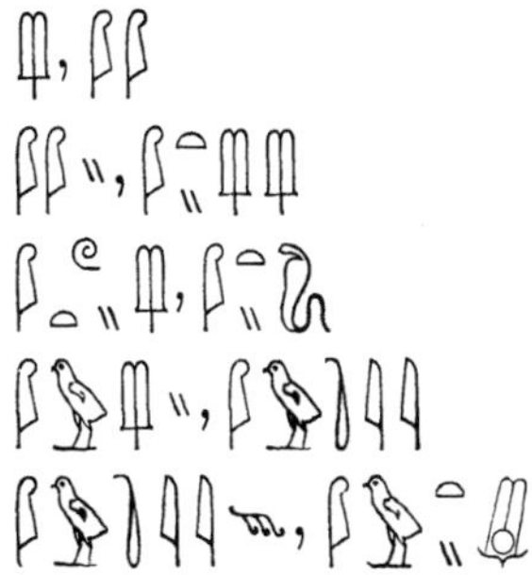	the two-feather crown, *e.g.*, that worn by Åmen.
shut		feathers, plumage.
shuti		merchant.

shutet . . . .

ṣhebu cakes, food.

shebeb throat.

Shebeb en Ḳesti name of a part of a boat.

sheben cakes, food.

shebenu mixed.

shep blind.

shepent vessel.

sheps to be holy, venerable, sacred, worshipful, majestic, awesone.

holy beings.

shept àb shame of heart, loathing.

shefu, *shefut* boils, blains, insolence, arrogance.

sheft ram (?), strength, power, terror; plur.

terrible of face.

sheft
shefit — strength, power, terror.

Shefit
Shefiti — the Ram-god, symbol of strength.

Shefshefit — strength, power, might.

shem
seshem — to walk, go, travel.

to calumniate, set the mouth in motion against a man.

shemiu
shemt — journeys, goings about, travellers.

shemu — the season of summer.

shemem — to be hot.

shemmet — fire, flames.

shemmet — poison.

shemā to sing, or play a musical instrument.

shemāit a singer.

shemā the south; stones of the south.

Shemāit the goddess of the South, *i. e.*, Nekhebit.

shems to follow, to accompany, be the member of a bodyguard.

shemsi follower, body-servant.

plur. of preceding.

chief servants of Osiris.

servants of His Majesty.

shen to revolve.

shen
shenit
shenu
shenn — circuit, circle, orbit; circuit of the earth.

shen — hair.

shenȧ — hair.

Shenȧt-pet-utheset-neter — the name of a sacred cow.

Shenȧt-sheps-neteru — the name of a sacred cow.

shenā — granary.

shenā — breast, body.

shenā — to turn back, repulse.

shenā — repulse, violence (?).

shenāāu — wayfarers (?).

shenā to turn back, repulse.

shenstet wickedness.

sheni hair, locks.

shenit storm.

sheniu chamber.

shenit chiefs, princes.

shenbet body.

shnemi

Shenmu the name of a town.

shennu a powder of some sort (?).

shennu snares (?).

shennu acacia trees.

Sḥennu the name of a town.

shens cakes, with shewbread.

shent flesh, skin (?).

shentu to curse, blaspheme.

shenti granary.

shenti heron.

shenti garment.

shentetu curse.

shenṭet a tree, the acacia.

shen-tȧ read.

Shentit the name of a goddess.

sher = and .

[*sherr* to be little.]

sherrȧu
sherriu } little ones, feeble men or gods.

sherȧt
shert
shertet } little one or thing, something of no value.

Sherem a proper name.

shersher winds, breath.

shert , , } nose, nostrils.

shert grain.

shert cake, bread.

shes (?) linen weavers (?).

shes , , linen, a linen garment.

shes  linen of the finest quality.

shes maāt  "cord of law", *i. e.*, with unfailing correctness and regularity.

shes  to be tied up, fettered.

shesui (?)  the two eyes (?).

shesep 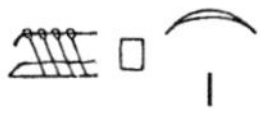 palm, a measure.

shesep 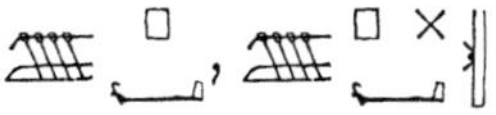 to take, undertake, accept, receive.

 receivers.

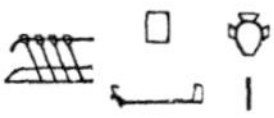 heart's desire.

shesep 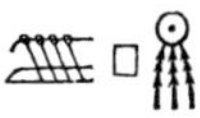 to shine, be bright.

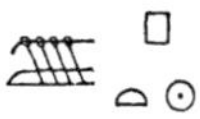 light. Note the forms  and 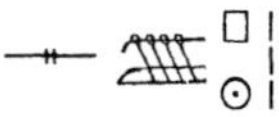 and SESHEP.

Shesep-temesu  name of a fiend (?).

shesau  skilled, able, intelligent, wise.

Shesmu	the headsman of Osiris.
Shes-khentet	a proper name.
sheta	tortoise.
sheta	to be hidden, secret, mysterious.
	hidden, hidden person or thing.
sheta	hidden thing, secret, mystery, something invisible and not understood.
	hidden places.
	hidden forms.
	hidden soul.
	hidden faces.
	hidden transformations.
	hidden things.

Shetait — the "hidden place"; a name of the Other World of Seker at Ṣaḳḳârah.

Shetat

Sheta-ḥer "hidden face"; a proper name.

Shetau-ā "hidden of arm"; a proper name.

Shetet-pet a proper name.

sheṭ to break up the ground, dig out, tear open, to deliver, strengthen, tie, bind up.

sheṭet lake, pool; plur.

sheṭit tank, cistern.

sheṭ to read, recite a book or prayer.

sheṭ 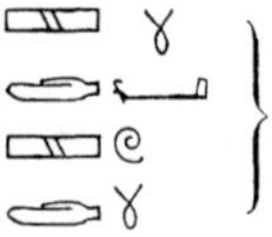 to swathe, to clothe.

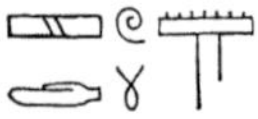 a garment.

 clothed, or covered, of arms.

sheṭu  leather straps.

sheṭḥu 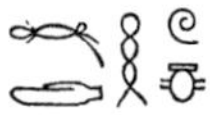 crushed grapes (?).

Sheṭ-kheru  the name of one of the Forty-two Judges in the Hall of Osiris.

 K.

k  thee, thou, thy; with sign of the dual 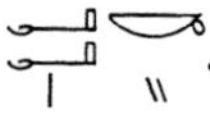.

ka  the double of a man or god, the personality of a man or god, self, the being of a man which is associated with the heart-soul , and is independent of the spirit-soul ; plur. .

Ka-ḥetep  a proper name.

kau 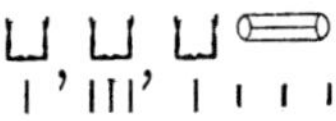 food.

ka  bull.

 the divine bull.

Ka-Åmentet  "Bull of Amenti"; a name of Osiris.

Ka-ȧn-erṭā-nef-nebȧ-f 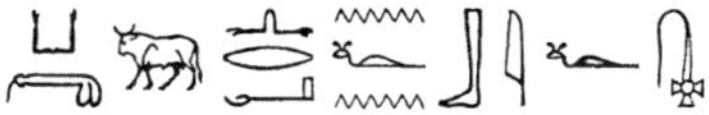 a proper name.

Ka-ur  "Great Bull".

Ka-ṭesher 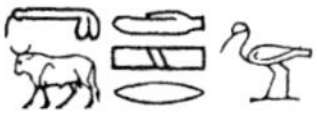 "Red Bull".

Ka  "Bull husband of the cows".

kaut 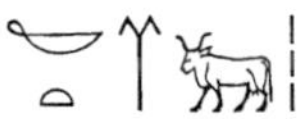 cows.

ka  to think, to cry out.

 thought.

ka  verily, prithee.

Kaa  the name of a god.

kaiu  cries (?), criers (?).

Ka-åri-k a proper name.

kaui a class of beings.

kabit lamentations.

karå shrine, chapel, sanctuary; , gods of the shrine.

Kaharsapusar-em-ka-ḥerremt a proper name.

Kasaika a proper name.

kat work, works, labours.

ki verily.

ki another. ... the one ... the other.

another man.

another chapter.

another person.

another time.

another reading, a variant.

kuȧ I.

kep to hide.

hidden place.

Kep-ḥer a proper name.

kefa to act with violence, expel, drive away.

kefa to remove the clothes, strip, undress. uncover.

kem to make an end of, to finish.

the end.

kem black.

Kem-ur the name of a town and of a lake.

Kemt  the "black" land, *i. e.*, Egypt.

Kemkem  the name of a god.

kenȧ  to speak.

Kenemet  the name of a town.

kenemet  night, darkness.

Kenemti  the name of one of the Forty-two Judges in the Hall of Osiris.

kenḥu (?)  night.

Kenset 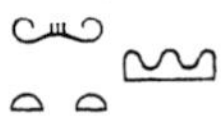 Nubia. The correct reading appears to be Sti, *i. e.*, the "land of the bow".

Ker 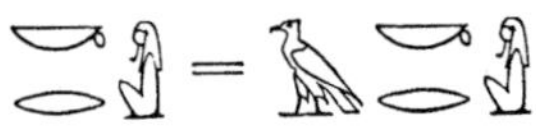 (?).

kerit 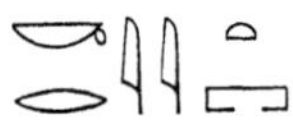 habitation, abode.

Keḥkeḥet  a proper name.

kes  to bow in homage.

kesu  homage, bowings.

Kesemu-enent  a class of divine beings.

kek, kekui 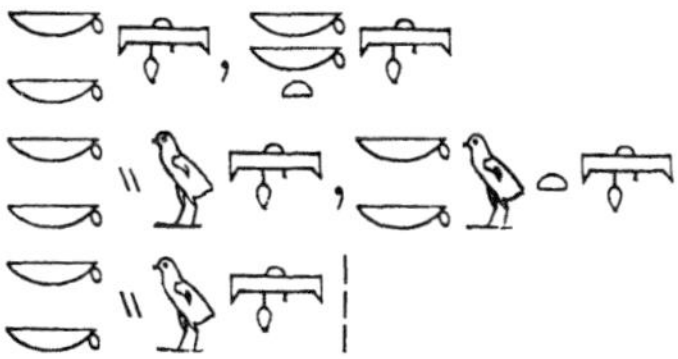 darkness, night.

ket  another.

ketuit 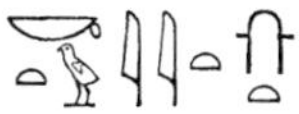 abode, habitation.

ketut  weapons, knives.

ket khu  other things.

ketet  little, bad.

⊿ Q.

qa 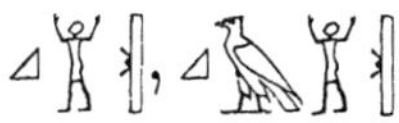 to be high, exalted, height.

 High God.

 Exalted one.

 doubly high, very high.

 exceedingly high.

 height of heaven.

 high, *i. e.*, loud-voiced.

 most terrible.

 high up on the standard.

 the god of the very high plumes.

Qa-ha-ḥetep  a proper name.

Qa-ḥer  a proper name.

qa  high ground, hill, staircase.

qa  to be rotten, putrefy.

qa  form.

qaat  bolts, fastenings.

qaȧ  form, image.

Qai  the name of a god.

qab  the innermost part.

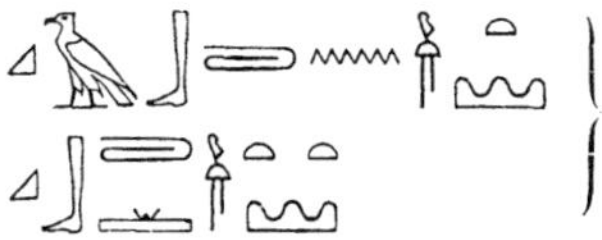 the centre of Ȧmenti.

qabt  a part of the body.

Qabt-ent-Shu-erṭā-nef-em-sau-Ȧsȧr   a proper name.

qamȧi  incense, unguent.

qamemt  to weep (?).

qart  a part of the Other World.

qart  bolts, fastenings.

Qaḥu  a proper name.

qaḥit  fire (?).

qasu, *qass*  to tie, bind, fetter.

 fetter.

 fetters.

qaqa  hill.

qā  be provided with (?).

qāḥu  arm and shoulder; dual 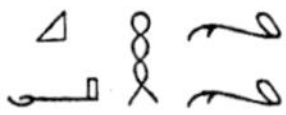, plur.  .

qāḥ 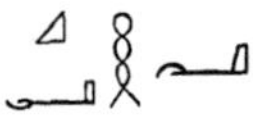 side of (?).

qu  limbs, flesh.

qeb 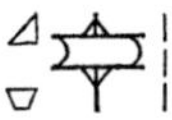 north wind.

qebbi, *qebti* 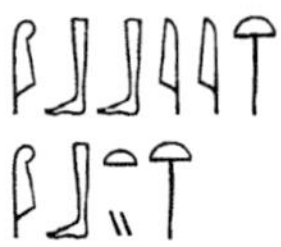 shade, shadow.

qeb ,  see .

qebḥ  to cool, refresh, be cooled, refreshed.

 place of cooling, the bath (?).

 the cool water of the First Cataract.

Qebḥ  the marsh of water-fowl.

Qebḥ-senu-f  one of the four sons of Horus.

Qebti  Coptos.

qefen  baked cake.

Qefenu  the name of a town.

qefṭenu 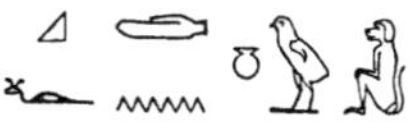 ape.

qema  to create, to fashion, to form.

qemama 

qemam 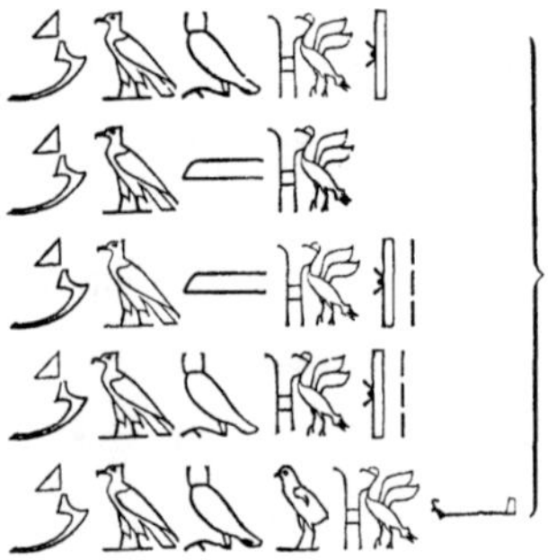 to create, to fashion, to form.

qemamu

 creatress.

 god of creation.

qemḥ  leaves of a tree.

qem-tu 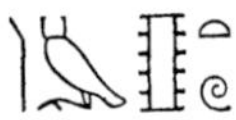 to overturn.

qemṭu  to say, repeat.

Qen  a proper name (?).

qen 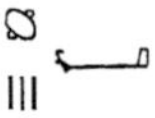 fat.

qen  to do evil, be evil.

qen  to be strong, bold, brave.

qenȧ 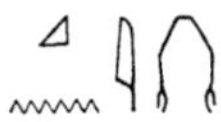 to embrace, embrace.

qenȧt  a kind of incense.

qeni — a kind of linen.

qenu — strong.

qenbet, *qenbit* — a class of officials, human or divine.

Qenna — a proper name.

qenert — grain (?) fruit (?).

qenqen — to beat, to strike.

qenqen — to feed, eat.

Qenqentet — the name of a lake in Sekhet-Åaru.

qer — the north wind.

qerå — storm, thunder, a proper name.

qerås — sepulture, burial.

qerfi — to tie, be tied.

Qernet — the name of a town.

qert, qerrt — cave, cavern.

qerti  the name of the two caves near Philae wherein the Nile rose; the name of one of the Forty-two Judges in the Hall of Osiris.

qeres 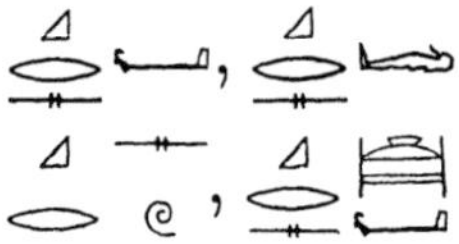 to bury; dead body.

qersu 

qerset 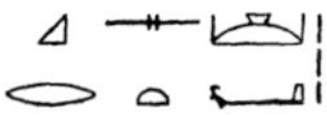 coffin, sarcophagus.

qerset 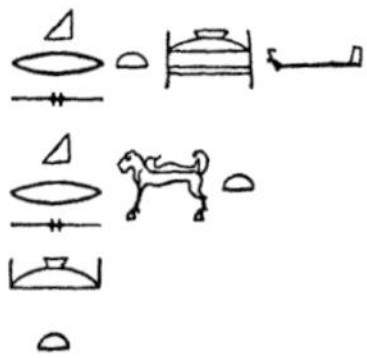 burial.

qerqer 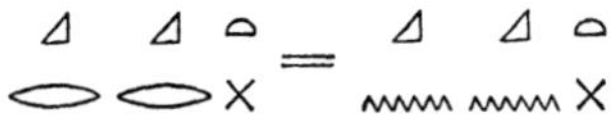

qert  bolt, fastening; .

qeḥḥtum (?)  castrated animals for sacrifice (?).

qes  burial (?).

qesu (for *qersu*) 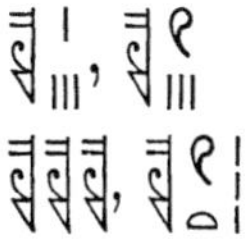 bones.

qesu (*qersu*) 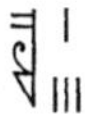 preserves (of birds).

Qesi  Cusae, the capital of the XIVth nome of Upper Egypt.

qesen  to be evil, bad.

qeq  see ȦM to eat.

Qetetbu  a proper name.

qeṭ 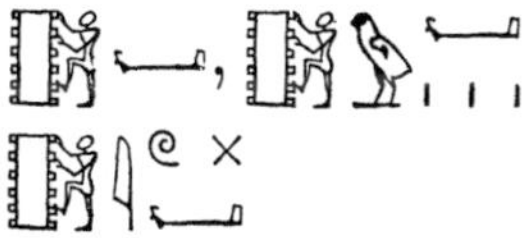 to build.

qeṭ 

qeṭu  to draw, sketch, make a plan or design; work of the artist.

qeṭu  sailors, mariners, crew of a boat.

Qeṭu  a fiend.

qeṭ — orbit, circle, like, similitude, character, dispositions.

likewise, also, totality.

qeṭt — slumber.

K̦.

ḳa — to besiege.

ḳa — filth, dung.

ḳa — to stink.

ḳaut, *ḳau* — calamity, calamities, misery, to suffer want, to lack something or anything.

ḳai — lake.

ḳau — a substance offered to the gods.

ḳauasha — to break.

ḳab — to depart (?).

ḳabti — the hair of some portion of the body.

ḳaf  ape; plur. .

ḳas  chamber.

ḳast (?)  . . . .

ḳat  claw, limb.

ḳatu  thoughts, meditations.

ḳuat  to besiege.

Ḳeb  (?)

ḳeb 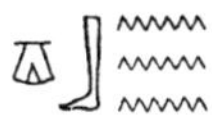 the celestial ocean.

ḳeba  to suffer, be in misery.

ḳeba  to cast an evil glance (?).

ḳeba  some wooden object.

ḳem  to find, discover.

 something found.

ḳemḳem to discover, find out.

Ḳem-ḥeru a class of divine beings.

ḳemut weak, evil beings.

ḳemḥ to see.

ḳemḥet eye.

Ḳemḥu the name of a god.

Ḳemḥusu a proper name.

ḳemḥut hair (?).

ḳen
ḳenn } weak, feeble, helpless.

ḳenu cattle.

Ḳem-ur
Ḳen-ur
Ḳer-ur } a proper name.

ḳenut deeds, documents, records.

Ḳenḳenur the name of a god.

ḳent — slit.

ḳer — moreover.

ḳert — but.

ḳer — to be silent.

ḳerḥ — night, darkness.

Ḳersher, — a proper name.

ḳer[ḳ] — to have, to hold, possess.

possessor.

possessions.

ḳer[ḳ] — lie, falsehood, deceit.

lie, falsehood, deceit.

Ḳer[ḳ]et the name of a town.

ḳeḥ weak, helpless, wretched.

ḳes one half.

ḳes side; dual , , both sides; plur. .

left side.

right side.

near, by the side of.

ḳesu to anoint, ointment.

Ḳesui the name of a canal (?).

Ḳestȧ one of the Four Sons of Horus.

ḳestȧ 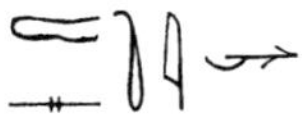 scribe's palette.

ḳesh 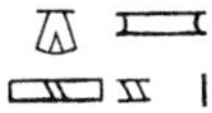 pool, lake.

T.

t 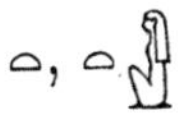 thy.

ta  the;  what is his, his.

ta  to be hot, to burn.

tau  flame, fire, hot, angry.

Ta-reṭ  the name of one of the Forty-two Judges in the Hall of Osiris.

ta 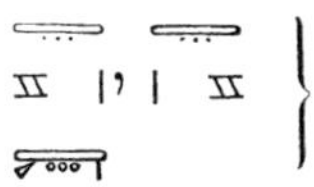 land, ground, country, the earth, the world.

taui 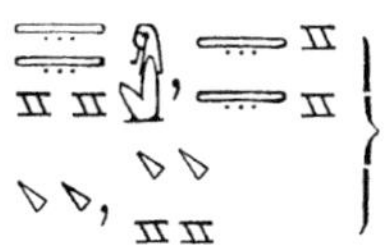 the "Two Lands", *i. e.*, Upper and Lower Egypt.

taiu  lands, countries, the world, all lands.

 the regions of the Other World.

 earth-gods.

Ta āb  "pure land", *i. e.*, the Other World.

Ta ānkhtet  "land of life", *i. e.*, the grave.

Ta ur 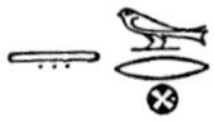 "great land"; a part of Abydos.

Ta en Manu  "land of Manu", *i. e.*, the West.

Ta en Maāt  "land of Law", *i. e.*, the Other World.

Ta en maākheru 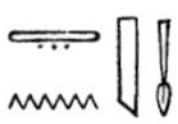 "land of triumph", *i. e.*, the Other World.

Ta Merȧ  "land of Merȧ", *i. e.*, Upper and Lower Egypt.

Ta Meḥ 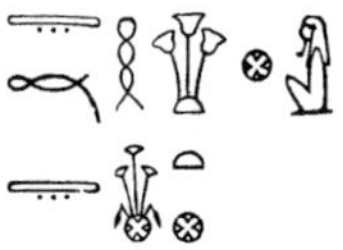 "land of the North", the Delta.

Ta mes tchetta  "land of eternity", *i. e.*, the Other World.

Ta Nefer 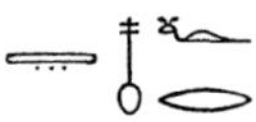 "beautiful land", *i. e.*, the grave.

Ta Nent 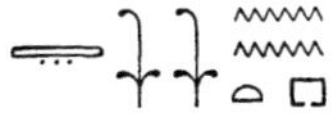 a portion of the Other World.

Ta neḥeḥ  "land of eternity", *i. e.*, the Other World.

Taiu nu neteru 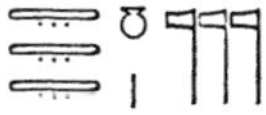 "lands of the gods", *i. e.*, heaven.

Ta remu  "land of fish".

Taui Rekhti
Taiu Rekhti 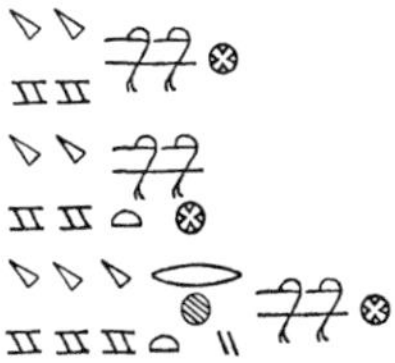 "lands of the Rekhti", *i. e.*, Isis and Nephthys.

Ta kharu  "land of the *kharu* geese".

Ta Sekri  "land of Seker", *i. e.*, the Other World of Memphis.

Ta She 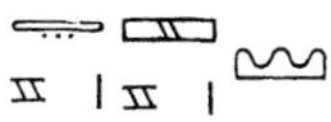 "land of the Lake", *i. e.*, the Fayyûm.

Ta shemā 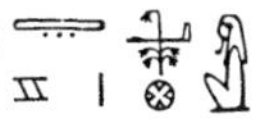 "land of the South".

Ta sheta  "land of mystery", *i. e.*, the Other World.

Ta Sti 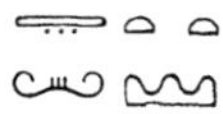 "land of the bow", *i. e.*, Nubia.

Ta qebḥ  "land of cool water", *i. e.*, the Cataract region.

Ta Ṭuat "land of the Ṭuat", *i. e.*, the Other World.

Ta Tchesert "holy land", *i. e.*, the Other World.

Ta en tchetta "land of eternity", *i. e.*, the Other World.

ta bread, cakes.

cakes made of fine flour.

white bread.

celestial bread.

bread of Nenet (?).

. . . . . .

Tait a proper name.

tait sail.

Tait the name of a goddess.

Tar the name of a fiend.

taḥenen to dip in water (?).

Ta-ḥer-sta-nef  a proper name.

Tatunen  the name of a god.

tȧt  emanation; plur. .

tiu  adorers.

tini 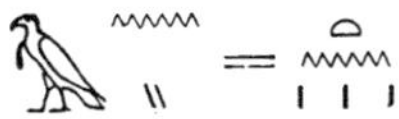 (?).

tu  a demonstrative particle.

tua  to adore.

tuȧ  I.

tui  a demonstrative particle.

tui  . . . . . .

tui  . . . . .

tuf  his.

tuni  . . . . . .

tur 
turȧ  to cleanse, purify, be pure, clean.

tuk thou.

tuḳ apparel.

tut to be like, similar.

tut type, form, image, statue, portrait figure.

as, like, similar.

tut to arrange, group together.

tebu to be shod, sandal (?).

teb sandal.

tebi, tebt , pair of sandals.

Tebu
Tebti } the name of a city.

tebteb to walk.

tebtebti the soles of the feet (?).

tep , head, the tip, point, or top of anything.

tep , upon.

tepi		he who is on, the first, best, or finest of anything.
		the best of the offerings.
		the finest linen.
		the choicest flowers.
		the earliest hour of every day.
		the earliest dawn.
		the earliest twilight hour.
	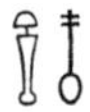	the greatest happiness.
	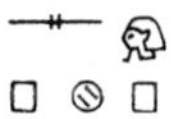	primeval time.
	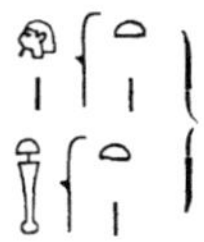	New Year's Day.
	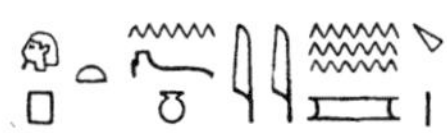	the best water in the lake.
		the original state of anything.
tep ā	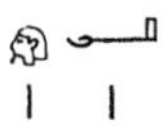	straightway.
tep ā		he of olden time, ancestor.

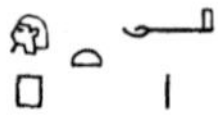 she of olden time, ancestress. plur.  ancestors, forebears.

ṭep re / *tepi re*  mouth, then what comes from the mouth, speech, voice, utterance; plur. .

tep reṭui  prescription, precept, command, chapter.

tep  unguent of finest quality.

tep  a kind of goose.

tept 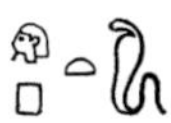 uraeus crown.

Tep-ṭu / *Tep-ṭu-f*  "he on the hill, or his hill"; a name of Anubis.

Tepa  the name of a cow.

tepȧ 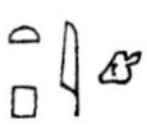 to snuff the air, breathe.

tepḥet	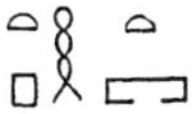	cavern, cave, den, hole in the ground; plur. .
tef		father.
tefa		that.
Tefnut	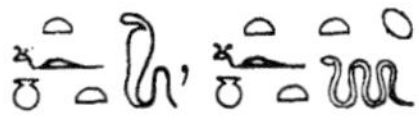	the name of a Water-goddess.
tem		to come to an end.
temt *temtu* *temti*	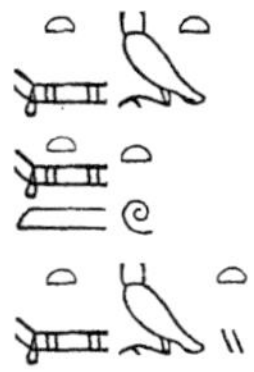	all, entirely;  wholly and entirely.
tem *temem*	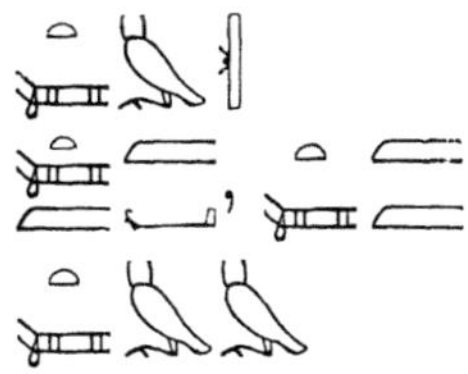	to be complete, whole, entire.
tem	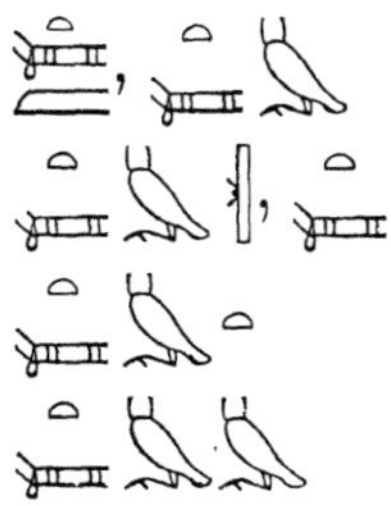	a particle of negation, no, not, without.

Tem, ***Temu*** — Tem, the "father of the gods".

Tem Harmakhis.

Tem Kheperȧ.

temam — basket (?).

temamu — stations (?).

temaāu(?) — winds.

temu, ***tememu*** — all people, mortals, mankind.

temem — part of a sledge.

tememu — parts of a net.

Temem-re — a proper name.

Tem-sep — the name of one of the Forty-two Judges in the Hall of Osiris.

temt 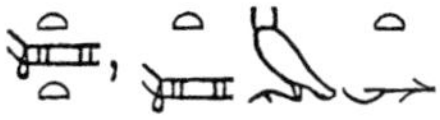 sledge.

ten  this.

ten 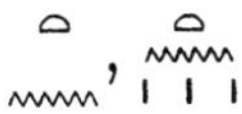 ye, you.

Teni  an ancient city near Abydos.

ten 
teni 
tenu 
what kind of? what manner of? whence? where?

ten  to be or become great, great, distinguished.

tenait  light.

tenu 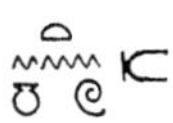 to divide, separate.

tenem 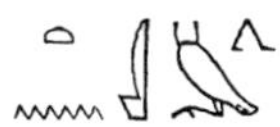 to turn back.

Tenemit  a proper name.

ter  a particle, then, etc.

ter — time, season; plur.

terui — the two seasons, *i. e.*, morning and evening, or sunrise and sunset;

teriti — the northern and southern halves of the sky.

teru — stream.

teh, *teha* — to march against, attack.

tehami — strider.

tehenen — to appoint, raise up.

tiḥṭut — prayers, offerings.

tekh — the pointer or tongue of a balance; "the pointer of the place of truth".

tekhni — hidden.

tekhtekh — to shake out the hair.

tesh — to depart, to go.

Teshtesh		an image which was dressed up as Osiris.
teka	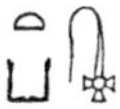	(with tekau and tekat)
tekau		fire, flame, lamp.
tekat	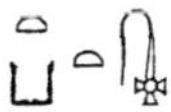	(with teka and tekau)
Tekem		the name of a god.
tekem		to approach.
teken		to enter, go in.
		those who enter.
tektek		to pass, walk, go.
teḳa		to be hot, to kindle.
teḳas		to walk, march.
tetbu		to smear.

T.

ṭa to pass away.

ṭa emission.

ṭaṭa to pollute oneself.

ṭaȧu the name of a garment.

ṭaȧr restraint.

ṭā, *ṭāṭā*, *ṭāṭāu* to give, grant, set, place, ascribe.

gift.

giver, giving, placing.

givers.

ṭāt ȧb heart's desire.

ṭā as auxiliary:

make to fear.

cause to do.

cause to be.

cause to become, etc.

Ṭāṭāu the city of Busiris or Mendes.

ṭit gifts.

ṭu, *ṭut* evil, evil thing, sin, fault, wickedness, sinner.

sin, evil.

ṭuu, *Ṭut* wickedness.

Ṭuṭu the name of one of the Forty-two Judges in the Hall of Osiris.

Ṭuis (?) the name of the rudder in the magic boat.

ṭuȧu ale (?), drink.

ṭu mountain; plur.

the two mountains.

two great high mountains.

Ṭu-en-Bakha Mount Bakha, the Mountain of Sunrise.

Ṭu-en-Neter-khert Mountain of the Other World.

Ṭut-f = (?).

Ṭu-menkh-rerek a proper name.

ṭu-ā to put forth the hand (?).

ṭua five; fifth.

ṭuau to do something early in the day.

ṭuat, **ṭuait** dawn, daybreak, to-morrow.

ṭua to praise, worship, adore; praise.

praisers.

neter ṭua  to offer up thanksgiving.

Ṭuamutef  one of the Four Sons of Horus.

Ṭuat  The Other World.

 the everlasting Ṭuat.

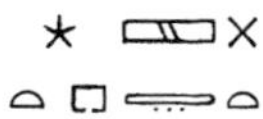 the hidden Ṭuat.

 the god of the Ṭuat.

 the beings of the Ṭuat.

ṭun 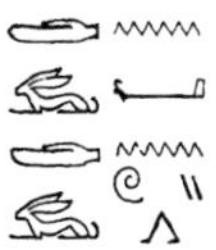 to lift up or stretch out the legs.

Ṭun-peḥti  the porter of the Second Ārit.

ṭur to be clean.

ṭurt . . . . . .

ṭeb horn; dual

ṭeb tomb (?).

ṭeb to be furnished or equipped.

ṭeb to wall up, to box in.

ṭebt box, coffer, coffin, chest, tomb; plur.

ṭebu frame, framework of a net.

Ṭeb-ḥer-kehaat the herald of the Fifth Ārit.

ṭeben, *ṭebenu* to revolve.

ṭebḥ to pray, make supplication.

ṭebḥu (?) / *ṭebḥet*	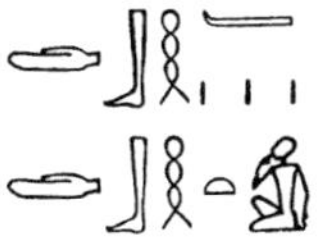	prayer, petition, supplication.
ṭebḥu	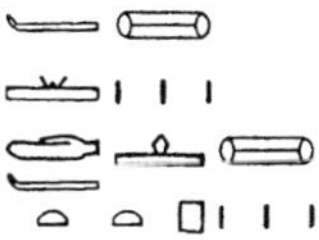	offerings, cakes, bread, etc.
ṭebḥu		funerary furniture.
ṭebḥ	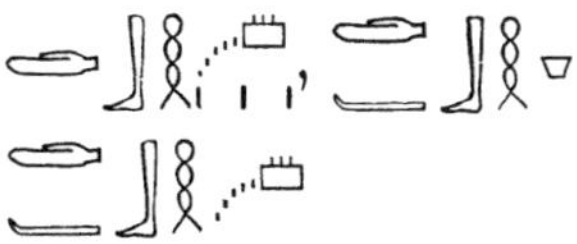	a grain measure.
ṭebt		block, slab, brick.
Ṭep	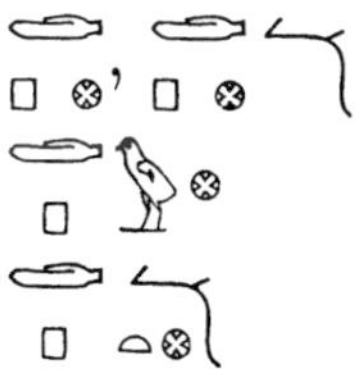	one half of the city of Buto,
ṭept	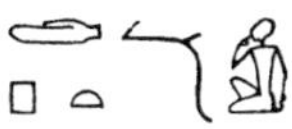	taste.
ṭepu		oar, paddle.
ṭept		boat.
ṭem		to cut, stab.
		with  a piercing voice.

ṭem, *ṭemt* knife, sword; plur.

two-edged knife, or sword (?).

Ṭem-r (?)*-khut-pet* . . . . . .

Ṭem-ur a name of Osiris.

ṭemamt a hairy covering, two locks.

ṭemam to make an end of.

ṭemam (*sic*)

ṭemȧ, *ṭemȧi* to unite, be united, touch, join.

ṭemȧ city; plur.

ṭemi shore, bank.

ṭemem entire, totality.

ṭemṭ  to collect, gather together, unite, all, entire.
ṭemtch

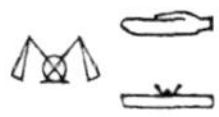 all, totality.

Ṭemṭiu  a class of divine beings.

ṭen  to cut off, or away.

ṭen  to place.

Ṭenȧ 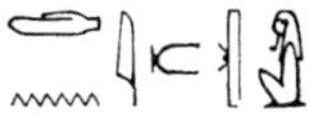 the name of a god.

ṭenȧ  to separate.

ṭenȧt  bank of a canal, piece of land.

ṭenȧt 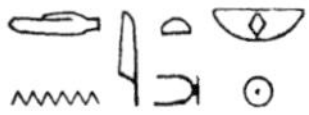 the weekly festival.

ṭenȧ  the name of a chamber.

ṭenȧ 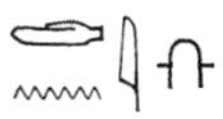 basket.
ṭenȧt 

ṭenȧu  lot, share, division.

ṭeni 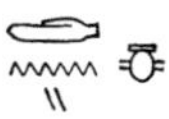 vessel.

Ṭeni	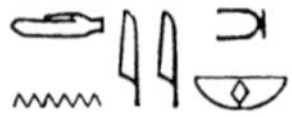	the name of one of the Forty-two Judges in the Hall of Osiris.
Ṭeniu		the god of old age.
ṭenu		to be distinguished.
ṭenb		to gnaw.
Ṭenpu		a proper name.
ṭenem		worms.
ṭenḥ	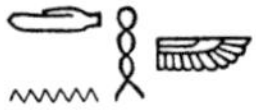	wing.
ṭenḥui		pair of wings.
ṭenḥṭenḥ	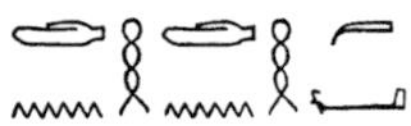	to fly.
ṭens		weights.
ṭent		abode.
ṭenṭ	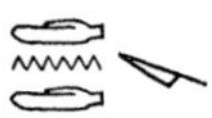	slaughter.
ṭenṭen	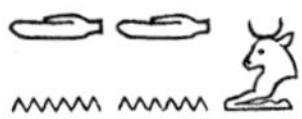	might, violence, valour.
ṭer	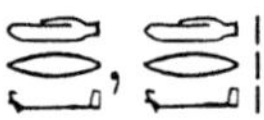	to destroy.

ṭerp	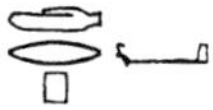	to offer.
ṭeref		wisdom, skill, book of wisdom.
ṭehant		forehead.
ṭehen		to salute humbly.
ṭehen	 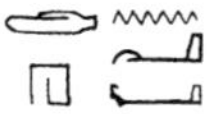	to place the forehead on the ground in token of homage.
ṭehen ta	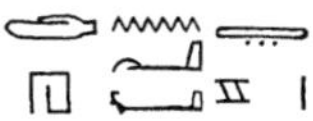	
Ṭehent	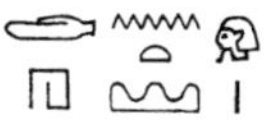	"brow of a hill"; a proper name.
Ṭeḥuti		the god Thoth, scribe of the gods, dweller in Khemenu 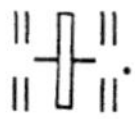.
Ṭeḥuti-Ḥāpi	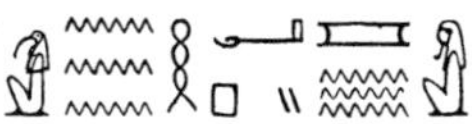	Thoth-Ḥāpi.
Ṭeḥutit	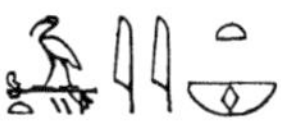	the Thoth festival.
teḥer	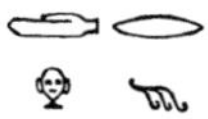	hair, feathers, foliage.
teḥerȧu		injury, harmful person, sickness (?).
ṭes	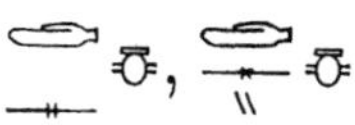	vase.

ṭes — to cut, smite.

ṭes — flint knife; plur.

ṭeser — sacred, holy.

Ṭesert-tep — a proper name.

Ṭesher — the name of a town and of its god.

ṭesher — to be red, become red, red, ruddy.

red ones, men or devils.

ṭesheru — gore, blood, redness (of clouds).

ṭesher — blood.

Ṭesher — the red land, *i. e.*, the desert.

ṭeshert — red flame.

ṭeshert — the Red Crown, *i. e.*, the Crown of Lower Egypt.

ṭeqer 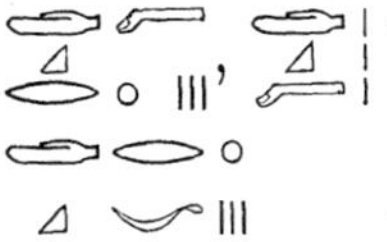 seeds, fruits.

ṭeḳa  to see.

 seeing.

 appearance.

ṭeḳaȧu  seeds, fruits (?).

ṭeḳ, ṭeḳeḳ  sight.

ṭeḳa  to hide.

ṭeḳa  plants.

ṭeḳas  to run, walk towards.

ṭetrit 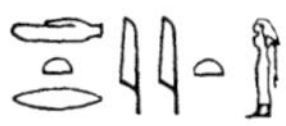 . . . . . Chap. XCIX, 12.

ṭet 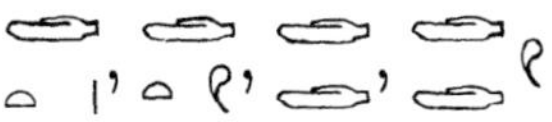 hand.

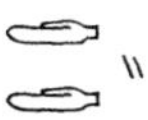 the two hands.

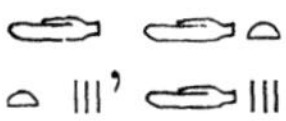 hands.

Ṭet-ent-Åst 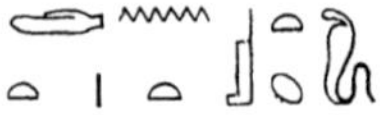 a proper name.

ṭet

ṭeṭṭeṭ 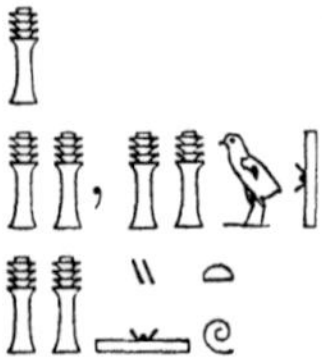 to stablish, be established, stable, permanent.

ṭeṭ  an amulet.

ṭeṭ 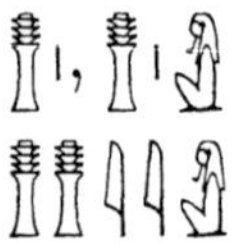 a figure, image, or tree trunk which was "set upright" during the festival of Osiris.

ṭeṭ  a building.

Ṭeṭu  the city of Busiris.

Ṭeṭt 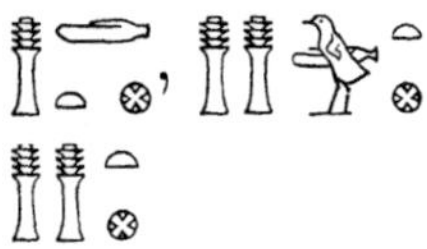 the city of Mendes.

TH.

th thee, thou, thy,

thȧ (*tȧ*) with verbs, etc.

Thȧnasa (*Tȧnasa*) a proper name.

thȧthȧ thighs.

thu thou.

thut ȧs behold!

thui . . . .

theb (*teb*) sandals.

Thefnut the name of a goddess.

thepḥet storehouse, cave, cavern, hole.

themes decree, writing.

		decrees.
then		this.
then		ye, you, your.
then		to be great, exalted, distinguished, worthy.
then		that.
Thena		a proper name.
Thenemi		the name of one of the Forty-two Judges in the Hall of Osiris.
Then-reṭ		the name of one of the Forty-two Judges in the Hall of Osiris.
thentchat		throne chamber.
therem		to make to weep.

thert a kind of tree.

theh to attack.

theḥenu unguent.

Theḥenu
Teḥenu the name of a country, Libya.

theḥent crystal (?), amber (?).

theḥen to be yellow, or green (?); .

theḥeḥ to cry out.

thes to be strong, give orders.

thes , to support, lift up, raise; joy.

thesu
thest supports, props.

thes to tie in a knot, knot, fetter.

knot.

thes vertebra.

plur. of preceding.

thesu word, speech, a saying, riddle.

conversely.

thesȧu to rule.

Thest-ur a proper name.

thesem dog, greyhound.

plur. of preceding.

thesthes a garment.

Thekem a proper name.

thet — the name of a red stone, or faïence, amulet.

thet — to take possession of, to seize, to carry off, conquer, acquire.

seizers, robbers.

ravisher of hearts.

ravisher of women.

Thet-em-āua — the name of a plank or peg.

thetthet — to destroy.

TCH.

tcha — see .

tcha — safe, sound, in good case.

tcha — to split, to cut.

tcha abyss.

tcha to transport, to sail with something.

one who transports.

transport.

Great Boat.

tcha to set out, go forth.

tchaau hair.

tchau (?) birds.

tchat an official.

tcha to seize, grasp, rob, ravish.

robber.

plunder.

"wing-carrier", fan-bearer.

tcha male, husband, phallus.

tchau		the west wind.
tchaui		Isis and Nephthys, the "two eagles".
tchaut		twenty; 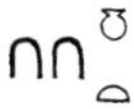 twentieth.
tchafu		flames.
Tchafi		the souls of Horus and Rā.
tchai		fiend.
tchaitiu		slaughterers.
tcham		papyrus.
tchamet		coverings, garments.
tchart		strength, strong.
tchat	 	strength, strong.
tchat	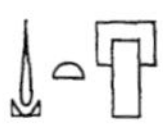	measure.

tchat 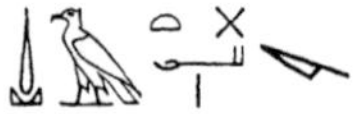 knife.

tchaut  foul things, filth.

tchaua 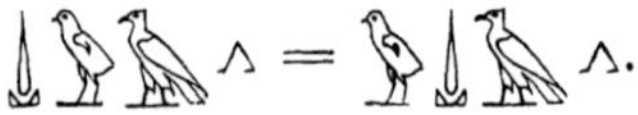

tchauu  amulet.

tchatcha  "head"; the name of the upper post.

tchatcha 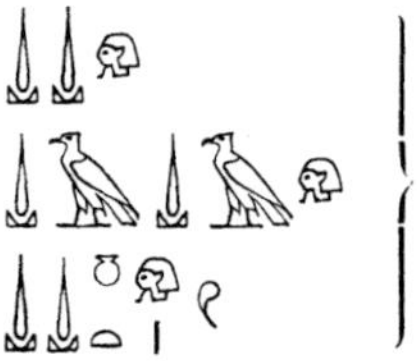 head, top of anything, summit.

tchatchat 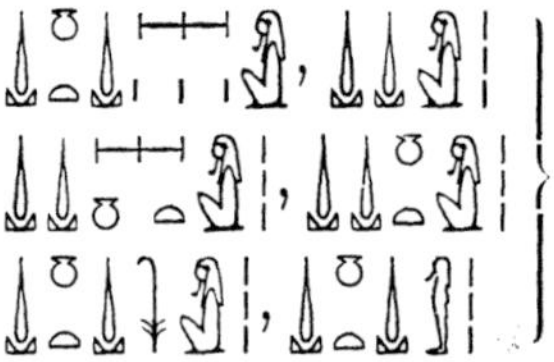 the "Heads", or "Chiefs", *i. e.*, the council of the gods in each great town of Egypt, and in the Other World. Every great god and goddess possessed a company or council of "Chiefs", *e. g.*, Osiris and Rā.

tchatchat 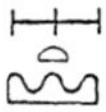 the domain of the cemetery in the hills; plur. 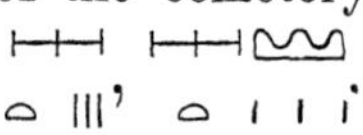

 the domain of eternity, *i. e.*, the grave.

the holy domain, *i. e.*, the grave.

the domain of Åmenti, *i. e.*, the grave.

city boundaries.

tchāāu staves.

tchābet burning coals.

tchām sceptre; plur.

tchām gold with a very large percentage of silver mixed with it, electrum.

tchār to go about in search of, to pry into.

tchārȧ fortress.

tchebā to seal, make a reckoning (?).

tchebā finger; plur. ; fingers which seize.

Tchebā-en-Sekri a proper name.

Tchebā-en-Shesmu a proper name.

Tchebāu-en-Ḥeru-semsu name of the paddles in the magic boat.

Tchebāui-en-tepu-ā-Rā a proper name.

tchefa the food of the dead, sepulchral offerings.

Tchefet a place and a goddess in the Elysian Fields.

Tchefit

tchefetch pupil of the eye.

pupil of the Utchat.

tchefetch to shed.

Tchen a proper name.

tchenḥu beams.

tchentchen to crush, break.

Tchentche[n] a proper name.

tcher to break.

tcher since, whilst, when.

tcher-ā straightway.

tcher-enti, ***tcher-entet*** since, because.

to the limit of, all, the whole.

tcher limit, boundary; plur. , boundless.

tcherȧu to constrain, fetter.

tcherȧ fort, stronghold.

tcherȧu heel, hoof.

Tcheruu	the god of boundaries.
tcheru	a bird with a shrill voice.
tcheri / *tcherit*	a bird, the incarnation of Isis and Nephthys.
Tcherti	Isis and Nephthys.
tcheres	abode, chamber (?).
Tcheḥes	the name of a serpent.
tches	self; myself, himself. thyself, themselves.
	with his own fingers.
	the god himself.
	with her own mouth.
tchesef	to snare.
	fowler.

tcheser — to make clear the ways, to put in good order, to be or make holy.

tcheseru — holy or beautiful things.

glorious, splendid.

Tchesert — the beautiful mountain, *i. e.*, cemetery.

Tchesert — a proper name.

Tcheser-tep — the name of one of the Forty-two Judges in the Hall of Osiris.

tchet — body, person; my own self.

tchet — house, chamber; the Ṭuat(?).

tchetta — eternity, everlastingness.

the god of eternity.

eternity and everlastingness.

tcheṭ  to say, speak, declare, recite words, converse.

em tcheṭ  saying, introducing a quotation.

tcheṭu  to declare, speak, etc.

tcheṭ-t 
tcheṭu 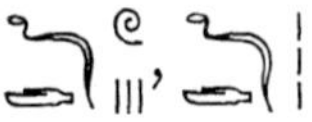 } words, orders, things said.

tcheṭ meṭu  "shall be recited" [the following].

 "another reading".

tcheṭ neḥes 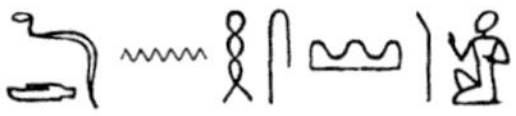 negro speech, or language.

tcheṭfet 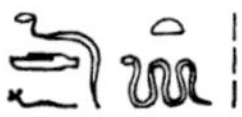 reptiles.

tcheṭḥu  a place of restraint.

tcheṭḥu 
 } to shut in, imprison.

tchetch  an instrument or standard.

Words and signs of uncertain reading.

	Chap. CXLV, IV, l. 16.
	Chap. CX, l. 5.
	Chap. CX, l. 35.
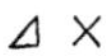	Chap. CXXXI, 5.
	Chap. XCIX, l. 38.

ENGLISH INDEX.